Anthony Wells is unique insofar as he is the only living person to have worked for British intelligence as a British citizen and US intelligence as a US citizen, and to have also served in uniform at sea, and ashore, with both the Royal Navy and the US Navy. He is a fifty-year veteran of the Five Eyes intelligence community. In 2017, he was the Keynote Speaker on board H.M.S. Victory in Portsmouth, England, to commemorate the 100th anniversary of the famous Zimmermann Telegram intelligence coup by 'Blinker Hall' and his Room 40 team in British Naval Intelligence.

The guest of honour was Her Royal Highness Princess Anne, with the Five Eyes community: past and present, represented from the United States, the United Kingdom, Canada, Australia, and New Zealand. Anthony was trained and mentored in the late 1960s by the very best of the World War II intelligence community, including Sir Harry Hinsley, the famous Bletchley Park codebreaker, official historian of British intelligence in the World War II, Master of St. John's College, Cambridge, and Vice Chancellor of Cambridge University.
Sir Harry Hinsley introduced Anthony to the Enigma data before it became public knowledge. He received his PhD in War Studies from King's College, University of London, in 1972. He holds Bachelor's and Master's Degrees from

the University of Durham, and a Master's degree from the London School of Economics. He was trained at Britannia Royal Naval College, Dartmouth, and received his advanced training at the School of Maritime Operations. He was called to the Bar by Lincoln's Inn in November 1980.

Anthony has four children and eight grandchildren and lives on his farm in Virginia. He is a Member of the Naval Order of the United States and was appointed an Honorary Crew Member of the USS Liberty by the USS Liberty Veterans Association. USS Liberty is the most highly decorated warship in the history of the US Navy for a single action, attacked by Israeli air and surface forces on 8 August 1967 in the eastern Mediterranean.

Anthony is the third chairman of the USS Liberty Alliance, succeeding the late Admiral Thomas Moorer, former chairman of the US Joint Chiefs of Staff and Chief of Naval Operations, and the late Rear-Admiral Clarence 'Mark' Hill, former distinguished US naval aviator and battle group commander. He is a retired US National Ski patroller and instructor, and a life member and former president of The Plains, Virginia, Volunteer Fire & Rescue Company. Wells is an FAA Commercial pilot with single and multi-engine, land and sea, instrument, and flight instructor Ratings.

Anthony was the technical director of Fleet Battle Experiments ALPHA and BRAVO in the Third Fleet, United States Pacific Fleet. He was the chief executive officer of TKC International LLC, a specialist company supporting the US Intelligence Community and Department of Defence, for twenty-five years. He held top secret SCI and special access clearances.

This book is dedicated to the men and women who have served, and serve today, in British Naval Intelligence. We owe them a lasting debt.

Anthony Wells

FROM BLINKER HALL TO ROOM 39: BRITISH NAVAL INTELLIGENCE 1880-1945

AUSTIN MACAULEY PUBLISHERS
LONDON • CAMBRIDGE • NEW YORK • SHARJAH

Copyright © Anthony Wells 2025

The right of Anthony Wells to be identified as author of this work has been asserted by the author in accordance with sections 77 and 78 of the Copyright, Designs and Patents Act 1988.

All rights reserved. No part of this publication may be reproduced, stored in a retrieval system, or transmitted in any form or by any means, electronic, mechanical, photocopying, recording, or otherwise, without the prior permission of the publishers.

Any person who commits any unauthorised act in relation to this publication may be liable to criminal prosecution and civil claims for damages.

The story, experiences, and words are the author's alone.

A CIP catalogue record for this title is available from the British Library.

ISBN 9781035851171 (Paperback)
ISBN 9781035851188 (Hardback)
ISBN 9781035851195 (ePub e-book)

www.austinmacauley.com

First Published 2025
Austin Macauley Publishers Ltd®
1 Canada Square
Canary Wharf
London
E14 5AA

Table of Contents

Preface   13

Abbreviations   14

Introduction   15

   The Impact of W/T and Intelligence on Naval Operations and Command   17

Chapter One   23

   The Need for a Naval Intelligence Organisation   23

   The Origins of the N.I.D.   26

   The Development of Radio Intelligence and its Significance for N.I.D. and Naval Operations   34

   Strategic Planning in Britain in the Early Twentieth Century   35

   The British Security Services and the N.I.D.   36

   The Flexibility of N.I.D. Organisation   38

   The Growth of 'Operational' Intelligence and the Jutland Experience   40

   Post-Jutland Intelligence Reforms   46

   Inter-War N.I.D. Organisation and Developments   47

   The Joint Intelligence Committee   51

   The Origins of Integration—Supreme Headquarters Intelligence Staff.   53

   Comparisons with American and German Intelligence   57

Chapter Two   62

   A Critical Appraisal of the Role of Selected Personalities Who Worked in Naval Intelligence   62

The D.N.I. in Wartime and His Role	62
The Recruitment of Civilians to the N.I.D.	63
Hall's Review of Main Intelligence Problem in 1914 and How He Solved It	66
Hall's Involvement with British Foreign Policy	67
Godfrey's Reorganisation of N.I.D. and Some of His Staff	75
Godfrey and the J.I.C.	78
Hall and Godfrey—Comparisons and Contrasts	81
Chapter Three	**86**
Naval Intelligence and Maritime Strategy	86
Naval Intelligence in the Nuclear Age	88
Intelligence and Gaining the Initiative	89
The Deployment of Forces	91
Locating and Identifying Forces	94
Air Reconnaissance	96
Intelligence and German Naval Strategy in World War I	101
Intelligence and the Unpredictable	104
The Dardanelles	105
The Norwegian Campaign	108
Intelligence and Tactics, and Tactical Situations	109
Politics and Strategy	114
The Degree of Flexibility of Intelligence and Naval Policy	116
Chapter Four: A Survey and Critical Analysis of the Relationship between Selected Naval Operations During the Period and Intelligence.	**121**
The Beginnings of Operational Intelligence in World War I	121
Radio Intelligence in World War I	123

The Battles of Coronel and the Falkland Islands	127
Zeebrugge; the Baltic (1919)	128
The Intelligence Position 1939-1940	130
Faulty Intelligence	132
Successful Intelligence	134
The Role of Technical Intelligence	135
The Invasion Threat, 1940	137
The Norwegian Campaign	138
Other Naval Operations and Intelligence in World War II	139
The German Operational Naval Intelligence Position 1943-1944	141
Chapter Five: The Methodology and Techniques of Naval Intelligence	**143**
Basic Method and Sources	143
Technological and World Political Changes	144
Intelligence in Peace and War	145
Radio Intelligence and Cryptanalysis	146
The Foreign Office and Naval Attaches	151
Capturing and Salvaging Enemy Ships	157
Prisoners of War, Deserters, Refugees, Resistance Groups, Friendly or Neutral Observers	158
Clandestine Intelligence	160
Aerial Reconnaissance and Aerial Photography	161
Commanding Officers' Reports and De-briefing	162
The Press and Radio	163
Topographical Intelligence and the I.S.T.D.	164
The Inter-War N.I.D. and Peacetime Intelligence	165
Pre-1914 N.I.D. Work	169

Chapter Six: Aspects of Naval Intelligence and Political Decision-Making — 175

    The British System of Politico-Military Decision-Making and its Relationship with Naval Intelligence — 175

    The Politico-Military Environment Within Which N.I.D. Operated — 182

    The Varying Emphasis Placed on N.I.D.'s Work Throughout the Period — 183

    Some Political Ramifications and Aspects of the Role and Work of Naval Intelligence — 191

    Naval Intelligence and Politics in the Inter-War Period — 200

Chapter Seven: Naval Intelligence and Specific Political Decisions — 205

    Foreign Policy, Strategy and Naval Intelligence Pre-1914 — 205

    Foreign Policy, Strategy and Naval Intelligence 1914-1939 — 209

    Politics, the War and Naval Intelligence 1939-1945 — 224

    The Naval Intelligence Officer and Politics — 238

Chapter Eight: British Naval Intelligence—A Perspective — 242

    Conditions for the Survival and Effectiveness of a Naval Intelligence Organisation — 242

    Naval Intelligence Personnel — 245

    The Political Appreciation of Naval Intelligence — 248

    Responsibility to the Public — 248

    Naval Intelligence in the Nuclear Age — 249

APPENDIX A: An Example of Hard Intelligence Data — 251

APPENDIX B: Directors of Naval Intelligence 1882-1945 — 252

APPENDIX C: N.I.D. Staff—1942 — 257

    Heads of Departments and Sections — 257

Sources — 259

Anthony Wells' Publications — 275

Literary Awards:	275
Articles	276
Classified Titles and Publications	282

Preface

This book examines, by reference to the political, institutional, organisational, personnel, operational, methodological and technical aspects of naval intelligence work, the developmental aspects of its history from 1880 to 1945. By analysing specific naval operations and discussing the strategic and tactical ramifications of intelligence, it seeks to throw light on the impact of intelligence on naval warfare in this period. In so doing, it reveals the place of intelligence in the general naval history of the period. It is not a definitive history, but rather a discursive analysis of those aspects considered the most important.

In the pre-1914 era, the N.I.D. was the heart of the emergent Naval Staff, involved in strategic planning at the highest level. World War I brought the need for an operational intelligence organisation, with the priority of locating, identifying, and deducing the intentions of major German units. Experience in war revealed the necessity for a clear definition of the relationship between the Operations Division and the N.I.D. The use of radio intelligence and cryptanalysis gave N.I.D. great operational successes and Admiral Hall the opportunity to involve N.I.D. in political issues.

The latter led to the review of N.I.D.'s role post 1918 and, in part, its run-down. The inter-war period witnessed N.I.D.'s decline as the most dynamic and influential Naval Staff department. Until the foundation of O.I.C. and the coming of war, N.I.D. was a backwater. World War II witnessed a revitalisation, a more structured and tightly controlled N.I.D., and the D.N.I. as an important echelon of the C.O.S. and J.I.C. organisations. N.I.D. regained its previous supremacy and was instrumental in the process towards intelligence integration at the end of World War II. It scored great operational successes.

The function of intelligence is demonstrated as being paramount in the naval organisation and critical to the interests of the State. Its maintenance was contingent upon variables which, throughout this period, were neither constant nor always recognised.

Abbreviations

D.N.I.	Director of Naval Intelligence
D.D.N.I.	Deputy Director of Naval Intelligence
N.I.D.	Naval Intelligence Department
F.I.C.	Foreign Intelligence Committee
Adm.	Admiralty
C.I.D.	Committee of Imperial Defence
J.I.C.	Joint Intelligence Committee
J.I.S.	Joint Intelligence Staff
J.P.C.	Joint Planning Committee
O.I.C.	Operational Intelligence Centre
C.O.S.	Chiefs of Staff
M.I.D.	Military Intelligence Department
S.O.E.	Special Operations Executive
P.W.E.	Political Warfare Executive
M.E.W.	Ministry of Economic Warfare
S.I.S.	Secret Intelligence Service
F.O.E.S.	Future Operations Enemy Section
I.S.T.D.	Inter-Service Topographical Department
U.S.N.	United States Navy
O.N.I.	Office of Naval Intelligence
O.S.S.	Office of Strategic Services

Introduction

During the last quarter of the nineteenth century, the Admiralty became acutely aware of the need for an organisation to collect, analyse, interpret, and distribute to the appropriate authorities data concerning potential enemies. This was part of the policy to systematise British Naval policy. The nature of the organisation which was initially created, in all its various facets, not least of all its role and importance in naval policy-making and action, has changed dramatically.

The development of that organisation reflects the increasing value attached to intelligence in determining the outcome of war at sea. However, it was by no means an organically evolving institution, expanding in proportion to any definable amount of intelligence required at any given time, or even equipping itself with techniques to keep pace with technological developments. It was a far more fortuitous interaction of events that has led to the creation of the defence intelligence organisation that the United Kingdom possesses today.

In tracing the growth of the intelligence organisation within the naval institution one sees emerging a doctrine of intelligence, albeit it's an unprecise and fluctuating one, but one which, by 1945, was firmly entrenched as a doctrine[1] and an organisation, naval intelligence had to fight for its place within the hierarchy of organisations that compose the Royal Navy, penetrating the infrastructure of a highly complex and sophisticated institution not in any logical way, but sometimes more by chance; at worst in a willy-nilly attempt to mould the course of action, at best in a forthright and prodigious drive to dispel the fogs of war.

The degree of success, measured both in terms of quality of intelligence and the impact it was to have, and the status intelligence acquired in the process, stemmed mainly from the guiding personalities of the time. It might be possible

---

[1] By intelligence doctrine is meant the well-tried rules, principles and procedures that make up the intelligence process.

to trace the ups and downs of naval intelligence in the twentieth century in graphical form, with the Directors of Naval Intelligence on one axis and their successes on the other.

But this would preclude a more fundamental appraisal of the various factors that account for its charismatic development, and would fail, for instance, to explain the inner subtleties behind the great successes of Admiral Hall's[2] pragmatic intelligence officers during the Great War, or the apparent failure of the intelligence machinery in the 1930s and its subsequent revival and conquests during World War II. Above all else such an approach would fail to trace the identification of the more elusive elements of intelligence which came to form a body of doctrine by 1945.

The principles of intelligence and the organisation which emerged were the result of an accumulation of vast experiences, and the often-costly interaction of individuals and groups. The monument for those who worked in naval intelligence from its early beginnings until 1945 is the lasting place that it has now gained for itself within the defence structure.

That was not achieved much earlier and is explained chiefly by the absence within naval intelligence of a doctrine, which in part could only be built up after years of experience, but which also could only be gained after the need to develop intelligence concepts, skills and organisation had been recognised. The problems were not apparent, and the immediate benefits not obvious.

There was no startlingly news about collecting information about actual or possible enemies. Nelson used intelligence information during the Trafalgar campaign. He and his great eighteenth century predecessors realised the need for continuous and timely data concerning the activities and possible intentions of the enemy, and the strength and capabilities of his forces.

---

[2] <u>Hall, Admiral Sir William Reginald</u>: 1870-1943; son of the first D.N.I., William Henry Hall; entered R.N. 1884; Commander 1901; Captain 1905; naval assistant to the Controller of the Navy, 1911-1913; Captain H.M.S. Queen Mary 1913; B. of Heligoland Bight, 28 August 1914; <u>D.N.I. 1914-1918</u>; CB 1915; KCMG 1918; promoted Rear-Admiral 1917; Vice-Admiral 1922; Admiral 1926; Hon. DCL Oxon. 1919, Hon. L.L.D. Cantab. 1920; MP (Con) West Derby Division of Liverpool 1919; principal agent of the Conservative Party, 1923; MP (Con) Eastbourne, 1925. Retired from politics, 1929. A drawing by Francis Dodd, Imperial War Museum.

The Impact of W/T and Intelligence on Naval Operations and Command

However, in the pre-wireless era, the commander at sea could only acquire such information when he put into port or a fast frigate located him. Similarly, naval authorities ashore had no knowledge of operational conditions because of communications. Even in the immediate operational environment, senior officers afloat were equally handicapped, since they were unable to exercise tactical control outside the limits of visibility.

With the advent of wireless telegraphy, and the later explosion of communication technology, the significance and role of intelligence changed accordingly.[3] But, it was not a smooth transition. In theory, the situation had changed overnight. The Admiralty, with intelligence and communication facilities, could obtain a detailed picture from a global to local and tactical levels, far more so than the commander on the spot, whether he was in a single ship or submarine, or as the leader of a large task force or group.

In practice, it did not work this way immediately. It was a slow process whereby it became recognised that commanders at sea should be supplied with as much intelligence as practicable and given general directives, but left with the individual right, and responsibility, to make the necessary tactical decisions in the light of their knowledge and interpretation of the situation. By 1939, this issue had been virtually resolved by the Admiralty.

Admiral J. H. Godfrey, Director of Naval Intelligence, 1939-1943, says this on the problem: "The British Naval tradition during the World War II was to issue intelligence 'raw', to leave commanders to make what use of it they could, and not to dress it up and make it look nice. The N.I.D. (Naval Intelligence Department) developed a method of distinguishing in the out-message between information, inference and comment which might well be perpetuated."[4]

The command situation was changed in order to meet the new requirements. Commanders-in-chief were now able to plan operations and dispose forces from ashore, and delegate the tactical handling of ships to force commanders. In the inter-war period, it became obvious that they had to be ashore, since there was a

---

[3] In July 1908, the Director of Naval Intelligence, Admiral Slade, presented a detailed and lucid paper to the First Lord and First Sea Lord on the effects of W/T on naval strategy and intelligence organisation. Slade MSS, Reel 3, National Maritime Museum.

[4] The Naval Memoirs of Admiral J. H. Godfrey—unpublished, typescript, Vol. V. Part I. p. 82-83, National Maritime Museum, Greenwich.

growing need for coordination, both on a purely naval and tri-service basis. Yet, the harmony between operational headquarters ashore and the sea-going command depended heavily on the viability of communications themselves, in terms of their tactical reliability, but also their vulnerability, an area now part of electronic warfare.

There were many crucial times during World War II when the maintenance of radio silence was essential, such as the operation against the Bismarck. Perhaps more important still the new structure of organising naval operations depended on the quality of information the Admiralty had at its disposal, which gave it the critical advantage over the man-on-the-spot. Instant communication from Whitehall with the front-line ship was fine, provided it was equalled by a system, and methods, for collating intelligence information, making sound decisions on the basis of this and issuing the correct orders.

Behind this then lay a fundamental problem and, as will be seen, a dilemma at times, over the whole system of naval command and control. Admiral Slade had a clear view of the situation: "…to sum up the whole case in a few words, the Admiralty from the far wider view of the operations that they possess, than that which is possible for the Admiral to obtain, can lead him up to a situation where he can strike, and is then given a free hand to do the best he can."[5]

Only in the light of experience has a coherent body of doctrine emerged, by which the naval institution can attempt to optimise its resources. The essential aims of British maritime strategy have not changed in essence since Mahan rationalised them, and nor have the inherent factors of sea warfare, not least of all the flexibility and mobility qualities of maritime forces, and also the very nature of the sea environment. The need to plan naval strategy, on global and local scales, to fulfil these aims, depends greatly on intelligence information.

In the contemporary context, the United Kingdom is concerned with the totality of factors that constitute a nation's make-up, both friendly and also a potential foe, that may explain to the defence planners and executives the way

---

[5] Slade MSS, Reel 3, National Maritime Museum, Greenwich. In World War II, Admiral Godfrey was wary of the Admiralty-based senior officer who used intelligence data and W/T, and his rank, to deprive the commander at sea of his right to make on-the-spot tactical decisions. He writes in his memoirs, "Wireless telegraphy allied to accurate intelligence at the centre play into the hands of anyone who by nature is a remote controller." Godfrey MSS, Vol. V. Part 2. p. 322-323, National Maritime Museum, Greenwich.

they should review their role vis-à-vis other nations. It is no longer regarded as satisfactory to know mere details such as paper strengths, morale, state of training, the reliability of equipment, weaponry, speeds, and endurances, or other traditional information such as the location of the enemy's vital interests and his main transport routes.

It is now necessary to go to a stage beyond this which encompasses the more subtle factors of the economic, social, geographical and political variables that may relate to an enemy at sea, and furthermore an appreciation of his history, habits, and doctrine that help towards an understanding of his naval organisation and role, and the place of this within the wider political context, as well as the predictability of the nature of a possible war at sea and the extent to which one can expect to break the enemy's will to resist, or in certain circumstances his reactions to the real threat of nuclear escalation.

The raison d'etre of the Royal Navy, therefore, rests largely on the accuracy of predictions. To prevent such predictions coming true or to meet them in the likelihood of their occurrence, at whatever level, must be intimately dependent on a continuous process of intelligence work, in peace and war. Intelligence can never be an infallible guide. At no time in the past has the course of a war been accurately predicted. Some factors and variables remain too complex and their inter-relationship too subtle to gauge.

No computer, using intelligence information, could have accurately weighed the effect of an intangible such as the enemy's offensive spirit in naval warfare during this period, although such intelligence appreciations were obtained and proved very valuable.

Intelligence organisations today aim to provide the best possible information available to those who make policy. A crucial part of intelligence must involve interpretation, requiring as it does special types of perception, at all levels. At one level, a faculty for imaginative insight into the decision-making processes of other societies and cultures, and a facility for surveying the complex of international affairs might be needed, and at another a calculated assessment of a unit commander's next move could be the need.

It follows, therefore, that if the intelligence officer is to select that which is significant for study and comment he must be constantly aware of policy interests and concerns. Without this awareness, there will always be a danger that the spectacular and the trivial will be presented as the important and significant. Good intelligence work will be a constant dialogue between the two authorities. This state of affairs was not quickly reached within the naval intelligence organisation.

Without good intelligence planning becomes surmise, and the commander is operating in a world limited by his own immediate facilities. In the early days of Wald War I, Jellicoe[6] had to keep strong forces at sea to meet the threat of any German forces that might be sent out to attack the east coast of England and North Sea trade routes. His general policy was based on very sound factors, but his immediate short-term planning and tactical dispositions was limited by lack of intelligence, resulting in wastefulness of effort and resources.[7]

Naval intelligence grew out of its initial limitations and became allied to the whole complex of major political decision-making in the sphere of foreign and defence policy, and their relationship with economic policy and the contingent issues of party rivalries and electioneering. The serious study of military intelligence is an essential part of the wider areas of politics, government and international affairs.

It has led one distinguished writer on intelligence matters to state: "…public discussion of intelligence must be inhibited by the inevitable content of the topic. However, it is undesirable and unhealthy that there should be no public debate or consideration of a subject that is crucial importance in national and international decision-making, and to which, after all, public funds are devoted."[8] In a democratic society, government has the responsibility to communicate, albeit perhaps in very general but nonetheless accurate terms, the

---

[6] Jellicoe, John Rushworth, First Earl Jellicoe, Admiral of the Fleet: 1859-1935; entered R.N. 1872; Captain 1897; Naval assistant to the Controller of the Navy, 1902; Director of naval ordnance, 1905; Rear-Admiral 1907; Controller and Third Sea Lord 1908; Vice-Admiral, commander Atlantic Fleet (flagship H.M.S. Prince of Wales) 1910; Second Sea Lord 1912; Admiral, C.-in-C. Grand Fleet, 1915; First Sea Lord 1916; dismissed by Geddes, Christmas Eve, 1917; Viscount Jellicoe 1918; Admiral of the Fleet 1919.

[7] Corbett J. S.: History of the Great War based on official documents: Naval Operations. Vol. I.

[8] Major-General Sir Kenneth Strong: Intelligence at the Top. Strong, Major-General Sir Kenneth William Dobson: b. 1900; 2Lt. lbt. Royal Scots Fusiliers 1920; military career 1920-1943—command of 4/5 bts. Royal Scots Fusiliers, Staff College, Camberley; military attaché Berlin; Feb. 1943-July 1945 head of General Eisenhower's Intelligence Staff; Director-General of Political Intelligence, F.O. 1945-1957; first Director of Joint Intelligence Bureau, MOD 1948-1964; Director-General of Intelligence, MOD 1964-1966.

reasons for its defence policy.

In the United Kingdom, it is assumed that people have a natural right to be told why arms are being purchased and the possible uses to which they might be put. It is an unchallengeable fact that there are too many public controls to prevent British arms being used for purposes other than those for which they were procured, without public consent by the rightful authorities. The reasons for particular policies are public concerns.

However, it will be seen that the detailed evidence for making long and short-range predictions, based on intelligence data is not necessarily communicated to the public, both because it may not be in the immediate public interest to do so for security reasons, but also because certain types of major political decisions involving foreign and defence policies do not require public resources to the minutiae of evidence to justify their having been made.

Thomas Hobbes wrote in *Leviathan*: "Fourthly, in Deliberations that ought to be kept secret (whereof there may be many occasions in Publique Businesse) the Counsels of many, and especially in Assemblies, are dangerous. And therefore, great assemblies are necessitated to commit such affairs to lesser numbers, and of such persons are most used, and in whose fidelity, they have most confidence."[9] One can apply Hobbes' dictum to the relationship of the Naval Intelligence Department with the decision-making authorities within the Admiralty, and the present-day Admiralty Board's relationship with the Defence Council.

That all this work can be challenged, if need be, within the forum of the House of Commons, completes the modern context of Hobbes' dictum. Although Machiavelli would probably have disagreed with the relationship the Naval Intelligence Department acquired (through its own internal relationship within the naval hierarchy, and hence external relationship within the defence structure) with the state, he would, speculatively speaking, perhaps have approved of the growth of intelligence.

Central to Machiavelli's political philosophy was his idea that a "prince ought to have no other aim or thought, nor select anything else for his study than war and its rules and disciplines; for this is the sole art that belongs to him who rules."[10] British Naval intelligence illustrates the growth of an organisation, and

---

[9] Thomas Hobbes: *Leviathan*, Chapter twenty-five.

[10] Machiavelli: *The Prince*, Chapter fourteen.

the development of principles and methods in order to perfect Machiavelli's art of war.

Chapter One

The Development of British Naval Intelligence as an institution, and an analysis of its organisation.

The Need for a Naval Intelligence Organisation

During the 1890s, the transformation of the Royal Navy began, from a Navy of small battleships and cruisers, and ships with auxiliary sail power, to a great fleet of nearly forty Dreadnought battleships and battlecruisers, numerous fast cruiser squadrons, one hundred and fifty destroyers, and a large submarine flotilla. The turning-point came in 1889 with the passing of the Naval Defence Act. By 1901, the effective range of the broadside was between two and three thousand yards, and the effective range of torpedoes was increased from two thousand to ten thousand yards between 1901 and 1914.

Certainly, technological change had had a major effect upon war at sea in the past. The use of the gun, and the broadside, had changed the pattern of sea warfare in the sixteenth century. However, the last quarter of the nineteenth century witnessed an unprecedented advance in naval construction and weaponry, and the pace of change that followed took the nineteenth century Navy by surprise.

In the wake of this advance arose needs to modify the administration, organisation, and training of the Navy, and to revise naval tactics and the finer practices of naval warfare. Controlling all of these factors, in theory if not always in reality, was Britain's role and commitments in the world, and how a technically changing Navy could fulfil its traditional global aims in the face of challenges to British supremacy from the east and west. The Royal Navy's era of unchallenged dominance in the nineteenth century was both a product and a cause of British economic and territorial supremacy.

From without came signs of opposition and from within, the ideological basis of nineteenth century British industrial society was changing, revealed in a multi-variety of political, economic, and social innovations. The Royal Navy was in the midst of dynamic change, and for a while it remained static. Central to this problem were the basic aims of British maritime strategy. Were they to change too? How were they to be achieved in a changing world situation?

In a changing world, technologically and politically, there was a growing need to establish within the Navy an organisation which could collect a stock of basic factual data, kept well up to date, with particular emphasis on current developments which might impinge on the naval and national interests, thereby enabling itself to make informed forecasts of the shape of things to come, the most important part of the intelligence process.

Before the international situation deteriorated and the pre-1914 arms race began, the rate of technological change and the need for greater intelligence of the technical accomplishments of foreign powers was incentive enough to create the Naval Intelligence Department.

The birth and growth of the naval intelligence institution stems then from an immediately recognisable need. However, it does not reflect any major change of role in the Royal Navy. Its emergence does exemplify the rapidly changing circumstances of Britain and her defence responsibilities. It is, in part, a question of levels. There are certain inalienable factors, self-evident, regarding Britain's defence and the role of her Navy within this, such as the economic factors regarding Britain and possible enemies.

In 1914, for example, and indeed in 1939 too, it was common knowledge that Britain could not live, let alone wage war, for more than four or five weeks after her sea lines of communication to the outer world were severed. This statement could be scaled down until one was left with the problem of predicting the smallest movements of enemy units at sea; going up the scale again, to the top, one could say, using the previous example, that the whole issue of the maritime war in 1914 thus depended on the battle-worthiness of the Grand Fleet, whose margin of superiority over its opponents was very slight, and for periods vanished when several ships were being docked at the same time.

Within the vast complex of levels, naval intelligence had to find its level of usefulness. For an embryonic institution, this had all the attendant dangers of penetrating a traditional and highly entrenched institution such as the Royal Navy. It could have no doctrine, since this depended largely on experience and circumstances. The circumstances of 1805 were widely different from those of the Dreadnought era. There were no significant parallels in history to be drawn on, and no one was able to produce a model for an intelligence organisation, based on a logic drawn from existing naval circumstances and experiences, or write a prognosis of future requirements.

The newly created Naval Intelligence Department not only sought concrete objectives, and means to achieve them, but also relationships with other departments. The logic of any modern institution demands that it has aims or objectives and a structure or organisation to meet these. This, therefore, implies clearly defined responsibilities and authority, supported by terms of reference. The relationship of such a body with other departments or units will be clear, boundaries of interest will be precise, and the role of each part in achieving the objectives of the whole organisation will be known to all.

Communications will be good. These elements were, in one sense at least, alien to the Navy of the late nineteenth century, until Fisher took it by storm.[11] These ideas were not verbalised, although the Navy in practice did follow some of these precepts, and highly successfully. To establish a viable position within the hierarchy of naval departments and to develop a working relationship and rapport with them was difficult in the extreme. This will become apparent when the relationship with the Operations Division of the Admiralty and the Naval Intelligence Department is examined.

Central to this problem was the ever-present and unquantifiable factor of personalities, and their interaction, a factor that at times was paramount. The penetration of a structure such as the nineteenth century Royal Navy by a new organisation could, and did on many occasions, lead to highly charged personal relations.

The concepts and practical details of war at sea were still firmly stated. The scope for diverging from these was indeed limited, often at the peril of one's career. Nelson had thrown the Fighting Instructions to the wind. Success was his justification. With the technological revolution that was overtaking the Royal Navy, there was an ever-growing need to re-think and establish new principles of war at sea to meet all the contingencies of a future war, and also for exercise

---

[11] Fisher, John, First Baron, Admiral of the Fleet: 1841-1920; entered R.N. 1854; Captain 1874; Rear-Admiral 1890; Third Sea Lord and Controller 1892-189; C.-in-C. North America 1897; C.-in-C. Mediterranean 1899; Second Sea Lord 1902; First Sea Lord 1904-1910; 1914-1915.

purposes. The need to establish the basis upon which such principles might be built was not self-evident.

As a result of these factors, the early years of the Naval Intelligence Department were stamped by an adherence to what are regarded today as limited and specialised areas of naval intelligence work. It also tended to become too unnecessarily involved with the work of the British counter-espionage service and the Special Branch, and at times became involved in activities which were well outside of its naval scope. On an inter-service-level, the Naval Intelligence Department was linked with its Army counterpart through the Committee of Imperial Defence.

The Origins of the N.I.D.

The British government and Sea Lords became acutely aware of the need for a body of uniformed experts providing intelligence after the Balkan crisis of 1878. War with Russia had been narrowly averted, and, despite threats from the Russians to occupy Constantinople, the Mediterranean Fleet had occupied the Straits. Naval attaches, especially in Paris and Rome, were pressing too for a central authority to control and decide policy for sources providing intelligence information. What they argued, and what the Balkan crisis had revealed, was the need for a coordination of intelligence information (as then understood), with naval planning in the widest context.

After preparatory committee work from May 1879 onwards by two successive First Lords, W. H. Smith and Lord Northbrook, the Board of Admiralty created the Foreign Intelligence Committee in December 1882, later to become the Naval Intelligence Department, (the N.I.D.).[12] The F.I.C.'s first Director was Captain William Henry Hall, the father of Admiral Reginald Hall, the Director of Naval Intelligence during World War I. The Naval Intelligence Department was officially created in January 1887.

The next Director after Hall, Admiral Bridge, had a special responsibility for collecting data on the movement of merchant and war ships and preparing plans for the protection of trade in the event of war.

---

[12] Details of the reorganisation and work of the Foreign Intelligence Committee and the creation and early work of the Naval Intelligence Department are to be found in: Adm. 5, 6074, 1462, and Adm. 116, 3106, and Adm. 1, 6505, 6634, 6731, 6772, 6818B, 6868 A/B, 6922, 8623/64. See especially Adm. 1/7166B—Instructions for the Director of Naval Intelligence, 24 January 1887.

The main catalyst in the creation of the Foreign Intelligence Committee (F.I.C.) and then the Naval Intelligence Department (N.I.D.) was the need for a systematic study to be made of the needs for the defence of trade. Before the F.I.C., there were no war plans as such for the defence of trade. To facilitate this, a body of knowledge would be required to analyse what British trade comprised (how much, where, along which routes, when, what sort of ships and cargoes), what would be needed to defend it, and, equally important, how, and related to these—who would pose threats, and what would be the nature of their threats.

We now know how in the latter part of the nineteenth century, the Admiralty began to shift its emphasis from the French and Russian torpedo boat and battleship threats to the menace of German naval expansion. It was around the threat to trade that discussion, planning, naval construction, and exercises gathered.

Early pressure had come from J. C. R. Colomb.[13] The work of Professor B. McL. Ranft[14] has shown how Colomb's attacks in Parliament on the Admiralty's lack of policy-making, which he attributed to inadequate intelligence, led to the increase of the government vote for naval intelligence from the £500 allocated in 1884 to between £4000-£5000 per annum and a staff of ten able young naval officers. This occurred during the debate on the naval estimates February-March 1887. As late as February, 1902, Colomb was still not convinced that the intelligence department had enough detailed information of the positions of merchant ships.[15]

Professor Ranft has also shown how the early F.I.C. produced papers on what would be required of the Navy in a French war and what strength it would need, and outlines of possible naval operations against Russia.[16] He concludes: "Hall's insistence on the necessity for constant intelligence about the movements of Russian cruisers in peacetime and for Commanders-in-Chief to have detailed

---

[13] See his article: Naval Intelligence and the Protection of Shipping in war. R.U.S.I. Journal. XXV. 1882. p. 553-590. <u>Colomb, Sir J. C. R.</u>: Captain, RM (9rtd.) 1869; MP Tower Hamlets (Con) 1886-1892; MP Great Yarmouth 1895-1906.

[14] See his unpublished Oxford D. Phil. Thesis: The Naval Defence of British Sea-Borne Trade, 1860-1905. 1967. p. 116-117.

[15] See his unpublished Oxford D. Phil. Thesis: The Naval Defence of British Sea-Borne Trade, 1860 1905. 1967. p. 141.

[16] Ibid. p. 184-185.

plans ready for protecting trade at the outset of war were indications of the increasing business-like working of the Admiralty at the time."[17]

Admiral Bridge[18] inherited a much healthier and indeed more powerful position from his predecessor, mainly as a result of the problems which arose during Hall's period of office and their solution. In 1884, Lord Charles Beresford,[19] a junior Lord of the Admiralty, had bitterly attacked the Foreign Intelligence Committee, demanding in the process the creation of a Naval Staff to prepare contingency plans for all war eventualities. This furore had been mainly exacerbated by the Penjeh crisis on the Afghan border, as a result of which the Fleet had shadowed the Russians in the Pacific.

Hall suffered a sardonic attack from the editor of the Pall Mall Gazette on 13 October 1886, who described the Captain as a "mere compiler of information, a contemporary gazetteer in breeches". Despite the vitriolic comments from the press and Beresford's personal attacks, constructive reform did emerge with the formation of the Naval Intelligence Department (N.I.D.), which was given very wide-ranging responsibilities.

Along with Colomb, Lord Charles Beresford had been one of the prime movers in pressing for a full N.I.D. to develop from the F.I.C., again with the main idea of gathering data to help prepare detailed war plans, especially for defending trade. His forceful contribution to the creation of the N.I.D. cannot be overstressed.

With the development of the N.I.D., there originated the idea of a Naval Staff, and in this sense the growth of an Admiralty-based Naval Staff is inseparable from the concepts and growth of a Naval Intelligence Department. Donald MacLachlan has written: "The Director of Naval Intelligence was the first, and

---

[17] Ibid. p. 187.

[18] Bridge, Admiral Sir Cyprian: 1839-1924; entered R.N. 1853; Captain 1877; D.N.I. 1889-1894; C.-in-C. Australia 1894-1898, China 1901-1904. Wrote two major books— The Art of Naval Warfare (London 1907), and Sea Power and Other Studies (London 1910).

[19] Beresford, Lord Charles, Admiral: 1846-1919; entered R.N. 1859; MP (Con.) Waterford 1874-1880; Captain 1882; MP East Marylebone 1885-1889; Junior Naval Lord 1886-1888; after resignation in January 1886, he became the most outspoken critic of naval policy; resigned seat in 1889 on return to active service; Rear-Admiral 1897; MP York 1897-1900; second in command Mediterranean 1900-1902; MP Woolwich 1902-1905; C.-in-C. Mediterranean 1905-1907; Channel Fleet 1907-1909 until ordered to haul down his flag after dispute with Fisher; MP Portsmouth 1910-1916.

was to remain thereafter the senior member of the Naval Staff directly responsible to the First Sea Lord. That fact probably gave him greater prestige with most naval officers than the activity of which he was in charge."[20]

The instructions given to Captain Hall read as follows: "to collect, classify and record, with a complex index, all information which bears a naval character, or which may be of value during naval operations, to keep up our knowledge of progress made by foreign countries in naval matters, and to preserve the information in a form readily available for reference." This development was very much against the later ideas and reforms of Fisher, who was totally against the idea of forming a Naval Staff.

He thought it would convert "splendid sea officers into very indifferent clerks." As an integral part of an embryonic Naval Staff, the early N.I.D. suffered from the logical problem that there were no well-established naval staff departments with which it could liaise. Hall found himself facing the dilemma of having no planning division with which to coordinate his intelligence work. As a result, N.I.D. tended to trespass into this area at the expense of its own intelligence efforts.

The extensive development of N.I.D.'s pre-1914 Naval Staff work will be reviewed in later chapters. A brief glimpse now will reveal the extent of its activities, and the degree of influence it exerted.

Professor Ranft's thesis, in analysing the strategic and tactical factors involved in the protection of trade, 1860-1905, and the body of thought relating to them, has shown how involved the N.I.D. was in the great controversy, and dilemma, over the relative effectiveness of convoy, as opposed to protecting the 'sea-lanes' and meeting points of trade routes, blockade, and seeking out and destroying the enemy's main units wherever he might be in a pitched battle. Central to this was the divergence of opinion over what constituted 'offensive' and 'defensive' naval warfare. Many thought convoy to be too defensive.

In a fully documented account, Ranft has examined in detail the political ramifications of these divergent policies, such as the significance attached to a Russian seizure of Constantinople, the place of Egypt and Alexandria in British Mediterranean strategy, and the strategic disposition of naval forces on the China and Australia station. On the latter issue, and specifically related to an N.I.D. memo of 1 May 1900, Ranft makes the very significant comment: "This is yet

---

[20] Donald MacLachlan: Room 39. p. 373. Before the modern idea of a Naval Staff was developed, the First Sea Lord considered himself to be the Naval Staff.

another example of correct strategic thinking in placing the protection of trade as the first priority which at the same time failed to face up to the practical difficulties of bringing an enemy to action and protecting merchant ships in the enormous expanses of the Eastern seas."[21]

He traces this theme through his thesis, and concludes: "The British failure to anticipate Germany's use of the submarine against sea-borne trade is more understandable. The suitability of the submarine for such warfare was unknown to the German themselves in 1914 and the diplomatic disadvantages of using it ruthlessly long delayed its full potential being realised. The failure to understand that the convoy would provide the only effective defence was due not to any exceptional stupidity on the part of those in control of the Admiralty but to the fact that their thinking on the subject was necessarily heavily conditioned by the complex and confused naval and commercial thinking about the defence of sea-borne trade which they inherited…"[22]

It is chastening to recollect that by the spring of 1917, merchant shipping losses were disastrous. Lloyd George wanted convoy introduced against the advice of the Admirals. On 26 April 1917, he ordered the Admiralty Board to institute convoys. The first convoy sailed on 10 May 1917. A. J. P. Taylor has written: "The institution of convoys was his (Lloyd George's) greatest stroke. It ensured that Great Britain would go on to victory, and would survive at any rate the World War I as a great power."[23]

D.N.I.s from Custance onwards (1899-1902) (see Appendix C for the list of D.N.I.s from 1882-1945) until the end of World War I were deeply concerned with the problems of invasion. In 1903, N.I.D. was considering the implications of the loss of the command of the sea in home waters and how this might affect an invasion threat. The Military Intelligence Department (M.I.D.) were concerned—the D.N.I., Battenburg (1902-1905) soon calmed their worst fears in a paper presented to the Committee of Imperial Defence (C.I.D.) in July 1903.[24]

Four years later, the D.N.I., Slade (1907-1909) still has the responsibility for drawing up counter-invasion plans with the Army. The First Sea Lord, Fisher,

---

[21] Ranft thesis. p. 215.
[22] Ranft thesis. p. 303.
[23] A. J. p. Taylor: The First World War. Hamish Hamilton. 1963. p. 177-182.
[24] Cab. 3/1/16A: July 1903. See also the M.I.D. paper, Cab. 3/1/13A.

leaves the matter entirely in Slade's hands.[25] Similarly, Fisher entrusted Slade with all manner of naval business—not just intelligence, but planning, policy-making, and general administration. Edmond Slade devised plans for a blockade against Germany, and how the Navy should treat neutrals and contraband, and he developed a naval strategy for a possible war against the United States (July 1908), placing great stress on the role Canada would play in such a war.

He produced papers dealing with possible attacks on Imperial territories, and he was particularly concerned with the possibility of Germany converting merchant ships for belligerent purposes. He wrote: "The merchant ships so transformed into men-of-war represent virtually a considerable accession of cruiser strength to the enemy on all stations." As with all his predecessors, Slade was concerned with the defence of trade. However, he does not appear to have advanced proposals for organisation in peacetime much beyond the early days of Colomb and Lord Charles Beresford in the 1880s.

On 16 July 1908, Slade wrote the First Lord and First Sea Lord: "In order that the Admiralty may be in a position to provide such protection as not only will enable trade to continue without undue interruption, but will also instil such confidence in the ship-owners as will encourage them to continue their regular sailings, it is first of all necessary tat accurate information as to what is taking place on the trade routes be at all times available." To help facilitate the latter, Slade created port intelligence officers to liaise with consuls, masters of merchant ships, shipping lines, the Admiralty and commanders of naval units.

In all manner of other naval business, Slade was active, such as analysing the state of shipbuilding in various countries, German and Russian operations in the Baltic, and the British Naval manoeuvres of July 1908.[1]

In all these activities there was strong continuity from the early 1880s until the end of the Great War, and in wartime of course there was an immediate need for timely and accurate intelligence. Throughout the Great War, the D.N.I. assured the Prime Minister, Cabinet, and Admiralty that the N.I.D. could give early and accurate warning of any German preparations to invade England.[2] What is more, the D.N.I. pre-1914 never really lost his status within the naval hierarchy on any occasion, or the respect of the First Lord.

In 1913, Churchill relied totally on the D.N.I., Admiral Henry F. Oliver (D.N.I. 1913-1914) to furnish him with the facts and figures in favour of eight not four further Dreadnoughts being built (the Chancellor of the Exchequer was

---

[25] Cab. 16/3A. 12 December 1907.

opposing this). Churchill even consulted Oliver about Fisher's recall as First Sea Lord (he had been retired in 1910). Oliver's biographer writes: "...Oliver...expressed grave doubts whether Fisher, with his dynamic personality and intolerance, would work in double harness with Churchill who, unlike most First Lords, would expect to be kept well informed and consulted about strategy and dispositions of ships."

With his staff of seven Royal Marine officers, two Fleet Paymasters, one Staff Paymaster, one Engineer Commander, two Commanders, and ten clerks (minute by later Naval Staff standards), Oliver enjoyed power and kudos second only to the First Sea Lord himself.[26] In marked contrast with the inter-war period, the D.N.I. was involved in the early and very basic discussions pre-1914 on the strategic uses to which naval aircraft could be put.

It was a former D.N.I., Rear-Admiral Sir Charles Ottley (D.N.I. 1905-1907) who, as the secretary of the C.I.D., instigated discussion and Naval Staff talks on naval air power in January 1912, and promoted the eventual production of papers by Captain Murray F. Sueter, the Director of the Naval Air Department in August 1912. When the First Sea Lord, Admiral of the Fleet, Sir Arthur Wilson and the First Lord, Churchill, began discussions on the future use and development of airships for naval purposes, it was the D.N.I. who produced reports for them on the Germans' Zeppelin naval airship policy.[27]

The initial limits that this new department had set itself is indicated by its early concentration of effort on reorganising the cypher system. This received marked attention with the appointment of Admiral Beaumont as the N.I.D.'s third Director of 1894.[28] Beaumont discovered the cypher records of a Captain Cator, R.N., who had produced work on cyphers when he was a lieutenant. These challenged the old Vigenere system of cyphers, and was concerned that all modern systems of encipherment were based on Vigenere's principles, (and therefore, no cypher secrets would be safe from a potential enemy in future), created a new cypher system for the Royal Navy, based on Cator's ideas.

---

[26] See Admiral Sir William James: A Great Seaman. The Life of Admiral of the Fleet Sir Henry F. Oliver. Witherby. 1956.

[27] Cab. 38/23/1, C.I.D. 172B.

[28] Beaumont, Admiral Sir Lewis Anthony: b. 1847; entered R.N. 1860; Rear-Admiral 1897; D.N.I. 1894-98; C.-in-C. Pacific 1899-1900; C.-in-C. Australia 1901-1903; Admiral 1906; C.-in-C. Devonport 1905-1908.

His work gave the British Navy a lead over the French and Germans, who were also busying themselves with cypher research.

The often-parochial attitudes of the infant N.I.D. must be seen in the light of its opposite number in the Army. During the Boer War, the Army had failed woefully to develop and use its Intelligence Branch, which was regarded very much like a reference library. By contrast, Admiral Custance,[29] Beaumont's successor as Director in 1899, created an organisation that saw itself as something going beyond the work of code-developing and code-breaking. Admiral Custance argued the case for the creation of a Naval Staff College and a War Course at the Royal Naval College, Greenwich.

The Admiralty Board sanctioned the latter in 1900, and senior naval officers began to discuss and formulate for the first time in a formal environment a maritime strategic doctrine, stimulated at that time by the publication of Mahan's book in 1889 (The Staff College was founded in 1919). In 1902, the N.I.D. acquired a Trade Division and a policy emerged for routing merchant ships in the event of war.[30]

Between 1898 and 1900, laws were passed in Germany increasing the size of the German Navy from a small coastal defence force into a High Seas Fleet. The arms race that ensued between the great powers forced the Admiralty to make improvement in naval intelligence. The free and easy methods of obtaining information through the reports of naval attaches abroad (who were able to visit foreign arsenals and dockyards and secure information largely on a quid pro quo basis) were now to all intents and purposes inadequate.

---

[29] Custance, Admiral Sir Reginald: 1847-1935; A D.N.I. 1866-1890; naval attaché Washington and Paris 1892-1895; D.N.I. 1899-1902; second in command Channel Fleet; an opponent of Fisher's Dreadnought policy; author of The Ship of the Line (London 1912).

[30] The work of this division proved of critical value in the 1914-1918 war. Although much of its earlier ideas and plans had to be modified in the light of war experiences (especially unrestricted U-boat warfare), and temporarily abolished in 1909, the research and planning done from 1902 onwards gave Britain an unparalleled start in the organisation of her trade in time of war. Details are to be found in Adm. 137, 408-446, and 2732-3045, Public Record Office. The records of the work of the shipping and intelligence officers (who helped decide routes, planned convoys, etc. in the light of known and possible enemy moves) are to be found in Adm. 137, 324, 359-361, Public Record Office.

It began to develop new methods, though still tending to concentrate on the revision of cyphering procedures, but, more important, the interception of German cyphers and codes were set in motion. The latter arose as much by chance than design. In October 1904, Fisher became First Sea Lord. He invited Alfred Ewing, then a professor of mechanical engineering at Cambridge, to become Director of Naval Education.[31] As a result of the close relationship between these two men, Ewing developed ideas of his own on the organisation of a code and cypher-breaking department.

As a result of Ewing's initiative, when war came in 1914, the Royal Navy possessed the nucleus of a cypher section, which was in fact already supplying the Operations Division of the Admiralty with intercepted German naval wireless signals, and had discovered the German method of cyphering.

The Development of Radio Intelligence and its Significance for N.I.D. and Naval Operations

It was around Ewing's cypher team in the Admiralty that the N.I.D. was first able to come to grips with its internal opponents, and also have a major impact upon the war at sea. Fletcher Pratt has written: "this was to have the most important effects on the German naval effort, and through it on the whole course of the war. Twice in the early days, the Germans tried slipping flotillas of destroyers down along the coast of Holland in an effort to raid the British troop convoys across the Channel. Each time Room 40 read their radio signals and knew of the project.

"The first time, fog and a storm forced the raiders back to harbour; the second time a fast and powerful British light cruiser waited across their path and sank four of the German ships before they could get away."[32] Somewhat ironically, the strength of this team depended largely on civilian members, whom Ewing had the good sense to import into the Admiralty because of a lack of expertise and flair amongst naval personnel. The key men who assessed the information

---

[31] Ewing, Sir James Alfred: 1855-1935; ed. Edinburgh Univ.; Professor of Mech. Eng. and Physics at Imperial Univ., Tokyo. 1878; Prof. of Eng. Dundee Univ., 1883; Prof. of Eng., Cambridge, 1890; DN EDS, 1903; invited by the D.N.I., Rear-Admiral Sir H.F. Oliver, to establish Room 40, 1914; Vice-Chancellor of Edinburgh University, 1916-1929. CB 1907; KCB, 1911; FRS 1887. Portrait by Douglas Shields (c. 1903) in the board room, Engineering Laboratory, Cambridge.

[32] Fletcher Pratt: Secret and Urgent. The Story of Codes and Cyphers.

pouring into the nerve centre of Ewing's organisation, Room 40 in the Admiralty, were all civilians.

Strategic Planning in Britain in the Early Twentieth Century

Outside the purely naval sphere, there had been concern long before the Great War began that there was not adequate attention given to long-term military planning based on sound intelligence. In January 1904, Lord Esher's War Office Committee reported: "The British Empire is pre-eminently a great Naval, Indian, and colonial power. There are, nonetheless, no means of coordinating defence problems, for dealing with them as a whole, for defining the proper functions of the various elements, and for ensuring that, on the one hand, peace preparations are carried out upon a consistent plan, and, on the other hand, that, in times of emergency, a definite war policy, based upon solid data, can be formulated." [33]

As a result of this committee's efforts, the Committee of Imperial Defence was founded on 4 May 1904, very much a Balfour brainchild. It is indicative of both the thinking of the time, and also of the structural nature of each organisation that the Committee of Imperial Defence was given a purely advisory role and no legal power at all. However, the committee immediately set about creating sub and ad hoc committees, their fundamental aim being the assessment of the military needs of the Empire, with special reference to Britain's defensive preparations to meet the new political groupings of Europe.

A review of the committee's work indicates that hardly a stone was left unturned. All manner of problems were reviewed—the position of possible enemy and neutral shipping, enemy trade, Britain's supplies, the control of railways and ports, the insurance of ships and cargoes against war risks, counter-espionage, censorship, the treatment of enemy aliens, cable and wireless communications, and so on.[34]

Lord Oxford paid the committee considerable compliments when he wrote: "It would not be an unjust claim to say that the government had by that date (August 1909) investigated the whole of the ground covered by a possible war

---

[33] War Office Committee Report. January 1904. Lord Esher Chairman.
[34] See Lt. Col. Sir Maurice Hankey: The Origin and Development of the Committee of Imperial Defence. The Army Quarterly. Vol. 14, April and July 1927.

with Germany—the naval position; the possibilities of a blockade; the invasion problem, the continental problem; the Egyptian problem."[35]

Parallel to these events, one sees a clearer identity for the N.I.D. emerging. In some areas, it lost a considerable amount of authority and influence gained between 1902 and 1909, for in the latter year, the N.I.D. Trade Division was abolished, and a new Naval Mobilisation Department was created from the War and Mobilisation Divisions of the N.I.D. Although stripped of several of its hitherto major functions, N.I.D. was back to its original roles of the Hall and Bridge eras, collecting and collating intelligence.

The D.N.I. had momentarily lost ground, and the First Sea Lord himself was without informed advice for his war plans. However, in 1912, the Director of Naval Intelligence's position was again reasserted with Churchill's reforms in the Naval Staff structure, with the quite clear separation of War Information, War Plans, and War Arrangements. In this new scheme of things, the First Lord raised the Naval Intelligence Department to the senior position within the Naval Staff, and the Director regained direct access to the First Sea Lord.

The British Security Services and the N.I.D.

Parallel to these developments in higher defence planning, there were reforms within the counter-espionage service, an organisation which was to have close connections with the N.I.D. during the Great War. The Boer War had revealed the poverty of British counter-espionage, and with a European power struggle emerging, a sub-committee of the Committee of Imperial Defence recommended the establishment of a new intelligence organisation on the military side, civilian in character and organisation, but one which was regarded as a supplement to the N.I.D.

The creation of M.I. 5 (counter-espionage) and M.I. 6 (espionage) received additional impetus as a result of the Agadir crisis of July 1911.[36] The respective heads were Commander Mansfield Smith-Cumming, R.N., and Colonel Vernon Kell of the South Staffordshire Regiment. There was always a naval officer in charge of M.I. 6 until Admiral Sinclair died in December 1939. Kell was to work closely with Scotland Yard, a combination which was to ultimately thwart the

---

[35] Lord Oxford: The Genesis of the War. See Chapter XV.
[36] See Donald McLachlan: Room 39. p. 383.

German espionage machine, though initially his work was hampered by British law, insofar as it gave protection to known German spies.

This situation was rectified in 1911 with the passing of the Official Secrets Act, which had hitherto been confused and defective. The law was put on a clear basis and extended so as to embrace every possible mode of obtaining and conveying to the enemy information which might be useful in war. However, the law did not affect M.I. 5's legal position. Whilst it could trace spies, it could not arrest them. Any arrests made had to be with the cooperation of Scotland Yard.

A son of an Archbishop of York, Basil Thomson, was appointed to act as the link man between M.I. 5, Scotland Yard, and the recently created Special Branch. These bodies became closely associated with the activities of the N.I.D., and it was the latter which grew to dominate the scene, notably during World War I with Hall's period as D.N.I. Hall's drive, energy, ruthlessness, and purposeful character rendered M.I. 5, M.I. 6, and the Special Branch echelons of the Naval Intelligence Department. Besides dabbing in counter-espionage, Hall wanted British agents in every part of the world where he had interests, and he wanted them under his direct control.

This reveals the absence of central policy and coordination of British intelligence efforts; that a senior naval officer could extend his influence beyond the purely naval sphere and even within that into areas that were purely civilian shows the urgent need for a clear-cut definition of boundaries of interest. The N.I.D., and certainly Halls regime, did fill a vacuum and his activities reflect the inadequacies of Britain's other intelligence bodies.

At the end of the nineteenth century, the British Secret Service tended to concentrate its efforts on detecting plots by Irish rebels against Britain, and the researches of Richard Deacon have shown that the Secret Service tended to concentrate too much on French and Russian activities instead of German, despite the changing European situation. However, he does show that in the long run, Britain easily had the best intelligence service of any foreign power inside Russia during World War I and immediately afterwards.[37]

Certainly Kell's and Cumming's departments scored successes; the discovery of Karl Gustav Ernst's 'post office' for the German Secret Service in London enhanced Kell's reputation, and the organisation the Special Intelligence Service established in the USA was a prototype for the future. During World War I, Sir William Wiseman, officially head of the British Purchasing

---

[37] See Richard Deacon: A History of the British Secret Service. (Muller, 1969).

Commission in the United States, controlled all Cumming's agents in that country, an organisation developed with some alacrity in the pre-1914 years.

There were unfortunate episodes too. In May 1910, two Royal Marine officers, Captain Trench and Lieutenant Brandon, acting for the N.I.D., set off to gain knowledge of the Frisian islands. They were captured and sentenced to four years imprisonment; seventeen months before their sentences expired, they were pardoned by the Kaiser to mark George V's visit to Berlin. However, it is a pertinent point that the efficacy of any British organisation must be seen in the light of the effectiveness of foreign intelligence services. The Germans were surely lacking in expertise and method too. It was not until as late as July 1914 that their master agent in Britain, Steinhauer, realised the significance of Scapa Flow for the British fleet.

The Flexibility of N.I.D. Organisation

When examining the higher echelons of defence planning pre-1914 and the organisation created to meet actual war requirements, one can detect their obvious failings and omissions, which is the prerogative of hindsight and experience, but in the same way as comparing the merits or otherwise of British and foreign intelligence expertise, when seen in terms of their results, reveals a more realistic criterion for appraisal, so too does a glance at the comparative war organisations of Great Britain and Germany. Churchill gives an analytical account of the formation of the War Council in the 'World Crisis'.[38]

His discussion there is in marked contrast to Ludendorff's comments in his memoirs concerning military planning and organisation in Berlin: "The machinery of government in Berlin gave the impression of being extremely clumsy. The various departments worked side by side without any real sympathy or cohesion, and there was infinite overlapping. The left hand did not know what the right hand was doing."[39] Whatever the eventual outcome of any strategic policy, it was equally critical that the organisation which would facilitate such policy being made would be such that as much evidence as possible would be brought in before the final decision was made.

This is central to the development of British intelligence work. Even though at times the war organisation either rejected or misused intelligence data, or was

---

[38] See W. S. Churchill: The World Crisis. Vol. II, Chapter IX.
[39] General Ludendorff: My War Memories. p. 263.

not aware of the need to collect such data, it was, above all else, sufficiently flexible and oriented so as to adjust itself to needs that were often apparent only after the event. In this area, Britain undoubtedly scored over her foreign allies and enemies.

Irrespective of military blunder or success, British Naval Intelligence was to flower as a result of this ability within the British military machine, at political, bureaucratic, and uninformed personnel levels, to recognise that there had been a need and its fulfilment had been found wanting, and therefore innovation must occur. In this sense, British Naval Intelligence had a hopeful future, since the developing logic behind defence thinking would naturally lead to a heavy intelligence requirement.

Causal relationships tend to become lost though in this grey area of institutional development, and one is left with the familiar hen or the egg problem. Did intelligence help mould defence organisation and planning, in terms of laying down various requirements, or was intelligence organisation methods, and its role in the defence hierarchy determined by non-related factors, and how, and to what extent did these two fluctuate? The answers to these questions will emerge when the activities of some of the outstanding D.N.I.s and their principal subordinates are examined later.

At this stage, the dominant factor to consider in relation to intelligence growth, is the flexibility of the higher defence planning organisation. Through the Committee of Imperial Defence, the Prime Minister and Cabinet received collective advice on which to base strategic decisions, instead of receiving separate and possibly contradictory advice from the sea, land, and later air, specialists. Working in close liaison with the Chiefs of Staff, the Committee of Imperial Defence furnished the government with a comprehensive survey of Britain's defensive situation as a whole, based in part on appreciations from the intelligence bodies, the Foreign Office, and other government departments.[40]

Although naval intelligence was to lose ground after the Great War, the primary concerns were still evident. For example, in February 1920, the government set up a sub-committee to overhaul Britain's pre-war arrangements in the light of accumulated experience, and by the summer of 1921, the

---

[40] N.I.D. and the C.I.D. worked in close harmony, as the papers of Sir George Clark, Secretary of the C.I.D. in its early years, show. See Adm. 116, 3095. Public Record Office.

Committee of Imperial Defence was in full swing again, conducting a full investigation into defence requirements.

In many ways then, a too mechanically organised N.I.D. could have inhibited its growth, and because of the flexibility within the defence machine, its growth became organic—continually adjusting and re-defining its roles and individual tasks through interaction with the other defence bodies. But it is people that make institutions and it was the ability and willingness of intelligence staffs, civilian and uniformed, to invest their expertise and authority in inter-functional exchange within the Naval Staff that produced this flexibility.

As a result of this interaction of personalities to meet changing needs, the organisation of naval intelligence never became permanently structured in one particular way. It merely remained a framework in which individual effort could be coordinated. The World War I was the catalyst which ensured the survival of these characteristics of the institution—the continual adaption to meet changing objectives, people, resources, and the environment in which the work was performed. It was the clarification of the N.I.D.'s objectives which led to logical planning, instead of what had at times prevailed in the pre-war years, namely periodic drives to achieve limited goals.

What Admiral Reginald Hall's era witnessed was the imminent need to identify and group work according to priorities—responsibilities were defined, authority delegated, and relationships established for the purpose of enabling people to work most effectively together in accomplishing the objectives set them. It was the process that created the organisation, rather than the bureaucracy of the organisation itself, which always remained in command.

The Growth of 'Operational' Intelligence and the Jutland Experience

In August 1914, the system of collecting and disseminating intelligence was still very primitive. Let us look at one very important area—the control of merchant shipping. The world was divided into intelligence areas, corresponding approximately, but by no means exactly, to the limits of the naval stations. In each N.I.D. area was one naval intelligence officer (under the command of the Admiral commanding his station, not the D.N.I.), who received reports from the reporting officers in his areas (these were usually the consuls and other principal British officials in ports). He was the link man with N.I.D. in the Admiralty and his area naval commander.

When war was declared, each naval intelligence officer was given control of the British merchant ships in his area or port(s). This control was much less than it later became, and, in the early part of the war, was almost wholly confined to the offering of suggestions to masters as regards their route and procedure and precautions they should take to lessen the chances of capture. If a trade route was deemed unsafe, a naval intelligence officer could close it, and until it was reopened, merchant shipping would proceed along it at their own risk. As far then as the physical defensive aspects of British merchant shipping organisation was concerned in 1914, this was almost non-existent.[41]

The Great War was the first great challenge to the N.I.D., for it was faced with the need to provide, for the first time, 'operational' intelligence on a large scale. Admiral Denning (D.N.I. 1959-1964) has defined operational intelligence as "that part of naval intelligence organisation which concerns itself solely with obtaining, deducing, coordinating, and promulgating intelligence which immediately affects any naval operation being, or about to be, undertaken by British or Allied, or any part of British or Allied, fleets."[42] Room 40, the keystone of N.I.D. in World War I, fought a dogged battle to win for itself the role implicit in Denning's statement.

Room 40's role was regarded by the Operations Division as a mere passer-on of information. It was not allowed to interpret, and this was certainly exacerbated by the absence of camaraderie between Room 40 and the Operations Division. In other words, total discretion was left with the Operations Division as to what interpretation should be placed on intelligence material and how, if at all, it should be used.

This, needless to say, rankled with intelligence workers, as did the refusal by the Operations staff to provide N.I.D. with full, up-to-date operational details, which in itself would help determine intelligence requirements and establish criteria for sifting intelligence and interpretation. This absence of a fundamental

---

[41] See the Naval Staff Monographs for World War I. Vol. 5. p. 34-35, 41-43, 104-105. Ministry of Defence (Navy) Library, Empress State Building, London.

[42] Denning, Vice-Admiral Sir N. E.: b. 1904; Captain 1951; Director of Administrative Planning MOD (N) 1952; Director R.N. College, 1956; Rear-Admiral 1958; Dept. of Chief of Naval Personnel, 1958; Director General of Naval Manpower 1959; D.N.I. 1960-1964; Vice-Admiral 1961; Chief Naval Supply and Secretariat officer, 1962-1964; Deputy Chief of the Defence Staff (Intelligence) 1964-1965.

relationship between the workers of Room 40 and operational staff officers could have, and nearly did at Jutland, lead to disaster.

One major consequence of this breakdown was the loss of confidence in intelligence data shown by sea-going commanders. At times, Room 40 was totally unaware of the destination and the use to which its intelligence material was put. Until the post-Jutland period, N.I.D. had its function withheld, mainly because the Operations Division reserved the right to be the sole arbiter for vetting intelligence material. When discussing Jutland, Professor Arthur Marder indicts the Operations Division for being too much of a one-man show.

Jackson Marder, the head of Operations Division,[43] shows lacked creative thinking, as his superior, Admiral Oliver,[44] the Chief of the War Staff, who tended to decide all. Marder lays the ultimate responsibility at the feet of the First Sea Lord, Sir Henry Jackson,[45] who was quite satisfied with Oliver. The First Sea Lord seldom visited the operations room and the pack of vital signals which were fed to the Operations Division by the N.I.D. were merely put on file by one Captain Everett and never consulted.

Procedure in the Admiralty tended to reflect procedure at sea. Certainly 'enemy reporting' and 'action information' was a universal fault in the British fleet. The fact that Jellicoe never knew that the enemy was passing astern of him at Jutland indicates bad reporting by the flotillas, but the records also indicate that Jellicoe did not insist on receiving the minutiae of enemy positions and strengths that would have enabled him to make the deductions Room 40 did, though admittedly from different sources. The necessity for acquiring such

---

[43] <u>Jackson, Rear-Admiral Thomas</u>: b. 1868; entered R.N. 1881; Commander 1899; Captain 1905; Rear-Admiral 1916; naval attaché, Tokyo, 1906; <u>D.N.I. Jan. 1912-Oct. 1913</u>; Director of the Operations Division, Jan. 1915-June 1917.

[44] <u>Oliver, Admiral Sir Henry Francis</u>: b. 1865; entered R.N. 1878; Commander 1899, Captain 1903; Rear-Admiral 1913; <u>D.N.I. 1913-1914</u>; DCNS and Chief of Admiralty War Staff 1914-1918; Vice-Admiral 1918; Vice-Admiral commanding Home Fleet 1919-1920; Second Sea Lord 1920-1924; Admiral 1923.

[45] <u>Jackson, Sir Henry Bradywardine, Admiral of the Fleet</u>: entered R.N. 1868; Commander 1890; Captain 1896; Controller and Third Sea Lord, 1905; Commander Third Cruiser Squadron, 1908; Chief of the War Staff, Admiralty, 1913; President of the R.N. College, 1916; Admiral of the Fleet, 1919; KCVO 1906, KCB 1910, GCB 1916.

information was not apparent until after Jutland, when it became part of maritime tactical procedure.[46]

What N.I.D. succeeded in proving as a result of Jutland was that intelligence has no value until it is placed in the hands of those who can act upon it, the distribution of intelligence therefore became as important as its collection. Jutland showed that the next worst thing to not having intelligence is keeping it shut up. This advance in N.I.D. was paralleled by a clearer statement of tactical procedure at sea—each unit was to receive all relevant information of its own forces and intelligence of the enemy, and was to be given definite instructions in pursuance of the operational objectives.

Moreover, in future, each unit commander was to keep his senior (and any other units concerned) informed of changes in circumstances and his own intentions (subject to electronic policy imposed at the time). This could not help but improve operational efficiency; 'information' and 'cooperation' were the new watchwords. In what ways then had Jutland revealed the paucity of these?

From the beginning to the end of the Jutland operation, N.I.D., Operations Division and Jellicoe failed to work in harmony. During the morning of 31 May 1916, an officer from the operations room asked Room 40 where the directional stations placed the German call-sign 'DK' (DK was the German C-in-C's harbour call-sign; when he put to sea, he took another call-sign and transferred DK to the W/T station in Wilhelmshaven. He did this to conceal the fact that the fleet was at sea). In Wilhelmshaven, he was told, and he asked no more. He wrongly concluded that the German flagship was there and passed a signal to that effect to Jellicoe at 12:20 pm.

That signal went without N.I.D.'s knowledge or confirmation. Professor Marder writes: "But for the error in the Operations Division, he (Jellicoe) would undoubtedly have steamed at high speed and arrived in the battle area somewhat earlier and so gained an hour or two of daylight."[47]

---

[46] N.I.D. was equally aware too of the urgent need for incoming intelligence data to be speedily transmitted. Hall was anxious that the Fleet in general and C-in-Cs should transmit any information considered relevant to the N.I.D. immediately. Between August and September 1915, measures were taken to improve the transmission of intelligence. See Adm. 137, 1100, p. 147-158. Public Record Office.

[47] Arthur J. Marder: From the Dreadnought to Scapa Flow. Vol. I. p. 43.

Hence when Beatty[48] reported sighting a German battle cruiser squadron at sea to Jellicoe, their faith in intelligence data was shaken, and they therefore tended to prefer on-the-spot reports throughout the rest of the battle. Jellicoe wanted knowledge of the Germans battle fleet's formation, approximate position, course and speed, and it was precisely on these points that the C-in-C was unable to obtain data from the Operations Division. Jellicoe's confidence in Operations was badly and permanently shaken.[49]

If Jellicoe himself is to be criticised for not having sufficient information available, then it must rest on his failure to organise immediate operational intelligence. The fourth Light Cruiser Squadron and a flotilla could have been used for this purpose and sent off to the southeast to collect information. Jellicoe could have insisted too that his subordinates signal enemy dispositions to him immediately. That Beatty, and several of the captains, erred in this, there is now no doubt.

During the fourth encounter, none of the destroyer captains involved took pains to inform the C-in-C of their life and death struggle, and during the sixth encounter, only one destroyer reported the fight and position to the C-in-C.[50] But Beatty suffered too; he never received the intelligence the Admiralty had wirelessed to Jellicoe during the night. He did not, therefore, share his C-in-C's appreciation of Scheer's whereabouts.

The second critical piece of intelligence information to reach Jellicoe, namely the High Seas Fleet's impending dash for the Horns Reef and home, was disregarded by him. Jellicoe simply distrusted the validity of Admiralty intelligence after the disastrous consequences of the 9.58 signal from the Admiralty to the Iron Duke. This was the result of three intercepted enemy messages which had been deciphered by Room 40 and passed on to the

---

[48] Beatty, David, First Earl, Admiral of the Fleet: 1871-1936; Lieutenant 1892; promoted Commander (aged twenty-seven) 1898; Captain 1900; Naval secretary to First Lord (Churchill) 1912; Vice-Admiral 1915, Commander Battle Cruiser Squadrons (flagship H.M.S. Lion); December 1916 acting Admiral, C.-in-C. Grand Fleet (flagship H.M.S. Queen Elizabeth); First Sea Lord, November 1919.

[49] See Jellicoe's own accounts in: The Grand Fleet and The Crisis of the Naval War. In the former he writes: "I should not for a moment have relied on Admiralty information of the enemy in preference to reports from ships which actually sighted him."

[50] See Geoffrey Bennett's account in: The Battle of Jutland.

Operations Division. The 10:41 pm signal gave the course and speed of the High Seas Fleet.[51]

If Jellicoe had acted quickly and plotted the enemy's track from the last known position, the Grand Fleet could have intercepted the High Seas Fleet. In fairness to Jellicoe, the Operations Division did not send all the information they had received from Room 40—that Scheer had called for airship reconnaissance of Horns Reef; in all, eight critical signals were not transmitted. On the basis of the 10:10 pm signal (airship reconnaissance) and the 11:15 pm signal (assembling of flotillas), Jellicoe could have made for Horns Reef in time to cut off Scheer from his base.

Jellicoe writes himself in the *Grand Fleet*: "Of course, if the Admiralty had given me the information as to the airship reconnaissance at the Horns Reef, I should have altered in that direction during the night."[52]

It is vital, as well as interesting, to compare Jellicoe's comments with those of Admiral Tovey,[53] referring to the intelligence data given to him at the time of the Bismarck operation: "The accuracy of the information supplied by the Admiralty and the speed with which it was passed were remarkable; and the balance struck between information and instruction passed to the forces out of visual touch with me was ideal."[54]

This reflects the quite dramatic change between role, organisation and effect between 1916 and 1941. So, in one sense then Jellicoe cannot be held blameworthy. Room 40 never knew Operations were not passing on their information to the C-in-C and, in any event, nor could they contact the Grand Fleet directly.

Arthur Marder writes: "Although Scheer was on the run, a decisive result might have been possible in the daylight hours of 1 June if the C-in-C had been

---

[51] The signal read: "German battle fleet ordered home at 2214. Battle cruisers in rear. Course SSE3/4E. Speed 16 knots."

[52] Jellicoe: The Grand Fleet.

[53] Tovey, First Baron of Langton Maltravers, Admiral of the Fleet John Cronyn: 1885-1971; Captain 1923; Naval Assistant to the Second Sea Lord 1930-1932; Rear-Admiral 1935; Rear-Admiral Destroyers, Mediterranean 1938-1940; Vice-Admiral 1939; second-in-command Mediterranean Fleet 1939; C.-in-C. Home Fleet 1940-1943; Admiral 1942; Admiral of the Fleet 1943; C.-in-C. Nore 1943-1946.

[54] Admiral Tovey: Sinking of the Bismarck, May 1941. London Gazette. 16 October 1947.

better served during the night with information from the Admiralty and his own fleet."[55] When Jellicoe realised what Scheer was doing, it was too late.

Post-Jutland Intelligence Reforms

Jutland forced reform through. From November 1916, the Grand Fleet received daily summaries of all enemy movements and changes (Throughout World War II, N.I.D.'s Information Section promulgated Weekly Intelligence Reports to the Fleet). Admiral Reginald Hall was convinced by Jutland that Room 40 should be an intelligence centre and not just a cryptographic bureau, passing signals to the Operations Division of the War Staff. By May 1917, Room 40 came directly under Reginald Hall's control, and in July 1917, Room 40 became a full section of the Intelligence Division, and began to send full intelligence reports to the Operations Division.

In December 1917, Room 40 and E1 (dealing with German U-boats) became subsections (ID 25a and ID 25b) of the German Section (14) of the N.I.D., under a single head. Above all else, this was to lead to a greater protection of British merchant shipping. Of equal importance at this time was the creation of the Convoy Section of the Naval Staff (25 June 1917), which was to work hand-in-hand with the N.I.D. Prior to this, the German and Enemy Submarines Section of the N.I.D. had been kept separate from Room 40 and its cryptanalysis, and all of these from the work of the Anti-Submarine Division of the Admiralty.

All of these organisations, united in the common goals of convoy protection and U-boat destruction were fully integrated. The significance of the separation of Room 40 from Sections E1 and 14 of the N.I.D. came out officially as late as the Naval Staff Appreciation of Jutland in 1922. This showed how, because of organisational failures and the secrecy attached to Room 40's work, a combined picture of the U-boat threat in particular had never emerged within the Naval Staff pre-1917.[56] Room 40 continued its general interception, deciphering and interpreting duties.

The destruction of the Zeppelin L-32 on 24 September 1916, yielded to the Admiralty the new German naval signal book. This had recently replaced the book captured from the 'Magdeburg' early in the war. This enabled Room 40 to continue to decipher many German messages, particularly impending

---

[55] Arthur Marder: From the Dreadnought to the Scapa Flow. Vol. 3.
[56] Arthur J. Marder: From Dreadnought to Scapa Flow. Vol. 4. p. 264-266, 295.

movements from the Jade.[57] Throughout 1917 and 1918, Room 40 continued to track Zeppelin reconnaissance over the North Sea. They were monitored as soon as they left their sheds and ample warning was given to the Grand Fleet of their arrival.[58]

It is a somewhat unfair criticism of the N.I.D. that it tended during World War I to rely on one major form of intelligence at the expense of others. This study will reveal the converse of this in later chapters. However, the activities of Room 40 may have had, indirectly, an unfortunate aftermath in the inter-war period. It is very difficult to prove a causal relationship between the decline of British Naval Intelligence between 1920 and 1938 and the overconfidence generated by the code-breaking activities of Room 40.

General Strong has written, when discussing military intelligence overall in the 1930s, "…As far as the Admiralty was concerned, a legend had been built up around a mysterious Room 40 and the highly secret operations of Admiral 'Blinker' Hall in World War I. Perhaps as a result, there was a tendency for Naval Intelligence to feel itself superior, in efficiency and influence, to the intelligence departments of the other two services; in fact, there was no justification at all for this attitude."[59] Strong was intimately concerned with inter-war intelligence organisation, and his observation is endorsed in other reliable published sources.[60]

Inter-War N.I.D. Organisation and Developments

The outstanding feature of intelligence in the United Kingdom between 1920 and 1938 is its indecisiveness. The problem stemmed from the failure to identify intelligence targets. Intelligence coming out of Germany in the 1920 and 1930s was scanty and uncoordinated. Those who regarded Germany as still one of the primary targets for intelligence were outnumbered by those who were anti-French and pro-German, and those who believed that Soviet Russia was the

---

[57] On 27 August 1914, the German cruiser 'Magdeburg' was wrecked in the Gulf of Finland. The Russians salvaged her and forwarded to London, copies of the German Navy codes found on her. By December, Sir Alfred Ewing's team in Room 40 had deciphered enough to give advance warning of sorties of the High Seas Fleet.
[58] Arthur J. Marder: From Dreadnought to Scapa Flow. Vol. 4. p. 10.
[59] Major-General Sir Kenneth Strong: Intelligence at the Top. p. 18.
[60] See in particular Donald MacLachlan: Room 39. p. 28

primary target. Besides lacking basic objectives, military intelligence in all three services suffered from organisational problems.

Strong writes: "The intelligence staffs of the War Office, the Air Ministry and the Admiralty had little contact with each other and there were no joint staffs. As a result, there was considerable duplication of effort and waste of resources. Estimates of German strengths and intentions were made quite independently by each Ministry, each for its own use."[61]

This comment is echoed by Richard Deacon in his 'History of the British Secret Service', (Muller, 1969) whose sources show a lack of cooperation between M.I. 6 and the N.I.D., and a failure on the part of the hierarchy of the Secret Service to give coherent guidance to the government, though the treatment given to intelligence data by inter-war politicians is a separate factor, dealt with elsewhere. The Prime Minister, in theory, still remained the titular head of the intelligence bodies, and the individual permanent heads had direct access to their respective Secretaries of State, M.I. 5 to the Home Secretary, M.I. 6 to the Foreign Secretary, and the military intelligence bodies to their Chiefs of Staff and Secretaries of State.

To meet World War II requirements, the Special Operations Executive, (S.O.E.) was founded, under the direction of Sir Winston Churchill, by Hugh Dalton, Minister of Economic Warfare. This combined under its command D section of the Secret Intelligence Service (S.I.S.). The S.O.E. was something of a disaster in many ways, despite the efforts of its three heads, Sir Frank Nelson, Sir Charles Hambro, and Major-General Sir Colin Gubbins. The relations between the S.O.E., the S.I.S., M.I. 5, and P.W.E. (Political Warfare Executive) were never cordial, and at times marked by an almost venomous mutual distrust.[62]

Between 1918 and 1937, there were eight D.N.I.s, and they must all have felt that the N.I.D. was a shadow of its former self. It was not until the mid-1930s that one can detect any sign of revitalisation in the N.I.D. after its post-war rundown. The latter was epitomised by the fate of N.I.D.'s Movements Section. In October 1920, it still had on its staff one Commander, one Captain RM, one Lieutenant RM and six clerks. By March 1927, it had only a marine in charge and two clerks. By December 1928, it had ceased to exist.[63]

---

[61] Major-General Sir Kenneth Strong: Intelligence at the Top. p. 18.
[62] See for example M. R. D. Foot: S.O.E. in France.
[63] Godfrey Memoirs: Vol. 5. Part 1. p. 342.

In 1935 came the first signs of change with the appointment of Vice-Admiral Sir William James as Deputy Chief of the Naval Staff.[64] He prompted the Admiralty Board to improve operational intelligence. In December 1936, the question of establishing an operational intelligence centre was first raised. The Spanish Civil War revealed deficiencies in passing intelligence to ships and other relevant departments, and in June 1937, a Lieutenant-Commander Norman Denning was brought into the N.I.D. to work out the organisation required for a wartime operational intelligence centre, and by November 1937, his ideas began to come to fruition.

Eventually, he was able to set up the O.I.C. (Operational Intelligence Centre) with three rooms in the Admiralty and the assistance of a signals expert. One of Denning's first major contributions was to improve the direction-finding and interception organisation for, as Denning said, it was possible for two separate divisions of the Navy to have different plots of enemy fleet locations. On Denning's advice, Rear-Admiral Troup (D.N.I. 1935-1939)[65] and HF/DF stations built in the north and an O.I.C. teleprinter system to set up, so as to allow instant communication with the stations, Coastal Command Headquarters, local naval units, coastal watchers and agents' signals.

It was located in the Citadel under Horse Guards Parade, where it is hoped it could survive a direct bomb hit. Denning's hard work had its reward at the time of Munich, when his O.I.C. had all German ships plotted. What Norman Denning aimed for with his O.I.C. was a resemblance of the enemy's operations room.[66] In January 1938, O.I.C. had acquired Room 30 in the Admiralty.

The slack of the years 1930-1935 was quickly taken up during the last four years of peace and the momentum gained after Jutland, during the height of the

---

[64] James was in charge of Room 40 for part of World War I and Deputy D.N.I. after 1918. James, Admiral Sir William Milbourne: b. 1881; Commander 1913; Captain 1918; Rear-Admiral 1929; Vice-Admiral 1933; Admiral 1938; Director of R.N. Staff College 1925-1926; Naval assistant to the First Sea Lord, 1928; Commander Battle Cruiser Squadron, 1932-1934; DCNS 1935-1938; C.-in-C. Portsmouth 1939-1942; Chief of Naval Information, 1943-1944.

[65] Troup, Vice-Admiral Sir James Andrew Gardiner: b. 1883; Commander 1916; Captain 1922; Rear-Admiral 1935; D.N.I. 1935-1939; Vice-Admiral 1939; retired 1939.

[66] Details of the improvements made in the N.I.D. communications system between 1935 and 1939 are to be found in Adm. 116, 4080. For example, the institution of a teleprinter service between the Code and Cypher School and the Royal Navy's W.T. stations at Flowerdown and Scarborough is detailed.

Hall era, and lost in 1918 was continued, such that by 1939 three basic, but very important concepts of intelligence, had been established: Firstly, the O.I.C. could 'interpret' intelligence data and, secondly, linked to this, the Operations Division could no longer just ask for bare facts, and, thirdly, N.I.D. was provided with full details of the Fleet, which would assist it in its interpretation of raw intelligence.

At long last, naval intelligence had been integrated with the Plans and Operations Divisions. Donald MacLachlan writes: "…the Naval Staff, in September, 1939, found themselves ready to go into action with a highly trained organisation for centralised control of the war at sea."[67] Later in the war, Italian and Japanese O.I.C. subsections were set up. Perhaps not as spectacular as Admiral Hall's N.I.D., the department of the Godfrey (D.N.I. 1939-1943)[68] and Rushbrooke (D.N.I. 1943-1946)[69] era was to be characterised by cool and well-planned professionalism, and not indulging in anything like the same amount of private espionage that Hall delighted in.

The arrival of Godfrey in office was to mark a total change in tone in the N.I.D. just as Hall's arrival had in 1914.

One of the outstanding failures of naval personnel administration during the inter-war period must remain the Admiralty's failure to select an intelligence-trained specialist for the task of D.N.I. and then allow their nominee to hold the job for only a few years. This led to many errors; for example, as early as 1936, German cryptanalysts had penetrated the wireless security of British ships in the Red Sea and this failure in naval security was not completely overcome until the middle of 1943.

Perhaps its worst effects were felt in the disastrous Norwegian campaign of 1940. The D.N.I. remained responsible for naval censorship and security, and he delegated these responsibilities to subordinate sections and heads.

---

[67] Donald MacLachlin: Room 39. p. 59.

[68] <u>Godfrey, Admiral John Henry</u>: 1888-1971; Captain 1928; Rear-Admiral 1939; Vice-Admiral 1942; Admiral 1945; Deputy Director, Plans Division, Admiralty, 1933-1935; Captain H.M.S. Repulse, 1936-1939; <u>D.N.I. 1939-1943</u>; Flag officer commanding Royal Indian Navy, 1943-1946.

[69] <u>Rushbrooke, Vice-Admiral Edmund Gerard Noel</u>: b. 1892; Commander 1918; Captain 1936; Chief of the Intelligence staff, China station, 1937; Captain H.M.S. Guardian 1939; H.M.S. Argus 1940; H.M.S. Eagle 1941; <u>D.N.I. 1942-1946</u>; Rear-Admiral 1945; retired 1947; Vice-Admiral on the retired list 1948.

The Joint Intelligence Committee

The greatest advance in intelligence organisation between the wars was the formation of the Joint Intelligence Committee (J.I.C.). The idea of such a committee had first been mooted in the Churchill Committee of 1922, but it did not make any real headway until the Chiefs of Staff Committee began discussions on the topic during 1935-1936 and eventually submitted a proposal to the Committee of Imperial Defence. On the 30 January 1936, the Joint Intelligence Committee was formed as a sub-committee of the Committee of Imperial Defence.

Within six months, a formal link was established between the J.I.C. and the Joint Planning Committee (J.P.C.). This was the first move towards an overall intelligence appreciation being conducted by a single body whose main concern was strictly concerned with intelligence data, rather than the much broader responsibilities of the Committee of Imperial Defence. It reflects a fundamental change in viewing the significance of intelligence data and what conclusions could be drawn at varying levels.

This is borne out by events—the J.I.C. became concerned with the long-range forecasting and strategic planning in global terms, whereas O.I.C. was immediately concerned with, for example, day-to-day U-boat hunts. What the J.I.C. did too was to reduce inter-service rivalries and created a joint service objective appraisal of common problems. Immediately after World War II began, the J.I.C. was made responsible to the Chiefs of Staff Committee, and it soon became very powerful—no Chief of Staff could ignore it.

In the event of a J.I.C. disagreement, the matter in question could be referred to the War Cabinet. Admiral Godfrey wrote in his memoirs: "Working under the Chiefs of Staff Committee, the J.I.C. issued intelligence submarines and directed the policy of various sub-committees…It dealt with administrative and other questions concerning the topography, prisoner of war interrogation, and photographic interpretation centres."[70]

The J.I.C. had direct links with all the British intelligence bodies and, although there were setbacks, the British were able to avoid the outstanding weaknesses of German intelligence, notably their failure to realise that the collection and judgment of material by four or five organisations working independently, continually preyed on by the jealousies of rival services and

---

[70] Godfrey Memoirs: Vol. 5. Part 2. p. 215.

watched suspiciously by the party and its security machine, was bound to be inefficient. Moreover, the British were aware of the need to communicate a limited amount of intelligence to service personnel.

In the spring of 1939, the Information Section of the N.I.D. was formed (N.I.D.19)—this informed all service personnel of the progress of the war, under proper security conditions, through weekly intelligence reports.

When examining the progress towards final service integration, of which 'Overlord' must be taken as one of the major points in time to take stock (when in fact integration was virtually complete), there were quite clear stages when this was halted. For example, Godfrey's early efforts to form a joint service topographical Intelligence Sub-Committee of the J.I.C. were frustrated. The R.A.F. and Army were against the idea, arguing that each service should cope with its own individual problems.

However, the obvious demands for such an organisation became so apparent that by February 1941, Godfrey had won the day with the founding of the topographical section of the J.I.C. under N.I.D. control. Internally within the Admiralty and the N.I.D., Godfrey strove to facilitate integration of functions. Godfrey's great success stemmed from this ability to see the problem and how it could be solved within a complexity of service hierarchies and institutional prejudices.

In his unpublished 'Memoirs', he states, with reference to the last months of 1939: "The incidence of responsibility between the operational, planning, trade, and anti-submarine divisions was as yet ill-defined."[71] He was a man who, having defined relationships and organisational structures, could set about giving them practical expression.

At times though, Godfrey felt that he may perhaps have pushed through integration too rigorously, at the expense of the N.I.D.'s operational efficiency. For example, in March 1942, it became known that the Germans were installing radar on Spanish soil near Gibraltar. Godfrey wished to act quickly but found himself restricted by the system of joint consultation he had developed. Admiral Hall would have organised a purely N.I.D. private venture. The D.N.I. could no

---

[71] Memoirs of Admiral Godfrey: typescript in the National Maritime Museum, Greenwich, and the Ministry of Defence (Naval) Library, Empress State Building, London. Several parts of Admiral Godfrey's Memoirs, unavailable in these two libraries, were loaned to the author by Vice-Admiral Sir N.E. Denning, KBE, CB.

longer practice counter-intelligence on his own authority, but merely recommend a course of action as the Naval Staff member responsible.

British Naval Intelligence gained the tremendous lead it had over the enemy and allies because Godfrey rapidly implemented the need to establish an organisation to link operational intelligence (O.I.C.), Plans and Operations. As early as February 1939, Godfrey had a Captain, R.N. running this vital section of N.I.D. Despite the uncertainties and failures of 1939 and early 1940 in the N.I.D., Godfrey had created in O.I.C. an organisation that allowed progressive expansion and change. At the heart of this system lay efficient communications, the responsibilities of the Signals Division of the Naval Staff, though communications security was the D.N.I.'s responsibility.

The O.I.C. had direct telephone and teleprinter links with all operational headquarters of C-in-Cs at home, the headquarters of Coastal and Fighter Commands, and the area Combined headquarters. Within O.I.C., there were liaison officers from Coastal and Fighter Commands.

Before making any evaluation of the effectiveness of the organisation which Godfrey and Rushbrooke commanded during World War II, one must establish acceptable criteria for such a measure. The first of these must be the effect which the 'hard' intelligence work of the N.I.D. had on the outcome of the war, generally and at crucial points during the progress of the war, as well as in specific operations. It does not follow that because the N.I.D.'s work was perhaps ineffective at times that its organisation was at fault.

Secondly, the work of the N.I.D. must be seen against the general background of British intelligence work during World War II, and thirdly, a comparison with enemy organisation is an indicator of relative advance or otherwise within the N.I.D.

The Origins of Integration—Supreme Headquarters Intelligence Staff

Perhaps the best point at which to judge Naval intelligence as an organisation during World War II is the period before and during D-Day. By this stage, the naval element in overall military intelligence organisation was fully integrated with the other services. The Supreme Headquarters Intelligence Staff at Bushy Park was divided into two divisions, one concerned with information about the enemy and the other with counter-intelligence. The former was directly modelled on the pattern of the O.I.C. and the latter reflected the experience of the security sections of the military intelligence departments, as well as M.I. 5 and the American counterparts.

This division waged a ceaseless war against enemy agents and spies. General Strong describes the intelligence group gathered together at Bushy as "...perhaps the best and most experienced operational intelligence staff ever assembled. It included Navy, Army, and Air Force officers and it can be said to have been the forerunner in many respects of the present Defence Intelligence Staff in the British Ministry of Defence in London, and perhaps of the similar United States organisation, the defence intelligence agency."[72] N.I.D. cannot, therefore, be separated from the new joint and combined organisation about which Strong writes.

What the D-Day intelligence machine reveals is the final recognition to synthesise all intelligence data, and above all else, it recognised the need for forms of intelligence that hitherto were not considered relevant to waging war. The D-Day and post D-Day planners at last recognised that the strength and possible actions of opponents cannot be calculated solely in terms of the now obvious factors, such as the number and disposition of ships, but in terms too of the more subtle economic, geographic, psychological and allied factors, and that it is the judicious weighing all this evidence that will help predict enemy movements.

At this level, intelligence had moved into the top flight of strategic decision-making. The later integrated Defence Intelligence Staff, which Britain acquired (1963) was the natural heir to Eisenhower's organisation at Allied Headquarters.[73]

In General Strong's opinion, the break-up of the Allied HQ joint British-American organisation in July 1945, at British instigation, was a great mistake, mainly because many of the post-war intelligence problems concerning Germany might have been avoided, and cooperation with the Russians might have been easier. Strong writes: "The British had chafed too long under joint control and were determined to free themselves from any hint of continued subordination to

---

[72] Major-General Sir Kenneth Strong: Intelligence at the Top. p. 131.

[73] See Mr Peter Thorneycroft's White Paper on the Central Organisation of Defence, (Cmd. 2097): "...the staff as a whole will be integrated. It will be responsible...for producing a defence intelligence point of view on matters which are of interest to the Ministry of Defence."

American influence, and I think that even at that stage American intelligence had determined to go its own way."⁷⁴

Certainly, one can surmise and say that the British attitude prevented what should have been the next logical step in the integration process of British intelligence, namely joint Anglo-American intelligence. Regrettably, Britain did tend to stand still. Despite the formation of the Joint Intelligence Bureau in 1945 (with Strong as its first Director), it was fifteen years before the various departments concerned with armed forces intelligence were finally combined in the Defence Intelligence Staff, and this was achieved in the face of determined opposition.

Strong, who had a long wait before he fulfilled his ambition to become the first Director General of Intelligence, Ministry of Defence, writes that: "The main force behind the moves for a new order was Lord Mountbatten, and the integration of intelligence staffs to form a single Defence Intelligence Staff took place as part of the general scheme. It is true that he received powerful political support, but without his knowledge and prestige, it would have been impossible to make progress."⁷⁵

No doubt Lord Mountbatten's great insight and drive had been mainly responsible for accomplishing the final act, but it had to have an organisational and psychological precursor.⁷⁶ It can be no mere coincidence that Vice-Admiral Sir Norman Denning became Mountbatten's and Strong's main support in forming the Defence Intelligence Staff. As a head of the O.I.C. during World War II and later on as a D.N.I., Denning had, no doubt, realised very early on in his intelligence career that O.I.C. was the paradigm of the intelligence organisation of the Armed Forces required as a whole. It took twenty-five years to happen.

---

[74] Strong, p. 217.

[75] Major-General Sir Kenneth Strong: Intelligence at the Top. p. 225.

[76] Mountbatten of Burna, First Earl, Admiral of the Fleet: b. 1900; Naval Cadet 1913; Commander 1932; Captain 1937; Rear-Admiral 1946; Vice-Admiral 1949; Admiral 1953; Admiral of the Feet, 1956; in command H.M.S. Kelly and 5th Destroyer Flotilla 1939; H.M.S. Illustrious 1941; Commodore Combined Operations 1941-1942; Chief of Combined Operations 1942-1943; Supreme Allied Commander South-East Asia 1943-1946; Viceroy of India 1947; Governor-General of India 1947-1948; C.-in-C. Mediterranean 1952-1954; First Sea Lord 1955-1959; Chief of the Defence Staff 1959-1965.

The tremendous strides N.I.D. and British military intelligence mad during World War II cannot be seen in isolation. Its contribution, in terms of 'hard' intelligence was far greater than the purely non-military intelligence departments in Britain, whose sources of data and aims assumed a more limited role, when viewed against Eisenhower's Supreme Headquarters Intelligence staff. M.I. 5, quite naturally, was preoccupied with security, and cannot sensibly be regarded as a major intelligence department, only insofar as it provided very specific types of data.

Similarly with the Secret Intelligence Service, which, although it provided hard data, this again was of a limited type for purely military purposes, though much of the information from that source fitted into the overall mosaic of military intelligence data, assisting in the long-range and more immediate predictions to be made, rather than being an end in itself.

In 1939, the S.I.S. was very weak when Hitler made his swift blitzkrieg across the continent, inflicting severe setbacks on the British spy network; for example, The Hague spy network was broken up by the Nazis. By the spring of 1940, Britain was left with practically no effective intelligence service in Europe. The S.O.E. never really succeeded either, and tended to become characterised by amateurism. There seems to have been considerable negligence in the selection of personnel, and the S.O.E. lay itself open to penetration by traitors, notably Guy Burgess, who acquired infamy later, an obvious homosexual and married to an Austrian communist, as well as double agents, posing as refugees.

It would be naïve to say it was just bad luck that the Abwehr succeeded in breaking the S.O.E. radio network in Holland, and eventually, through radio signals from the U.K., built up a picture of the whole S.O.E. organisation in Holland. Clandestine intelligence gathering of the S.I.S. variety is very limited, as are the economic warfare activities of an organisation like the S.O.E., and certainly as far as naval intelligence was concerned in World War II, it would be quite misleading to ascribe a dominant role to the agent. Harold Nicolson wrote, in an uncannily accurate way: "…in diplomacy, at least, the part played by intelligence, by which is often meant the Secret Service, is very small indeed."[77]

Apart from diplomacy as such Nicolson's comments apply to naval intelligence when assessing the value of different sources of intelligence data. General Strong writes: "…my experiences of military intelligence leads me to accord them (spies), in general, a fairly modest place in the hierarchy of sources

---

[77] See Harold Nicolson's comments in Journey to Java.

even though their courage, ingenuity and tenacity frequently stirred profound admiration and clearly still rouses interests on account of the human aspects."[78] This viewpoint has been reinforced more recently by the researches of Captain Stephen Roskill, in his work on the life of Sir Maurice Hankey.

In the first volume of his biography, he writes: "…the common illusion, fostered by the popular press and by imaginative writers, that an Intelligence organisation depends on sensational and daring coups, such as the rifling of the safe of a foreign diplomat or the seduction of officers by beautiful but dissolute women is far from the truth. In fact, such coups are extremely rare, and when they are brought off their effects are often exaggerated.

"Rather does successful intelligence work depend on the painstaking collection of small pieces of information from scores of different sources, on classifying them for reliability by comparative processes, and on fitting the pieces together, as with a giant jigsaw puzzle, until a broad and accurate picture finally emerges. Hankey's work in the Mediterranean conformed very precisely to that pattern."[79]

Comparisons with American and German Intelligence

The advance made by N.I.D. during the last three years of peace and during World War II must be seen in the light of developments within the German and American organisations. The Americans quickly made up their losses after Pearl Harbour, but in 1939, they were very much behind the British. Their equivalent to O.I.C. was very ineffectual and its close ties with the State Department inhibited its main work. This situation was so bad that the members of the O.N.I. (Office of Naval Intelligence) hesitated before asking the State Department if it would put them in touch with American Naval officers who had worked in American consular agencies as intelligence workers.[80]

American Naval intelligence was symptomatic of the general malaise in American military intelligence pre-1939. General Eisenhower wrote: "The selected body of officers which had, between the two World Wars, truly absorbed the teachings of our unexcelled system of service schools was

---

[78] Strong: Intelligence at the Top. p. 133.
[79] Captain Stephen Roskill: Hankey. Man of Secrets. p. 81.
[80] Donald MacLachlan has examined the American record. He gives details of O.N.I.'s diminutive position. See p. 224, Room 39.

splendidly prepared, except in the field of practical intelligence training, to carry on the vital task of operational planning."[81] Eisenhower's criticism is echoed in other sources. The Navy Department, unlike the British Admiralty, impeded all constructive planning in the intelligence field, a fault which lay both within and outside the control of the formal American defence structure.

Certainly, the American public always viewed with repugnance everything that smacks of the spy; during the inter-war period, no funds were provided even to establish the basic requirements of an efficient intelligence system—a body of fact-finders. The only indication of active American Naval intelligence was the maintenance of attachés in most foreign capitals, but few of these were familiar with the essentials of intelligence work. The lowliness in rank of those who worked in American Naval intelligence pre-war is one indicator of the failure to emphasise the intelligence function.

Any intelligence information which did reach the Naval Staff could not be satisfactorily handled as there were too few people adequately trained and capable of analysing such material.

Unlike its British counterpart, the American Naval Intelligence Division failed to develop a clear plan for its own organisation, nor did it establish a workable scheme for classifying the type of information deemed necessary for determining the purposes and capabilities of potential enemies. But this did not apply solely to the U.S.N. The United States Army had problems too, as the official history indicates: "…there were insufficient facts on which to base strategic estimates; and there were no trained personnel for either strategic or combat intelligence."[82]

General Marshall eventually came to grips with M.I.D.'s problems, but not until as late as May 1942, when he appointed Major-General George V. Strong as head of the M.I.D. The solution of the U.S.N.'s dilemmas will be dealt with later. In 1939, the N.I.D. in Britain outstripped the Americans—it had created an organisational structure that enabled it to perform several clearly defined functions and, equally important, the structure of each individual's job in N.I.D. was such that it allowed him to be able to improve his performance.

The advance made by N.I.D. appear even greater still when compared with the German intelligence machine. After having examined the German documents, Donald MacLachlan interviewed Grand Admiral Donitz in November 1966.

---

[81] Dwight David Eisenhower: Crusade in Europe. p. 41.

[82] See a history of the Military Intelligence Division. MID, WDGS, ML, 725/1, AGO.

This is the impression he obtained: "It seems likely that the working of operational intelligence as understood in the Admiralty was not known to the German naval staff. Donitz and his officers received their intelligence material in digested form on the end of a teleprinter, they tried to combine in one office the product of operations with the study of the enemy's intentions and forces; which is a very different thing from having intelligence and operations working closely together but separated in command and organisation."[83]

This somewhat chronic organisation soon showed itself in German naval operations. On a purely inter-service basis alone, the teething troubles of N.I.D., in say for example, trying to achieve a satisfactory relationship with Coastal Command were mild compared with the experience of Raeder and Donitz. Where in the Third Reich did the causes originate?

There was never any German naval intelligence organisation that, on immediate inspection, resembled the British and American bodies. There were two intelligence agencies within the Nazi state—the Abwehr (German Secret Service) and the Sicherheitsdienst (SD) (the Gestapo Intelligence Service). Neither of these bodies had a history comparable with the N.I.D.'s. During World War I, the Germans had been fairly active in Spain, using it as a listening post for what was happening in France, checking British warships in Gibraltar, and supplying German U-boats and auxiliary cruisers in Spanish harbours with intelligence provided by agents.

Their activities were highly restricted, and it was not until 1 January 1935 that German intelligence was born with the appointment of Canaris (age forty-seven) as Chief of Intelligence. He was a brilliant and resourceful man. The Abswehr under Canaris was perhaps the only body within the Nazi state that offered an ideal refuge for manoeuvre against the regime, mainly because its unique position rendered it immune to the spying of the gestapo. In such a totalitarian state, intelligence data could possibly have acted as a sobering buffer between grandiose territorial plans of expansion on the one hand and political and military realities on the other.

Canaris tried to do this, but he was always fettered by the absence of sound political intelligence data, which remained the domain of the S.D. However, Canaris was clever enough not to take this situation too tragically. He recognised (as Hall had done) that the boundary between political and military intelligence is a fluid one. Canaris was sure enough of himself to be certain that he could

---

[83] Donald MacLachlin: Room 39. p. 123.

manoeuvre with sufficient dexterity so as to ensure that not only he himself should be well-informed on foreign political affairs, but also that, on occasions, he should be in a position to furnish his military superiors with such news as might be of use to them.

This is supported by Canaris' most authoritative biographer, K. H. Abshagen: "It was Canaris' ambition to be able, at all times, to lay before the Wehrmacht leaders the fullest—or in any case the most realistic—statement concerning military, political, and economic conditions in any given country."[84] What is more, Canaris was able to inform the generals and admirals of the next moves of the SS and the gestapo, a point emphasised by most historians of the Nazi era.

The two principal differences between N.I.D. and Abwehr policy and organisation have become apparent; firstly, there was never any official recognition of the need for a dialogue between the political decision-makers and the intelligence gatherers and interpreters, and their masters—the military planners and commanders. Canaris attempted to cement this breach. However, secondly, this was indicative of the general problem of the military in the Nazi state—Hitler had no real high regard for the professional expertise of his Commanders-in-Chief, and it was part of his Weltanschauung to disregard hard military facts when making political plans.

Whatever interpretation or school of thought one adheres to when examining the causes of the World War II, there is no doubt that there was a gulf between the megalomaniac Hitler on the one hand, and the more rational militarists and planners on the other who, whatever their political sympathies and aspirations for Germany, viewed the situation in terms of hard military facts and probabilities. This is seen, for example, during the summer of 1938 when Canaris did not confine his warnings to the generals and admirals.

He overcame his personal dislike of Ribbentrop and endeavoured to convince the Minister of Foreign Affairs that there was danger of a general European war if Czechoslovakia were openly attacked. This was of no avail. K. H. Abshagen gives a lucid insight into the Abswehr's role when he writes: "Officially, the Abswehr knew nothing, or very little indeed, of the real strategic plans. Canaris' department was much better informed about the enemy and his plans. Thus, the influence of the Abswehr on operations was slight and, at best, of an indirect character. The stories that represent Canaris as one of the prime directors—or even as the leading spirit—of the German war machine are as far

---

[84] K. H. Abshagen: Canaris. p. 105.

from the truth as the reports that, through the Abswehr's treason, German plans of campaign reached the enemy's hands. Of such plans, save, possibly, in the merest outline, the Abswehr had no knowledge at all."[85]

On all fronts, Canaris' work was checked, and often, for professional reasons, he would refuse to perform certain tasks. To illustrate the former point, Hitler totally ignored Canaris' warnings at the time of the Norwegian campaign, when the Abswehr predicted that strong British Naval forces would be waiting in Norwegian waters for the German force invading Norway. In the event the British were not there, and although Canaris' reasons were very sound, it did not enhance his reputation with Hitler.

(Canaris knew British intelligence in neutral Sweden was highly efficient, and he quite rightly assumed that Swedish captains who visited Stettin and the other German Baltic harbours would report to British agents on their return to Sweden the massive build-up of an invasion force. The British did, in fact, receive such information.) On the latter point, Canaris refused to allow the Abswehr to become an instrument of clandestine warfare, just as the N.I.D. had lost this role after World War I. For example, on Canaris' instructions, the order of General Keitel to the Abswehr to plan and execute the assassination of the French general Weygand was disregarded.[86]

In the light of American and German experiences, one can clearly see how N.I.D. had more fully conceptualised its role and structured itself accordingly, albeit somewhat pragmatically at times. N.I.D. had defined its general purpose—set itself tasks, acquired for itself authority, and inter-service political-military relationships, and the standards it set itself, and the controls placed upon it were well defined and understood. Admiral Godfrey knew quite clearly to whom he was responsible, what discretionary powers he had, and the limits he could go to before consulting his superiors.

By 1945, N.I.D. had clearly defined boundaries, preventing duplication of effort and the political in-fighting that must ensure in any large organisation as a result of trespassing on other departments' territory.

---

[85] K. H. Abshagen: Canaris. p. 159.

[86] K. H. Abshagen: Canaris. p. 192.

Chapter Two

A Critical Appraisal of the Role of Selected Personalities Who Worked in Naval Intelligence

The various Directors of Naval Intelligence since 1882, when Captain William Henry Hall became the first D.N.I., until the last Director, Admiral Denning, ended the line of D.N.I.s in 1964, have varied immensely in the eighty-two years British Naval intelligence was a formal organisation. They have varied in their general backgrounds and experiences, in the ways they viewed their roles, the methods and personnel they selected, and above all, the impact they had on war at sea.

In any analysis of the organisational development of N.I.D., these principal dramatis personae cannot be seen just as the heads of an increasingly more important department, but as men who personally fashioned the detailed policies and growth of naval intelligence in defence planning and operations. They were men who had the opportunity to be intimately concerned with the minutiae of their department's work, and make day-to-day decisions which they, as professional naval officers, could see as perhaps being more meaningful for the operational Navy than the work of many of their Naval Staff colleagues.

It was a post which, seized with vigour and resolve, had greater potential than perhaps many of the other senior staff appointments.

The D.N.I. in Wartime and His Role

In war, the D.N.I. assumed a far more significant and powerful role. The two World Wars must, therefore, act as yardsticks for assessing the achievements and advances of naval intelligence, since only then could operational intelligence be applied in the full war context. In every sense this was true. Unlike his opposite numbers in the Army and the Air Force, the D.N.I. was at the heart of the struggle against Germany. The Admiralty, unlike the War Office and the Air Ministry, was an operational headquarters, controlling the fleet at sea—the D.N.I. was a central figure in this.

This is not to undervalue peacetime intelligence, far from it. Amongst the many factors which historical interpretation attributes to Britain's military dilemma in the last years of peace before World War II must be the factor of poor intelligence information. That there was not a Hall or Godfrey to give a fillip to the N.I.D. in the inter-war period is a reflection of many factors; that men of their quality were not easy to come by; that the D.N.I. appointment was not considered a good career job for an Admiral in peacetime, that the work of the N.I.D. was possibly misguided or lacked dynamism.

From this, one can surmise that the Navy was more fortunate to have men of Hall's and Godfrey's calibre available at the right moment in time. However, it was purely fortuitous that they were appointed and not someone else. This was especially true in Hall's case. Certainly, there was no pre-appointment training for the D.N.I. By definition, he was of wide naval experience and fairly senior, but there was no recognised career pattern for a future or existing D.N.I. The worst thing possible was for the job to go to a man in his last naval appointment before retirement.

In retrospect, it should always have gone to a man with a real future, and someone who had had experience of intelligence work previously. This rarely happened.

The Recruitment of Civilians to the N.I.D.

However, the D.N.I. above all else had to understand what the men at sea wanted and needed, and they had to have the tactical and strategic knowledge to judge what was in the enemy's mind. Few D.N.I.s were ever lacking in this. But there was nothing like a modern job specification for the appointment of D.N.I. and certainly no training system for him and his subordinates. As a result of this, the means by which personnel were acquired were unsystematic and often largely dependent upon personal contacts.

The needs of World War I rapidly meant the recruitment of many civilians to the N.I.D. This was mainly due to naval personnel not possessing the necessary aptitudes and skills for intelligence work, or was, at least, the reason given for the recruitment of so many civilians. Certainly, the conventional selection procedures for service officers did not pertain to tasks performed by the N.I.D., as the skills required were so different from those of normal career jobs. The point should be made that the service should have begun to formally train selected officers in intelligence work, as indeed N.I.D. did later in its growth.

Prince Louis of Battenburg (D.N.I. 1902-1905)[87] was a firm advocate of a specially trained intelligence staff, and he also saw the D.N.I. as an Admiralty Board member, second only to the First Sea Lord. His son, Admiral of the Fleet, Earl Mountbatten of Burma, was to become a firm protagonist in favour of service personnel populating the key posts in naval intelligence. Certainly, when he was in a position to mould the future of defence intelligence in Britain, his emphasis was on a service personnel hierarchy, save in the area of highly specialised technical skills.

That the service did resort to recruiting civilian personnel on a large scale in both World Wars was as much due to the pragmatic way intelligence was developing, and the way in which needs tended to emerge, rather than the complete absence of skills in naval personnel. It was far easier to acquire a barrister from civilian life, familiar with assessing evidence and presenting it in a logically digestible form, than to attempt to develop these skills in a naval officer, who no doubt spent most of his career performing less academic tasks.

The N.I.D. was always sensible enough to navalise its civilians as possible and where professional naval knowledge was required for tasks performed by civilians, naval personnel were always on hand to give the necessary information and help with interpretation.

There can be no doubt that the two doyens of British Naval Intelligence during the period were Admiral Sir Reginald Hall and Admiral John Godfrey; a comparative examination of their work will show how epochal their periods of office were, contrasting markedly with the inter-war period, and it will also provide a means by which to contrast the major developments in naval intelligence.

Godfrey's view of the inter-war D.N.I.s is summarised in this somewhat pointed comment in his memoirs: "Four of the D.N.I.s were not more than average: one was an outstanding technical and gunnery specialist but not a thruster…one got on the wrong side of M.I. 5. Of the eight, only one, Hall's successor, was of the calibre that could establish a great department and had he

---

[87] Battenburg, Prince Louis, Admiral of the Fleet: entered R.N. 1868; joint secretary naval and military committee on defence, 1894; A.D.N.I. 1900; D.N.I. 1902-1905; second in command, Mediterranean 1907; C.-in-C. Atlantic 1908; Second Sea Lord 1911; First Sea Lord 1912; resigned October 1914.

held the office for five years, he might have achieved something worthwhile; but he was wanted for another post, and lasted a year and a half, and was relieved by a nonentity."[88]

The era of Hall is a vanished world when compared with the defence intelligence structure of today. Captain Roskill has emphasised this point: "Today, when the Foreign Office exerts a paramount influence over all intelligence activities, it may seem extraordinary that until about 1919, the D.N.I. should have held virtually all the threads in his own hands, and should have decided on the time and manner of using the knowledge the he possessed."[89]

Admiral Hall's period of office marked a time of identification for the N.I.D. This is not to say that the department had wasted time in the pre-1914 period. The founding of the Committee of Imperial Defence drew out the activities of the N.I.D.; for example, Rear-Admiral C. L. Ottley, the D.N.I. 1905-1907, was deeply involved in that committee's activities.[90] The C.I.D. gave impetus to the N.I.D.'s activities.

In June 1905, for example, following discussions in the C.I.D., the War Office and Admiralty formed a joint committee to review and make recommendations for the defence of the principal naval bases at home and overseas. In 1906, Lt. Colonel Maurice Hankey (who worked in the N.I.D. from 1902-1908) was sent on a fact-finding mission of all the principal British bases abroad to assess their fortifications, role and powers to withstand attack.[91]

The first seeds of strategic intelligence gathering were sown in the last eight years before the Great War. In December 1906, the Ballard Committee, the brainchild of the First Sea Lord, Fisher, set to work.[92] He had decided to form a small and select body to draft in great secrecy naval war plans in the event of a war against Germany. This committee immersed itself in the strategic problems which would arise. In the light of the nature of the Great War, it is more than

---

[88] Godfrey Memoirs. Vol. 8. p. 156. On pages 157-158, Godfrey deals further with the collapse of the Hall tradition and the organisational rundown in the 1920s and 1930s.
[89] Captain S. Roskill: Hankey. Man of Secrets. Vol. I. p. 80.
[90] Ottley, Rear-Admiral Sir Charles: b. 1858; entered R.N. 1871; Captain 1899; naval attaché Washington, Rome, Tokyo, St. Petersburg and Paris, 1899-1904; on staff of the Committee of Imperial Defence, 1904; D.N.I. 1905; Secretary of the C.I.D. 1907-1912.
[91] See Captain Roskill's account of Hankey's activities in the N.I.D. 1902-1908 in his: Hankey. Man of Secrets.
[92] See J. Ehrmann: Cabinet Government and War 1890-1940. (C.U.P. 1958).

ironic to note how the ideas of the committee never came to fruition, based as they were, in the best traditions of the Elder Pitt, on a blue-water strategy, and not, as developed, a European land-based strategy.

The N.I.D. appreciated the susceptibilities of Germany's economy to blockade, and the ability the Navy possessed, in conjunction with the Army, to strike at the enemy in overseas theatres at times and places of British choice. These two factors were closely allied to the need to protect Britain from invasion and to protect British merchant shipping against a sustained attack. Mahan's message had had a profound effect upon many members of the Naval Staff.

Hall's Review of Main Intelligence Problem in 1914 and How He Solved It

Although much thorough, painstaking and valuable work had been done then before 1914 on the strategic deployment of British Naval forces, it was not until Hall came into office in November 1914, succeeding Rear-Admiral H. F. Oliver, that attention was paid to detailed intelligence gathering and interpretation. His appointment was as much by chance as design. His health broke down whilst he was Captain of H.M.S. Queen Mary at the same time as the D.N.I. vacancy occurred.

Hall was a veery remarkable man, insofar as he adapted from being a sea captain to developing into a great D.N.I. He quickly defined the problem—he saw that although on 4 August 1914, the British fleet was at the height of battle efficiency and at its war bases there was still no means of obtaining intelligence of the German fleet's movements, and without that intelligence, the British Navy would be almost powerless. It is true that Britain possessed sound information on Germany's war potential but the problem of how to monitor satisfactorily the German fleet's activities had not been studied.

Central to Hall's success as D.N.I. was his development and extensive use of the wireless tracking and deciphering skills of Room 40. He quickly realised the potential of Ewing's team—that wireless traffic was the only ready method of collecting information of enemy movements.[93] The use of ships for observing

---

[93] It should be noted that before Sir Alfred Ewing, there was no effective decoding service, and though Hall took great pains to keep the work of Ewing's small band highly secret, all of the other great powers had been operating deciphering departments in peacetime for several years. Admiral Sir William James gives details of this in his book,

enemy ships in their harbours (as Nelson had done with the French) was no longer possible with the advent of the submarine. A British warship running the gauntlet off the Jade stood a very good chance of being sunk by an enemy submarine.

Wireless traffic became of paramount importance. Signals could give the position of a ship, its direction and speed, and from this information might be deduced the operation involved. Moreover, the message itself might be deciphered, giving valuable information. Room 40's directional wireless plotting and signal deciphering became the keystone of Hall's success. It supported virtually all of his areas of activity, whether tracking German U-boats or helping to draw the United States into the war against Germany.

Hall's Involvement with British Foreign Policy

The most marked contrast that separates the Hall and Godfrey eras is Hall's involvement with British foreign policy. After 1919, the N.I.D. had its function strictly limited to naval affairs. The Foreign Office felt that Hall had too often taken matters into his own hands, as a result usually of Room 40 intercepting diplomatic messages which should have been passed immediately to the Foreign Office. After World War I, it was decided that future D.N.I.s would never be allowed to wield the power enjoyed by Hall.[94] However, it was a result of

---

The Eyes of the Navy. He shows how especially efficient were the Russian and French organisations.

[94] A committee, under the chairmanship of Rear-Admiral J. C. Ley, was appointed to review the role and system of naval intelligence. Its findings led to a re-definition of N.I.D. responsibilities and organisation. Details of this are contained in Adm. 137, 1630. At one stage in 1918, the D.N.I. and D.D.N.I. titles were abolished, but were soon revived on 5 April 1918 (see Adm. 137, 1630, p. 78.) However, it should not be assumed that Hall's system was radically changed after 1918. Many of the reforms which Hall put forward himself, as a result of wartime experiences, were implemented.

His recommendations for establishing base intelligence officers, tightening up the system for handling and distributing intelligence data (on a 'need to know' basis) for security reasons, as well as improving operational efficiency, and major improvements in the organisation of the N.I.D. were all implemented. See Adm. 137, 1630 Ps. 12-14, 131-134, Public Record Office. The organisational details of the N.I.D. in the first years after World War I, when the organisational and role adjustments had been made after the Hall era, are to be found in Adm. 116, 1842, Public Record Office.

initiative and drive and the ability to develop and exploit a situation that had enabled Hall to acquire the power he did.

The uniqueness of the events of war threw up the unpredictable situation, which a man of Hall's character and calibre was able to successfully exploit. Shortly before World War II began, there were almost panic moves to build up the N.I.D. by an infusion of new talent, not merely because of the peacetime run-down, but also because there had been a deliberate move to restrict the N.I.D.s activities after the experience of Hall's regime. Why then did Hall acquire this reputation and were the Hall critics justified?[95]

Firstly, Hall's political activities—he had a major hand in secret negotiations with Turkey, whom he wanted to detach from the Central Powers, and, he hoped, thereby preventing the need for a Dardanelles Campaign. Through his agents, he hoped to either persuade Turkey to break with Germany and to promote revolution against Enver Pasha and his 'Young Turk' party then in power, or at least persuade the more moderate members of the party to make peace with Britain. His agents were intercepting telegrams between Germany and Turkey, and Room 40 was deciphering them.

At one stage, Hall ordered his agents to offer £500,000 for the complete surrender of the Dardanelles and the removal of all mines, and he had a plan to offer £4M to the Turks if they joined the Allis. Fisher himself intervened and stopped the talks. The critical point is that Hall was bartering with public money without any form of official approval. The Foreign Office had no knowledge of his activities. Admiral James writes that he took this sort of responsibility on himself because he considered that the essential point in all such transactions was that they should be known to as few people as possible.

Perhaps Hall's greatest single piece of political intelligence work was his handling of the Zimmermann Telegram, intercepted and deciphered by Room 40. Its priceless contents told Hall the Germans had made the great decision to begin unrestricted submarine warfare and that they were preparing to bring Mexico into the war on their side in the event of the United States joining the Allied side.

---

[95] The most detailed documented account of Hall's time as D.N.I. is still Admiral Sir Williams James's The Eyes of the Navy. He makes additional comments on Room 40's activities in 'Room 40', an article in the Edinburgh University Journal, XXII, Spring 1965. p. 50-54. The papers relating to Hall's political activities were destroyed at the end of World War I. This was confirmed by the Head of the Naval Historical Branch, Rear-Admiral P. N. Buckley, CB, DSO.

Retrospectively, Hall's handling of the situation was brilliant; his sense of timing was perfect.

Hall did not pass the telegram to the Foreign Office because he felt that it might be handled by someone who might be unfamiliar with Room 40's activities and who might compromise part or all of its activities by revealing the telegram's contents in the wrong way and at the wrong time, thus giving away Room 40's secrets to the Germans. Hall personally handled the American Ambassador, Dr Page, and had the impression created throughout the world that the telegram had been obtained on Mexican soil.

What galled the Americans so much was the way the Germans had used the American Embassy as an errand boy to transmit a message that contained a plot against its own territorial integrity. Admiral James comments: "This piece of effrontery can never have been equalled in the history of political intrigue."[96] The part the telegram played in bringing the Americans into war had been assessed elsewhere.[97] President Wilson told Congress that the intrigues of the German government had served to "convince us at last that that government entertains no real friendship for us and means to act against our peace and security at its convenience."

Hall had surely done a great deal for Anglo-American relations, at the same time preserving Room 40's secrecy and his own integrity. However, the British Foreign Office was less pleased with Hall than Woodrow Wilson. Admiral James quotes a letter from Dr Page congratulating Hall on being made a K.C.M.G., in which Page quotes from a letter he had received from the President: "You will, at an early time, take some private occasion to assure Admiral Hall of my very great appreciation of what he had done and of the spirit in which he had done it." Surely no greater compliment could have been paid to Hall?

The above example does illustrate the extent of Hall's influence; his position was never seriously challenged at the time. The American Embassy in London was still fed by Room 40 with information concerning the United States; the source was the Berlin-Mexico, Berlin-Buenos Aires, Berlin-Madrid wireless traffic. As a result of the Zimmermann Telegram, there was a certain amount of

---

[96] Admiral Sir William James: The Eyes of the Navy. p. 137.

[97] Barbara Tuchmann in her, The Zimmermann Telegram, gives a fully documented account of the political aspects of the telegram. The most recent authoritative account of the cryptographic details can be found in David Kahn's, The Codebreakers (Weidenfeld and Nicolson, 1966.)

surprise and resentment that a Director of Naval Intelligence had been handling affairs that were the sole concern of the Foreign Office.

In mitigation, it may be said that as Hall's staff was the only body in existence who could work on cyphered messages and suspicious letters and that, as Room 40 worked as a team, it was never practicable to detach part of the staff to work in the Foreign Office. Hall's decisions must surely stem from complete confidence in his own judgment, and as the guardian of Room 40's secrets, he would not take the risk involved in permitting messages in their original cyphered form to leave the Admiralty.

Nonetheless, he made critical decisions which were never to confront Admiral Godfrey. Hall could and did pass on to government departments (in a form that did not disclose the source) everything in the deciphered messages that he thought they should know. The few men holding responsible positions, who knew how Hall was obtaining his information, trusted him implicitly.

Hall's power was unique because there were no lines of demarcation between the N.I.D. and the Foreign Office. This stemmed from the fact that the N.I.D.'s role, functions and responsibilities were ill-defined. Only the experiences of World War I revealed these. The exigencies of war, throwing up daily crises and emergencies called for decisions. Hall was prepared to make those decisions on his own authority. Godfrey was never faced with this predicament because his boundaries were more clearly defined for him.

The part Admiral Hall played in the Roger Casement affair illustrates his deep involvement in non-naval matters. However, it was Rom 40 which again provided the basic information which enabled Hall to act. Room 40 picked up signals indicating Casement's impending arrival in Ireland, and signs of a revolt planned for Easter Day and later postponed until the Easter Monday. As a result, Casement was captured and interrogated by Hall and Sir Basil Thomson, the head of the British counter-espionage service.[98] Hall was unofficially responsible for diverting sympathy from Casement when the appeal against the death sentence was heard on 17 July 1916.

---

[98] Throughout the war, the partnership of Hall and Thomson was of incalculable value to the Allies. Both had a remarkable flair for the strange tasks that so often confronted them; both could quickly take the measure of a spy or traitor, and both were adept at extracting information from prisoners. Sir Basil Thomson gives details in his book: The Story of Scotland Yard. Grayson and Grayson, London, 1935.

Hall released to the Americans the notorious Casement Diaries, indicating that he had possibly had homosexual tendencies. This had a profound psychological effect upon pro-Casement American public opinion. Whatever view is taken of Hall's action, and most writers have been highly critical, the point remains that Hall was in a good position, almost unassailable, to become so involved.

Hall's breadth of action is shown by the role his department increasingly came to play in counter-espionage work. Hall hoped that as a result N.I.D. would be more intimately related to another source which might add to the overall picture of the German position, which his department was attempting to produce. Under Hall, the N.I.D. worked hand-in-hand with Scotland Yard, M.I. 5, and the War Office Intelligence department. On 5 August 1914, twenty-two German agents were arrested by Scotland Yard, who had been watching them for some time. Only three German spies escaped back to Germany at this time.[99]

Hall ensured that German spies were tried in secret, so that false information could be fed back via German agents in neutral countries to Germany. After the Dogger Bank engagement, for example, faked photographs were sent to Germany of supposedly damaged British warships. They were ostensibly sent by a German spy; somewhat amusingly money was sent in return. Hall also persuaded the government of the necessity of censoring all mail.

The German master spy, Franz von Rintelen, was tracked down and arrested through Hall's organisation. Rintelen had recruited saboteurs from amongst the German-Americans—these fomented strikes in United States munitions factories supplying arms for the Allied cause, and they had arranged for incendiary devices to be placed in the holds of ships carrying munitions to Europe. Hall's man in Washington, the Naval Attaché, Captain Guy Gaunt, R.N. eventually undermined the Rintelen organisation.

On his return to Europe, von Rintelen's ship was stopped by a patrol boat off Ramsgatge and von Rintelen was arrested. He was interned for the duration of the war.[100]

---

[99] Roger Hilsman gives a detailed account of this in his: Strategic Intelligence. p. 20.

[100] A detailed account of von Rintelen's activities is given in his autobiography: The Dark Invader. Peter Davies, London, 1933. He pays a great personal tribute to Hall's skill and organisation. Captain Gaunt's greatest success was to plant some Czech agents in the Austrian Consulate-General in New York, and they obtained for him copies of

Hall was not totally successful everywhere. In South America, his agents had great difficulty in countering the activities of German agents because of the neutrality of the countries in which they worked. German activity was centred on interfering the ships' cargoes bound for Britain. Hall became gravely concerned with the sabotage of grain ships. At best, he was able to keep German activity to an acceptable level.

Admiral Hall rapidly built up his own espionage service. He realised the value of the agent, particularly in the principal neutral countries—Holland, Switzerland, Spain and Sweden. His development of this form of intelligence collection was solely upon his own initiative—there was no external control upon his activities. This was natural enough as there was no central Defence organisation which could monitor N.I.D.'s activities, in terms of evaluating the quality of the data it produced.

On the espionage front, Hall again tended to become involved in other than purely naval affairs. For example, he managed to persuade Anthony Drexel, an American sportsman of some note, to allow his yacht, The 'Sayonara', to be used for espionage purposes. On one mission, the yacht was used to link up with the Sinn Feiners in Ireland and obtain details of their plans, and Hall hoped to find out where Sir Roger Casement intended landing on his return to Ireland from Germany and prevent him from unifying the anti-British Catholic element in southern Ireland.

However, Hall's main espionage effort was directed towards purely military targets. From the moment he took charge of the N.I.D., he organised a network of agents and local residents sympathetic to the British cause in every quarter where sooner or later British forces might engage the enemy. In July 1915, for example, he set up intelligence service in Greece and the Levant, and his agents there reported details of any troop movements and naval activities to Room 40. In 1991, the N.I.D. planned the relief of the Serbian Army from starvation. The Royal Navy landed stores and food on the Dalmatian coast.

Hall selected his agents with great care. One of his most distinguished was the writer, A. E. W. Mason, who worked for Hall in neutral Spain. He achieved some remarkable successes and repeatedly destroyed the plans of German agents; he was able to win over to N.I.D.'s services Juan March, the powerful head of a

---

several critical documents being sent by the Austrian Ambassador to Europe Gaunt's other main adversary in the U.S.A. was the German Ambassador, Count Berstorff, who was fomenting anti-British feeling and openly supporting the pro-Irish organisations.

smuggling ring operating in southern Spain. After World War I, Mason managed to persuade M.I. 6 to keep the Gibraltar-Tangier network going, an organisation which became very useful in World War II.[101]

The contribution which the N.I.D. made to the war at sea was perhaps nowhere more self-evident than in the campaign against the U-boats. Here, Hall mustered every available source of information and it was a result of successes here that Hall was able to show that Room 40 was not just a cryptographic bureau, but an intelligence centre.[102] The staff of Room 40 became characterised by a flair for linking together items of information which, at first sight, did not appear to be inter-related. Every plan, and daily intelligence summary, paid close attention to minute detail.

Against considerable internal opposition Hall's organisation held its own, although its successes and failure could never be publicly aired. Public opinion never became aware of the part intelligence had played in naval operations. For instance, on 15 December 1914, the Germans raided the east coast of England. Room 40 warned Operations and a battle cruiser squadron was sent to intercept Hipper. Bad weather prevented contact and the bombardment of Scarborough followed, soon to be followed by a public outcry against the incompetence of the Royal Navy.

Sir Winston Churchill discusses the implications of this action in his *World Crisis*: "We could never admit for fear of compromising our secret information, where our squadrons were, or how near the German raiding cruisers had been to destruction."

The reputation which N.I.D. acquired depended on the quality of its staff. Both Hall and Godfrey relied heavily on civilians from the professional world for the main tasks of analysis and interpretation. Even Sir Alfred Ewing's staff of codebreakers were civilians, mostly academics from Osborne and Dartmouth Naval Colleges.

A glance at the backgrounds of the men who joined Hall and became N.I.D. leaders gives a strong impression of the academic, analytically-oriented mind Hall quickly realised was vital for successful intelligence work: Sir Philip Baker Wilgraham, fellow of All Souls; Thomas Inskip, K. C., later to become a Lord Chancellor; Harold Russell, a barrister; Algernon Cecil, a distinguished historian;

---

[101] A. E. W. Mason's work for N.I.D. is detailed in R. L. Green's biography: A. E. W. Mason.

[102] The confusion over signal intelligence at Jutland further enhanced Hall's case.

George Prothero, editor of the *Quarterly Review*; L. G. Wickham-Legg, a fellow of New College, Oxford; James Randall, a City wine merchant; Claud Serocold, a City figure who became Hall's personal assistant; Lords Herschell and Abinger; and Ralph Vaughn Williams.

Ewing made George Young (later Sir George Young) head of the diplomatic crypto section.[103] It was these men who sifted the information pouring into Room 40 and produced the daily intelligence summaries. Hall recruited three professors to prepare handbooks providing intelligence appreciations of new territories as the scene of military operations changed; these were Professor Dickson of Reading University, Professor Calder of Manchester, and Professor Stevenson of Glasgow.

It took Hall some time to overcome the prejudices of the Naval Staff against receiving information from civilians. Operations Division were very much against accepting intelligence reports from men without sufficient professional naval knowledge. They were highly critical of their major role in the cryptanalyst section, where it was claimed civilians could not possibly understand all the implications of naval signals. Hall stood firm and eventually won the day because Room 40's staff were able to prove themselves by sheer success.

In the process, Hall made many enemies. However, his many friends and subordinates realised what a great manager of staff Hall was.[104] When discussing the personnel shakeup in the Admiralty in 1917, Professor Arthur Marder writes: "Also kept on was Captain Reginald Hall, the D.N.I. (promoted to Rear-Admiral in April 1917) considered by many as one of the few great brains of the war, which, indeed he was."[105] Marder's words are eloquent testimony to Hall's great contribution to the naval side of the Great War.

British Naval intelligence, as with other aspects of Britain's defence system, entered the doldrums during the inter-war period. Rear-Admiral John Godfrey,

---

[103] By October 1914, Young informed Hall that he had details of German plans to raise revolt against British rule in India and Afghanistan, and about German sabotage in America and the Far East.

[104] In "Eyes of the Navy" Admiral James gives details of Hall's staff and his staff problems, and his clashes with other senior naval personnel and high-ranking civil servants. Further details and a different viewpoint of N.I.D.'s staff composition and the politics of naval intelligence are given in A.W. Ewing's: The Man of Room 40. The Life of Sir Alfred Ewing. Hutchinson. London, 1939.

[105] Arthur J. Marder: From the Dreadnought to Scapa Flow: Vol. 4. p. 61.

(D.N.I. 1939-1942), the man who was to revitalise naval intelligence at the crucial time, recalls in his memoirs an assessment he made whilst Deputy Director of Plans at the Admiralty in 1934:

"I was conscious of a certain lack of design which we did our best to mitigate by creating a future of our own devising, but one uncorrelated with politics and the temper of the country, or with the personality of cabinets and prime ministers…Thus, the planners found themselves working in a strange atmosphere in which past, present and future, facts, inferences and wishful thinking, became intermingled, and all sense of resolute purpose was blurred. Again, our prime ministers were peace-loving pacifist of passivist—and could not bear to think of war or the threat of war."[106]

Godfrey's Reorganisation of N.I.D. and Some of His Staff

When Godfrey took up his appointment on 3 February 1939, he came as a breath of fresh air to the N.I.D. He quickly assessed the problem and sought immediate solutions, in marked contrast with his predecessors as D.N.I., since the halcyon days of Admiral Hall, perhaps the most notorious between 1919 and 1939 being Admiral Sir Barry Domville (D.N.I. 1927-1930), a member of the sinister pro-German organisation, the Link, who was arrested in 1940 under Regulation 18b.[107] Admiral Godfrey writes in his memoirs of the impression he quickly acquired of the place of intelligence in the Admiralty, on assuming office in 1939.

"None of the Assistant Chiefs of Staff or Directors of operational divisions knew anything about intelligence. I myself knew precious little. There was no particular reason why we should have done, because the subject was swept out of sight during the twenty years of peace. A half-hearted attempt was made to

---

[106] Admiral John Godfrey: Memoirs; typescript is in the National Maritime Museum, Greenwich, and the Ministry of Defence (Naval) Library, Empress State Building, London.

[107] Comvile, Admiral Sir Barry Edward: 1878-1971; entered R.N. 1892; Commander 1909; Captain 1916; Rear-Admiral 1927; Asst. Sec. C.I.D. 1912-1914; Director of Plans, Admiralty, 1920-1922, D.N.I. 1927-1930; Vice-Admiral commanding third cruiser squadron, Mediterranean, 1931-1932; President RNC, Greenwich, 1932-1934; Admiral and retired list, 1936.

establish an intelligence course at Greenwich alongside the Staff College, but it petered out."[108]

In order to turn the N.I.D. from a static peacetime organisation to a dynamic wartime one, Godfrey brought in civilians of distinction and talent, men such as the young city stockbroker Ian Fleming (who became personal assistant to the D.N.I.), the solicitor Edward Merrett (Godfrey's private secretary), Ewen Montagu, Patrick Beesly and the Oxford Don, Frederick Wells. Godfrey quickly laid down that any intelligence data leaving the N.I.D. must be strictly separated from opinion, so that it would retain its authority and reliability. Initially, therefore, Room 39[109] tended to concentrate on radio intelligence.[110]

Godfrey rapidly organised his department on a section basis, with section heads directly responsible to him. The hierarchical structure he created was a direct reflection of the developing functions and techniques of the N.I.D. (see Appendix A for a diagrammatic representation of the N.I.D. sectional structure during World War II). The structure therefore was subject to considerable change, particularly during the early years of the war. The various sections grew at very different speeds, and some sections that were very prominent in 1943/1944 were hardly thought of in the 1940/1. As a general description, it would be true to say that N.I.D. was split into twenty sections, N.I.D. 17 being the 'coordinating' section, and N.I.D. 14 was the secretariat of the D.N.I.

The organisation Godfrey left in 1943 was continued by his successor as D.N.I., Rear-Admiral Rushbrooke (D.N.I. 1943-1946). The initial kingpin of the N.I.D. was N.I.D. 8—the operational intelligence centre; within this section the submarine tracking room tended to dominate. In January 1941, Commander Roger Winn, R.N.V.R. (later Captain, C.B., R.N.V.R.) became its head. It was Roger Winn who played the vital role of plotting the U-boats, working in close conjunction with Commander Richard Hall, R.N., who was responsible for plotting the mass of allied shipping.

---

[108] Godfrey Memoirs.

[109] This was the centre of N.I.D. during World War II, located in the Admiralty, and the successor to the Room 40, of Admiral Hall's day. Donald MacLachlan writes: "…legend and performance both played a part in giving Room 39 its reputation." Room 39, p. 4. He described it as "the bridge of the N.I.D. ship." Room 39, p. 10.

[110] In 1941, British warships captured two German weather ships, the Munchen and the Lauenburg, both yielding crucial German naval cyphers.

Roger Winn built up a biography of each U-boat, working in close liaison with the Chief of Staff to the C.-in-C. Western Approaches in Liverpool, the Chief of Staff to the A.O.C.-in-C. Coastal Command and with no. 15 Group, R.A.F. He also had a direct link with the Director of anti-submarine warfare and the head of Operations Division. Winn was assisted by Lieutenant-Commander Patrick Beesley, R.N.V.R., and Lieutenant-Commander Peter Kemp, R.N., the D/F expert in N.I.D.8. Winn was to prove himself an ace detective—predicting the U-boat's next move once it had given its position away.

As a result of brilliant successes, Winn's position increased in strength, particularly in terms of O.I.C.'s relationship with Operations Division. By 1943, Admiral Edelsten, the Assistant Chief of Naval Staff, ruled that no ship or convoy was to be routed without consulting Winn first and not to be routed against his advice. Once Winn had made a decision, he stuck by it. Donald MacLachlan describes the activity of the Citadel U-boat-merchant shipping plot as "like watching a precious patient fighting hour-by-hour for life."[111]

Perhaps one of the most outstanding pieces of routing during World War II was the assembling of four hundred ships off Gibraltar for the 'Torch' landings in 1942. The Hall-Winn organisation was given thirty-six hours in which to plan the movement of the slow convoy from the Bristol Channel and the fast one from the Clyde on a course for west of Biscay to avoid the U-boats coming and going from their French bases.

Like Hall, Godfrey chose his men well. Ian Fleming, who worked for Combined Operations as well as N.I.D.[112] had a gift for jollying along senior officers, and getting the job done. For example, his no. 30 assault unit was a great success—nicknamed 'Fleming's private Navy', it began tentative operations in the Middle East under the dual command of Dunstan Curtis, a Coastal Forces officer, and Quentin Riley, a pre-war polar explorer, mainly conducting beach

---

[111] Donald MacLachlan: Room 39. p. 120.

[112] It was some time before N.I.D. and Operations Division realised the value that Combined Operations had for providing intelligence data. It is possible to surmise that a much greater wealth of data could have been obtained much earlier in the war, and might conceivably have shortened it, if Combined Operations had been used more thoroughly. It was Fleming who gave the N.I.D. the breakthrough in the field. However, it is important to remember that Combined Operations had a difficult enough time itself in its infancy—there was a good deal of opposition to it and its first chief Admiral, Sir Roger Keyes.

reconnaissances and probing enemy territory. Godfrey always used Fleming whenever an intermediary was needed to perform a daring task which required an informal approach.

Perhaps the best example of this was Godfrey's and Fleming's visit to Washington to persuade the Americans to establish an intelligence organisation on N.I.D. lines and to foster Anglo-American intelligence cooperation. The visit was a great success, in part due to Fleming's brilliant diplomacy. In his capacity as Admiral Godfrey's first assistant, he was the key man in ensuring that N.I.D. ran smoothly—he was much less of an analyst but rather an organiser of the first order.

Above all else, he is remembered by those who worked in the N.I.D. as an R.N.V.R. officer who always set high standards of judgment and behaviour; this was vital in a Naval Staff department where civilians and 'hostilities only' officers were playing such a large part and who were under constant scrutiny by the rest of the Naval Staff made up predominantly of career naval officers.

Another of Godfrey's key men was the British Naval attaché in Stockholm, Captain Denham, R.N. It was he who gave the first reports that led to the chase of the Bismarck.[113] An Oxford Classics Don, Frederick Wells, was brought in by Godfrey to head N.I.D. 6—the Topographical Intelligence Section. He was a perfectionist who, together with men like Lieutenant-Commander George Gonin, R.N. (the key man behind the research into the beaches and tides for the D-Day landings), scored brilliant successes. Denham and Wells were typical of both the uniformed and civilian staff Godfrey collected about himself.

Godfrey and the J.I.C.

Godfrey, unlike Hall, was involved in the activities of a large, inter-service, intelligence body, the Joint Intelligence Committee (J.I.C.) whose range of activities, and authority, paralleled those of the Committee of Imperial Defence. Godfrey played a prime role in a long-range strategic decision-making, as well as managing the day-to-day affairs of the N.I.D. However, in many ways, the N.I.D. was to have a much more profound effect upon the outcome of the war

---

[113] After the war, Captain Denham found in the German naval archives a signal from Canaris, Chief of the Abwehr, to the German Naval High Command, dated the morning following his report to the Admiralty. It read: "Have positive proof the British Admiralty have received report of outward passage of Bismarck and Prinz Eugen."

than the deliberations of the J.I.C. Prime Minister Churchill said quite clearly from very early on in the war that he did not have full confidence in J.I.C. reports, and in fact preferred to see agents' reports personally before they went on to J.I.C. for analysis and interpretation.

On numerous occasions, Churchill made major decisions before J.I.C. could provide an answer, or, quite often, totally against J.I.C.'s advice (advice that more often than not had to be tentative as hard intelligence data was lacking). Churchill's attitude to J.I.C. naturally undermined its whole role and impact on military and political policy-making.[114]

The J.I.C. was faced with a great dilemma, one that never disappeared—the dilemma of having to provide the policy-makers at Cabinet level with information which would form the basis for a major decision, yet at the same time, never having sufficient factual data available with which to make a totally decisive report (which is what Churchill always demanded), not because J.I.C. was incompetent, but because more often than not it meant reading the minds of the Soviet and Nazi leaders beyond the bounds of other prima facie evidence.

Fortunately, the J.I.C. never committed professional suicide for an intelligence committee by giving political and military leaders an interpretation without conclusive evidence, even at the cost of severe criticism from the top,

---

[114] For example, in early 1941, British agents reported German troop movements in the Balkans. However, other evidence suggested that Hitler and Stalin were uniting further rather than Hitler preparing to stab Stalin in the back. The J.I.C. based this assessment on several factors—the continued Luftwaffe attacks on Britain (i.e., no reduction in the air power used against Britain, and therefore, no indication of any likely intention to move squadrons to a possible eastern front); supplies were still being sent in great quantities from Russia to Germany (i.e., there was no indication of the hardening of Russian attitudes or a forthcoming diplomatic debacle); both were dedicated to breaking up the British Empire (J.I.C. reasoned that both Stalin and Hitler would have the good sense to realise that together they would have a much greater chance of accomplishing this).

Quite naturally, J.I.C. could not come up with a firm answer to Churchill's leading question—was Germany going to invade the Soviet Union, and when? It was not until 5 June 1941 that J.I.C. began to have any real evidence in favour of Hitler's move eastwards, and it was not until 12 June that J.I.C. felts its evidence was conclusive. Churchill himself states in his, The Second World War, Volume III, The Grand Alliance, p. 354-361, that he had disagreed with J.I.C.'s early prognosis and had, in fact, decided in March 1941 that Hitler intended to invade the Soviet Union.

particularly Churchill himself. Besides the great responsibilities and worries of the N.I.D., Godfrey then was fighting political battles within the J.I.C. and, during the early stages of the war, within the Admiralty itself. Godfrey was not alone in his problems. Across the whole board of British intelligence organisations there were the natural and almost predictable clashes between intelligence heads and their masters.[115]

Unlike Hall's N.I.D., Godfrey's involvement in clandestine intelligence collection and espionage was reduced very quickly to zero; N.I.D. was not at all concerned by this. Much of the paraphernalia of clandestinity was turned over to the Special Operations Executive (S.O.E.), formed in 1940. Prior to this, all 'irregular' projects were performed by M.I. 6 initiated by the Directors of Naval and Military Intelligence. This reflects quite strongly Godfrey's and the defence administrators' attitudes to the functions of N.I.D. when compared with Hall's— the former saw N.I.D.'s function supplying the fleet with hard intelligence.

However, before S.O.E. was formed, Godfrey, with Fleming in close support, organised a series of clandestine operations, such as cutting off the Swedish iron ore supplies to Germany, blocking the Danube, and crippling the Rumanian oil refineries. Some of these projects could hardly be called naval and were surely in the best traditions of Admiral Hall. Godfrey personally instigated many of these projects before Churchill issued his order to 'set Europe on fire'. In his memoirs, Godfrey recalls how Churchill, when First Lord of the Admiralty,

---

[115] The head of M.I. 6 himself, Colonel Steward Menzies (he succeeded Admiral Sinclair at the beginning of World War II as the head of the British espionage service) was not separate from these. Many of his plans, he stated after the war, were thwarted in certain Foreign Office quarters for fear of offending the Russians, such as his plan to negotiate with the non-Nazi military leaders to organise the removal of Hitler, hoping thereby to shorten the war with a negotiated peace. The 'unconditional surrender' theme of the Casablanca Conference sounded the death knell of such a plan.

He came in for much criticism from Churchill, or so he would have posterity believe, because of M.I. 6's failure to produce the goods all of the time—a predictable occurrence since he had inherited an organisation which was singularly ill-equipped to collect and assess intelligence data from the Third Reich. Churchill's success as a war leader in part stemmed from his considerable ability to inspire and drive his subordinates—this often meant chiding them to obtain the desired results. That he did so was to Britain's advantage and perhaps, one can surmise, his subordinates may have felt unjustly treated at times. Richard Deacon gives a vivid, documented account of Menzies' problems in his: History of the British Secret Service. Muller. 1969.

made only a few incursions into clandestine activities, mainly because of the lack of money and the restraints placed upon him by the Foreign Office.

Hall and Godfrey—Comparisons and Contrasts

In surveying the British Naval intelligence scene from the Hall to Godfrey eras, one can see certain central points and landmarks emerging. Firstly, by 1943 (when Godfrey left office), there was an established intelligence doctrine within the N.I.D., that is a body of rules, principles, and procedures which have been well tried, such as those to which a recruit to N.I.D.'s staff would be introduced. There was never a hint of the doctrinaire creeping in—these doctrines were very much subject to modification as circumstances changed.

It was these doctrines which formed the basis for N.I.D.'s structural organisation (see Appendix A), though it was in part a dialectic process between organisations, established doctrine, and the demands of the times which produced change within the N.I.D. There can be no doubt that by 1940, Britain possessed the most efficient naval intelligence machine of all the powers.[116]

That it suffered a run-down during the inter-war period is true, and at times, its existence as a worthwhile, legitimate intelligence body is questionable, yet despite the political-military debacles of the 1930s (see Chapters Six and Seven for N.I.D.'s involvement in political-military decision-making in the 1930s), it was able to retain its integrity and, under Godfrey's leadership, to reassert itself.

What Hall had succeeded in doing from the time of Jutland onwards, and what Godfrey quickly reinforced, was to impress on the Naval Staff the tremendous need for intelligence, and intelligence defined as 'evaluated information' (a workable definition which has its origins in the Jutland

---

[116] Pearl Harbour was to prove the total absence within American intelligence as a whole (let alone the Office of Naval Intelligence itself) of a central point where all the bits and pieces of information could be fitted together into a coherent whole. The role and efficiency of the O.N.I. of the United States Navy were poles apart from the N.I.D. in the British Admiralty. See Roger Hilsman: Strategic Intelligence and National Decisions, 1956, p. 23-30, for a detailed, fully documented account of O.N.I. pre-Pearl Harbour, and the official enquiry and findings into naval intelligence following the disaster.

experience), and the independent, yet not autonomous, organisation which was needed to produce such material.[117]

Admiral Hall realised too that if N.I.D. was to succeed (i.e., its functions to be accepted and these functions to be successfully implemented), this would depend greatly on the 'power' N.I.D. could wield, and also the requests (or demands) it received from Plans and Operations Divisions. Hall won most of the really important political battles, though in his desire to ensure N.I.D. made its mark, he perhaps, at times, overstretched himself.

Herein lies the paramount difference between Hall and Godfrey eras: the latter saw N.I.D.'s primary roles as providing estimates and warnings, based on a fully documented analysis, in report form, and providing day-to-day operational intelligence (N.I.D. 9—Operational Intelligence Centre), whereas Hall went far beyond this, seeing the D.N.I. role as a part policy-making one (and at times taking the initiative himself). Hall's activities probably meant the permanent demise of this role, insofar as after 1919, there were quite deliberate and stringent moves to restrict D.N.I.'s activities.

However, it is legitimate to surmise that experience would have undoubtedly shown that intelligence and policy-making cannot go hand-in-hand. One compliments the other, but they must be quite separate bodies. Why have policy-makers if intelligence officials are performing their functions? But the crucial argument must surely be that 'good' intelligence never in fact can be 'good' if it is inhibited in its interpretive stages by a political end—the danger being that the intelligence might be twisted to fit the policy.

What Hall did very early on as D.N.I. was to make naval intelligence into something more than just a body of assembled facts and figures—naval intelligence under Hall became 'evaluated information'—the process of analysing and interpreting raw data, not the mere collection of often unrelated

---

[117] A lengthier definition of intelligence is given by Donald MacLachlan in his: Room 39. Naval Intelligence in Action, 1939-1945. Wiedenfeld and Nicolson, 1968, p. XIII: Intelligence, he writes, "…should consist of details tested as to source and balanced against the facts, reviewed in the light of experience and the memory of a man or department, weighted and presented in the form of appreciation, defended and amended under criticism, finally distributed or promulgated—as the Navy calls it—to be acted on. It is remarkably like the process of the law, beginning with the clue that leads to arrest, passing to the charge, the trial, the jury's decision and the conviction. As such it connotes the most painstaking and judicious brainwork."

and seemingly meaningless facts. Admiral Godfrey and his staff continued, albeit perhaps more professionally, the Hall tradition of naval intelligence workers being scientific in their approach—establishing hypotheses and testing them against a mass of raw data, and having a well-defined link with Plans and Operations Division.

To accomplish both of these aims, these two great D.N.I.'s saw the necessity of recruiting civilians to perform tasks for which both deemed naval officers were not trained, and skills they could not acquire overnight, which the naval appointing system demanded. To Godfrey, an officer appointed to N.I.D. for two years without some degree of background experience would be of little real use. However, it was professional advisers to the analysts and report-writers that naval officers were invaluable.

The Hall-Winn partnership in the operational intelligence centre is sure proof of this. As a result of recruiting civilians both Hall and Godfrey suffered, initially, considerable criticism. There was a natural feeling of resentment, and indeed insult, that civilians should be filling posts some felt were the preserve of uniformed officers. The basic argument against the scholar-intelligence worker at the Admiralty stemmed from the premise that the kind of knowledge that is useful in solving intelligence problems comes almost entirely from practical, first-hand 'experience', not from academic abstractions.

There was undoubtedly almost a ring of anti-intellectualism in the argument of the more determined critics. What Hall and Godfrey realised, and had the courage to state, was that the interpretation of 'experience' requires scholarly analysis, and further proved that the judicious combination of civilians (or civilians temporarily commissioned for the duration) and experienced naval officers working side-by-side worked very well, and eventually destroyed their most vehement critics' arguments.

Since the end of World War II, there has been a swing away from this system, not because of a reversal for Godfrey's ideas but, somewhat paradoxically, because of the greater emphasis placed on intelligence work in peacetime, and also because of the movement towards integration in the post-war period. It became easier to structure intelligence work and careers so as to make greater demands on uniformed personnel rather than civilians.

At the time of writing a review of the upper echelons of the United Kingdom Defence Intelligence Staff showed only two civilians in critical positions, and these technically-oriented ones—the Director of Scientific and Technical

Intelligence, and the Director of Economic Intelligence. In the critical days of World Wars I and II, both Hall and Godfrey had the insight and determination to bring into the N.I.D. the best outsiders they could muster.

In another vital area, Godfrey re-introduced a principle which Hall had fought to establish—that not only must the intelligence organisation analyse and evaluate as well as collect raw data, and be in a strong position to pass this to Plans and Operations with effect, but that, in quite another sense, it must be totally independent, separate from the masters it seeks to serve, so that the material N.I.D. acquired and processed would not be distorted by the views of those who make naval plans and direct naval operations. N.I.D. always 'guided', yet never became so involved so as to lose its objectivity or integrity of judgment.

In their desire to remain independent, neither Hall nor Godfrey forgot their main duty—to place before the naval decision-makers the very best data, unvarnished and unbiased, even though at times Hall may have become somewhat autonomous. Both were dedicated quite unequivocally to a large-scale operation of collection, analysis, and interpretation, and at the same time, developing and maintaining a dialogue with those who needed information and were able to ask the right questions of the N.I.D.

As a result of this process, British Naval intelligence by 1945 had acquired a dominant position, but one which in no sense was unbalanced. N.I.D. never claimed infallibility—it never claimed anything other than the necessity to provide objectively based and deeply considered information, to the utmost of its ability. World War II witnessed the healthy separation of any direct relationship between intelligence and policy-making.

Admiral Godfrey's era saw the emergence of a doctrine of British Naval intelligence which is perhaps best characterised by Sherman Kent, when he describes the doctrines of the ideal intelligence organisation: "Its job is to see that the doers are generally well-informed; its job is to stand behind them with the book opened at the right page, to call their attention to the stubborn fact that they be neglecting...Intelligence cannot serve if it does not know the doers' minds; it cannot serve if it has not their confidence; it cannot serve unless it can have the kind of guidance any professional man must have from his client."[118]

---

[118] Sherman Kent: Strategic Intelligence for American World Policy. Princeton, N.J. 1949. p. 182.

That the N.I.D. in 1945 was markedly like the intelligence organisation Kent describes must surely be the lasting testament to Admiral Hall and Admiral Godfrey, and the staffs who worked under them.

Chapter Three

An Analysis of the Interaction between Naval Intelligence and General Navy Policy, and Strategic and Tactical Practice at Sea.

Naval Intelligence and Maritime Strategy

The primary roles of the Royal Navy between 1880 and 1945 did not change dramatically. Although the balance between the major factors which affected Britain's role in the world and her international relations changed, such as colonial commitments, shifts in the world and European balance of power and political ideologies, internal socio-economic changes, and major shifts in the trade balance of the world, there was, nonetheless, a consistent school of thought throughout the period as to how Britain could use sea power.

The validity of this policy, in relation to a hypothesised view of what Britain's best interests were, is a major question, but one which is seemingly impossible to answer if one considers the totality of the major historical factors, the isolation of which would itself be a most difficult task, and one open to the disagreements of the historian, each wishing to emphasise his own interpretation.

What an analysis of the interaction between naval intelligence and general naval policy, and strategic and tactical practice at sea will do is to reveal how the men who were responsible for providing an appraisal of Britain's maritime position and how she should use her Navy—the men of N.I.D., saw the problems, and possible solutions to them. It will show the relationship between those who made plans and executed policy, and those who provided the intelligence.

In one sense, it could be said that the student of war has a ready-made eye-witness into the minds of those who made naval history, that N.I.D. was the all-knowing seer, foretelling the shape of things to come, giving Plans and Operations unequivocally accurate reports upon which to base their decisions, and therefore, like the historian, providing objectively based information, gleaned from every relevant source, but, unlike the historian, contemporaneous with the events themselves.

N.I.D. was never able to fulfil this idealised role, some of the reasons for which have already been indicated, but one of the chief reasons lies in the nature of events themselves, a factor totally outside the control of even the most efficient intelligence organisation. Intelligence can give sound predictions, or merely just hard data without interpretation, which may be of use, but it can never give absolutely clear direction, because of the inscrutable nature of events themselves, which is their essence.

The N.I.D. was concerned with the Royal Navy in relationship with those factors which N.I.D. isolated—it was a dialectic process between the intelligence man and his world. It is at this point that it can be said that, ultimately, however, scientific intelligence is in its approach and methods, it can never escape from the innumerable factors of which it is a product, so as to render itself separate from events in time. The changing N.I.D. was as much a product of dynamic change in time as the course of events it sought to influence.

Only the historian can attain a degree of uninhibited insight into events denied to those who helped make them; only he, because of the benefit of hindsight, can bring some degree of order from the apparent chaos of past events. However, the historian, like the intelligence worker, will tend to consider factors he considers important, but the means by which he selects those factors will be measured by more concrete criteria than those which were available to the intelligence worker—events that have occurred, rather than events that might occur.

Captain S. W. Roskill has written: "The need for intimate collaboration between Plans, Intelligence and Operations will be evident…it is no exaggeration to say that together they formed the trinity on which the execution of our maritime strategy chiefly rested."[119] Experience, the basis of Roskill's observation, has proven this statement to be true. The levels which are implicit in this statement are what one might call levels two, three, four, etc. Level one consists of the basic aims of British maritime strategy. These are the a priori aims upon which any naval policy and operations, in war and in peace, must rest if naval forces are to have a legitimate raison d'être.

Throughout this period, the Royal Navy has been committed to several basic aims—to defend Britain from invasion, to defeat all enemy attempts to prevent

---

[119] Captain S.W. Roskill, R.N.: The War at Sea. Vol. I. p. 21.

merchant ships, and to be able to launch attacks from the sea on enemy or enemy-held territory. All of these aims involved the need to deny the use of the sea to the enemy, entailing therefore the ability to seek out and destroy an enemy.

The levels below the basic aims will be the means by which these aims can be achieved in peace and war. The validity of the basic aims are major political-military decisions, and the means to achieve them the responsibility of the Admiralty; both will be dependent upon accurate information with which to make the necessary decisions—making long and short-term plans, and how best to conduct naval operations.

Naval Intelligence in the Nuclear Age

The advent of the nuclear deterrent, under whose umbrella any conventional war must now be fought, has upset this approach. Professor L. W. Martin has written: "Weapons must henceforth be exercised within a framework of nuclear deterrence and the limitations that this imposes upon the weapons that may be employed in any particular situation."[120] He reinforces this point later in his book: "…the limitation of war in the nuclear age is imposed by the necessity to avoid the general use of nuclear weapons."[121] In the modern age, a new single factor has thus been thrown into the international balance—nuclear weapon technology, moulding now all levels.

It is a unique situation, where weaponry is not only deciding the feasibility of various types of warfare, but also controlling the very premises upon which the very existence of maritime forces are based. However, in the pre-1945 non-nuclear era, there was a different pattern of military logic to be applied to maritime strategy. This logic has, in part, been challenged. How valid, for example, are such old factors as surprise (whether it be strategic or tactical surprise, or the use of a new weapon), secrecy, concealment, deception, speed, audacity, and the need to out-manoeuvre and, if possible, out-number?

How relevant is the concept of breaking an enemy's will to resist one of the explicit aims of global strategy? The new era has called for a different pattern of intelligence, since the very nature, and cost, of the nuclear threat has led to a very different approach to the predictability of a future nuclear war, particularly one that might originate in western Europe. The possibility of the nature of the war

---

[120] L. W. Martin.: The Sea in Modern Strategy. p. 14.
[121] Ibid. p. 44.

itself is changing the whole pattern of maritime strategic thought, the parallels with the past being mainly the planning for limited conventional warfare in marginal territories and the traditional exercise of diplomacy through the use of sea power.

In the event of the latter, naval intelligence must play its traditional roles, such as, for example, providing operations with intelligence appreciations, consulting with commanders on the analysis of action reports, and making recommendations for where transit patrols and area searches should be conducted. In any limited war, there would still be the need to deploy specialised forces to defeat attacks on merchant shipping by similar enemy units.

Such deployment would require an intelligence backup, just as would any attempt to attack an enemy at his source or conduct a distant blockade, attack his merchant ships, both of which might entail an intelligence appreciation of suitable strategic bases to be used. In this sense, there is strong continuity between the pre-nuclear and nuclear ages.

Intelligence and Gaining the Initiative

One of the paramount principles of naval strategy and tactics is to gain the initiative. Once an enemy has the initiative, intelligence assessments become increasingly difficult, for the enemy is calling the tune when to strike, in the way and place of his choosing; he has, in other words, created conditions favourable to himself. Intelligence is, therefore, always more reliable when one has the initiative and is launching the offensive because the task is simpler. However, experience showed that it was the in-between stage in any naval war where intelligence had an equally important role to play, that is the stage before either side had shown its hand, and the offensive and initiative had still to be decided.

Similarly, this applied to a period of stalemate, following a period of intense activity. When will the enemy next take the offensive, or when will it be advantageous to next hit the enemy? In general, it is true to say that any strategic deployment of naval forces, without sound intelligence, can turn operations into nothing more than wild goose chases. For example, in 1939 and early 1940, Admiral Forbes' Home Fleet was kept at sea without any concrete knowledge of the whereabouts of the enemy or what his intentions might be.

There was, at this stage, no satisfactory data upon which successful operational policy could be devised. The threat of invasion in 1940 made it absolutely necessary to have knowledge of what the enemy might do, and plans for stalling that invasion hinged on the accuracy of such intelligence. Similarly in World War I, in August 1914, Jellicoe established a line of cruiser patrols across the North Sea to Norway. He had no precise information on enemy intentions but geography itself dictated to him the initial deployment.

The above applies to the tactical as well as the strategic level (such as the deployment of Forbes' fleet). How, for example, could minelaying operations be successful unless the routes of enemy shipping were known? It took the N.I.D. some time before its knowledge of German minelaying activities became known. Conversely, how could Allied shipping be satisfactorily protected against enemy mining?

Strategic and tactical intelligence, and the contingencies this creates for naval planning and operations, in peace and war, has a strong political element, particularly in peacetime when, at worst, naval activity (based upon intelligence reports) can precipitate the very conflict that it was the original aim of statesmanship to avoid. However, at that stage, intelligence has passed from the hands of those who collect, analyse and write reports to those who act upon it.

The realisation of the great value of such intelligence was not initially appreciated during the earlier part of the N.I.D.'s history. For example, in the pre-1914 years, there was no serious appraisal made of the effects (strategic and tactical) of submarine warfare, least of all the effects which a policy of unrestricted submarine warfare might have.[122]

In 1914, British Naval Intelligence was not alone in its unpreparedness for a naval conflict. The Germans were far less concerned with gathering strategic or tactical intelligence, and were concerned with gathering strategic or tactical intelligence, and were concerned that Britain gave the appearance of great preparedness. The German Naval Attaché in London, Captain von Muller, reported that England was prepared for full naval war, and was not sure which way England would move in the event of certain hostilities by German land forces (presumably he referred to the violation of Belgian neutrality).

---

[122] It was not until Hall came into office in 1914 that full-scale appraisals were made of German submarine policy. For example, on 3 September 1915, the N.I.D. reported that there were no signs as yet that German submarine captains were changing their tactics. Merchant ships were instructed to carry out the policy originally promulgated by the Admiralty. There was no concrete sign (just suspicion) of a forthcoming policy of unrestricted U-boat warfare. This report and supporting documents are in Adm. 137, 1100, p. 170-173, Public Record Office.

There was a good deal of dissatisfaction within the German Navy of the lack of planning; Captain von Rintelen wrote in his book: "The tactics now employed against England, of merely waiting to deal with whatever move the enemy made, were not at all to our liking."[123] Von Rintelen's worst fears of the German Navy's lack of control were proven correct when hostilities began. At the time of the Battle of Coronel and the Battle of the Falkland Islands, the German Admiralty had no knowledge of Admiral von Spee's whereabouts or intentions, or the nature of the British threat.

Von Rintelen wrote: "Our hearts beat quickly when he (von Spee) destroyed a British squadron off Coronel. We did not know whether he would turn after the battle?"[124] and, "The unexpected news of the battle of the Falkland Islands threw us into deep depression."[125]

The Deployment of Forces

Von Rintelen's comments highlight one of the major strategic problems of World War I—the sound development of forces so as to fulfil defensive and offensive roles in the light of knowledge of enemy strengths and intentions. In this vital area, the work of the N.I.D., and particularly Room 40, gave Britain the advantage. At no stage during World War I could it be said that Scheer's intelligence sources compared in efficiency with the British Admiralty's. For example, on 21 April 1915, the German High Seas Fleet put to sea in the belief that Admiral Tyrwhitt's[126] Harwich force was about to attack the Zeppelin sheds at Tondern, behind the island of Sylt.

Room 40 was able to give enough warning of this move for the Grand Fleet to be ordered towards the Skaggerak. However, before they could arrive on the 22, Scheer concluded that Tyrwhitt's attack had been called off and ordered his ships back to the Jade. Jellicoe held on towards the Horns Reef, hoping to draw Scheer out, but had to withdraw because of dense fog.

---

[123] Captain von Rintelen: The Dark Invader. p. 24.

[124] Ibid. p. 41.

[125] Captain von Rintelen: The Dark Invader. p. 41.

[126] <u>Tyrwhitt, Sir Reginald Yorke, First Baronet, Admiral of the Fleet</u>: 1870-1951; entered R.N. 1883; Commander 1903; Captain 1908; Commodore Destroyer Flotillas 1914; Rear-Admiral 1918; Vice-Admiral 1925; C.-in-C. China station 1927; Admiral 1929; Admiral of the Fleet 1934.

It was this prior warning of enemy movements that gave the Royal Navy tactical advantage, and ultimately enabled it to dictate a dominantly one-sided naval strategy for the duration of the war. More often than not, the Germans were operating in the dark, as is shown by the following example. On 30 May 1915, Hall's men in Room 40 confirmed enemy movements. They had deciphered a signal from Scheer to his fleet. It read: "Hostile forces may proceed to sea"; this was followed by another signal ordering the High Seas Fleet to be assembled in the outer Jade by 1900 (In fact, these signals were made more threatening to the Admiralty by a deciphering error: Room 40's version read: "German forces may proceed to sea.").

During the afternoon, Room 40 supplied further information, and as a result of this, the Admiralty signalled Jellicoe and Beatty at 1740: "Germans intend some operations commencing tomorrow via Horns Reef. You should concentrate to eastward of Long. Forties ready for eventualities." As a result of Room 40's intelligence, the Grand Fleet sailed four and a half hours before the first units of the High Seas Fleet left the Jade. Admiral Scheer had no knowledge of the Grand Fleet's movements.

On this occasion, his submarines on reconnaissance failed to provide him with the correct intelligence as to what as at sea and its possible course. N.I.D.'s intelligence gave the initiative to the British fleet—where the enemy could be attacked, and what his possible intentions and strengths might be. In the knowledge that such intelligence was of a consistent quality, and regularly available, the Admiralty was eventually able to evolve a more rational strategy for bringing the major German units to battle, and in the event, gave them the great advantage of tactical surprise.

Nelsonian strategy would not have worked in this era and, at worst, without intelligence, Jellicoe's forces could have patrolled the North Sea on the off chance of a confrontation. N.I.D. provided the timely warnings that made wild goose chases rare occurrences. It was unfortunate for the Royal Navy that Germany's later strategy did not allow it to optimise the benefits of intelligence, and use this in the full-scale battle many dreamed of. The Germans were not prepared to run the risk of major losses to the High Seas Fleet in an attempt to damage the Grand Fleet to such an extent that the blockade would be broken.

Geoffrey Bennett summarises the situation thus: "When U-boats had shown that they could do so much damage to Britain's jugular vein, the High Seas Fleet was kept in being to prevent a close blockade of their U-boat bases, to occupy

British destroyers which otherwise would have been used to combat them, and to ensure that the Allies could not use their main elements of naval power for operations, such as amphibious landings on the north-west coast, which would have directly endangered the homeland."[127]

It was not until the post-Jutland period that Scheer evolved this strategy. Until 1916, he had hoped to lure the Grand Fleet to sea for a pitched battle; his principal means for achieving this were raids on English east coast towns. However, there can be no doubt that intelligence played an important part in giving tactical advantage, and ultimately strategic control. The Dogger Bank action illustrates this well; intelligence gave the Royal Navy tactical advantage, and from this came strategic control of the North Sea, and therefore, reduced the chances of the enemy being tempted to chance further raids on the east coast.

German naval historians have not been loath to criticise Scheer's strategic policy, or the organisation of which it was a product. Vice-Admiral Friedrich Ruge, referring to World War I, has written: "…there had been no corresponding progress in strategic and operational ideas or the employment of a powerful fleet, which possessed not a single overseas base for refuelling its coal-burning ships, whose endurance never exceeded 5,000 miles."[128] The N.I.D. was not unaware of the latter facts. However, it did lack crucial information about Germany's long-range strategic planning.

It did not, for example, realise the significance of the absence of a German operational war staff, or acquire data on German overall military strategy, or political strategy, which events, if anything, proved to be lacking too. As a result, the High Seas Fleet waited in the Heligoland Bight and the Grand Fleet at Scapa for the battle which did not come. In designing the High Seas Fleet, Tirpitz had made the fundamental error of designing a surface fleet whose ships, for want of the necessary endurance, could not break out of the North Sea and operate against trade.[129]

Within the limitations of German strategy, the N.I.D. was able to give the necessary warnings, but in a stalemate situation, this became of no avail if the enemy was not British strategic thinking pre-1914 was, in general terms, prepared for the German threat. Sir Julian Corbett gives erudite testimony to the

---

[127] Geoffrey Bennett: The Battle of Jutland.
[128] Vice-Admiral Friedrich Ruge: Sea Warfare, 1939-1945. A German Viewpoint. p. 15.
[129] This was a lesson the Navy of the Third Reich was quick to learn.prepared to commit his forces to battle.

work of the Committee of Imperial Defence and the N.I.D. pre-1914; "...the fundamental new problems had been fully realised and provided for by unceasing study." [130] The N.I.D. had appreciated that for the first time, the Royal Navy would be facing an enemy north of the Dover defile.

This would mean that the enemy had the North Sea and Denmark Strait to break through if it was to cause major damage, though it was realised the east coast ports and sea routes were now vulnerable. In consequence, it was realised that the Grand Fleet would have to be located in Scottish waters. Hence, the choice of Scapa Flow. N.I.D. had accurate technical information about the High Seas Fleet. Admiral Hall knew Britain outgunned and outnumbered the Germans, though he knew too that they had far superior armour. This information was fed to Plans and Operations for use in strategic and tactical studies.

Locating and Identifying Forces

Where British Naval intelligence failed badly in the last months of peace in 1914 and early in the war was in identifying and locating German warships in distant waters.[131] This was to cause considerable frustration for the operational planners. As late as July 1914, the whereabouts of the main German units on the China Station were still unknown (fortunately, this was to be greatly improved during the last weeks of peace). During that month, the Gneisenau was reported to have left Singapore. This information was inaccurate. The Gneisenau was mistaken for the gunboat Geier.

The other two light cruisers belonging to the German Pacific Squadron, Nurnberg and Leipzig, were believed to be somewhere on the west coast of North America. Sir Julian Corbett gives this account: "...this ship (i.e., the Nurnberg), a sister of the Leipzig, had left San Francisco and 21 July for Honolulu. She arrived on the 27 and sailed again on the same day for an unknown destination. She had, in fact, been ordered to join Admiral von Spee. This, of course, was unknown to the Admiralty, and the prevailing impression was that both the

---

[130] Sir Julian Corbett: History of the Great War based on official documents by Direction of the Historical Section of the Committee of Imperial Defence. Naval Operations. Volume I. Chpt. I.

[131] Compare this with the O.I.C.'s performance at the time of the Munich crisis and throughout 1939.

Leipzig and Nurnberg would operate along the trade routes on the east coast of North America."[132]

The weakness of Admiralty intelligence about the location of enemy forces and their strengths found its nadir at the battle of Coronel. The British force had divided itself into two inadequate squadrons, and in the event found themselves facing superior odds. Along with the exploits of the Karlsruhe and Emden, the battle of Coronel exposed British command of the Atlantic to real menace. Where, if at all, had intelligence failed?

Admiral Craddock was surely right in pursuing von Spree's force.[133] He rendezvoused his squadron off Cape Virgins. On the way to Punta Arenas, where he hoped to obtain further intelligence, he was continually intercepting call-signs between German warships and merchantmen. These could not be deciphered. On arriving at Punta Areas, the British Counsel there told him the Germans were probably using Orange Bay as a base. Craddock's misfortune was as much a result of poor communications as lack of intelligence, which, in this case, cannot really be separated.

Links with the South Atlantic were slow and uncertain. This is shown by the fact that the Admiralty did warn Craddock on 30 September of what the Germans might be about, but this never reached the Admiral. This signal informed him that the Gneisenau and Scharnhorst had bombarded Papiete and sunk the French ship Lelee on the 22, and were last reported steering northeast.

After the disaster at Coronel, the Admiralty were quick to remedy the situation.[134] What the Battle of the Falklands shows is that the British Admiralty succeeded in bringing an overwhelming superiority of forces, at the right time, in the right place, against the enemy. This was based on sound intelligence, but intelligence gleaned from Craddock's tragic action at Coronel. In strategic terms, the Battle of the Falklands meant that command of the outer seas had been won,

---

[132] Corbett: Vol. I. p. 145.

[133] Craddock, Vice-Admiral Sir Christopher G.T.M.: 1862-1914; CB 1902; MVO 1903; commander training squadron 1912; Rear-Admiral 1910; KCVO 1912.

[134] After Coronel Admiral Sturdee was made C.-in-C. to seek out and destroy the German force. His command was unprecedented—embracing a wider stretch of sea than had ever yet been committed to a single admiral. He sailed as Commander-in-Chief, South Atlantic and Pacific. Sturdee, Admiral Sir Frederick Charles Doveton: b. 1859; entered R.N. 1871; Captain 1899; Rear-Admiral 1908; A.D.N.I. 1900-1902; Rear-Admiral First Battle squadron 1910; Admiral 1917.

and Britain was virtually free to throw practically the whole weight of her Navy into the main theatre.[135]

The location of enemy naval units was as much a major intelligence function in World War II as it was during the Great War. However, in the interim, the development of air power brought an additional means by which the enemy could be located—air reconnaissance.

Air Reconnaissance

This became essential for successful sea or air strikes against an enemy which had now deployed himself on a greater scale and truly global basis. Without air reconnaissance, any air attacks, operations against major enemy units in port, in transit, or in action, would have been greatly thwarted, and the outcome of the war at sea placed in jeopardy. This was patently true of the anti-U-boat campaign. There was a direct link between N.I.D. (U-boat tracking room) and H.Q. Coastal Command. The two worked hand-in-hand, and through H.Q. Western Approaches the whole convoy organisation and anti-U-boat war was conducted.[136]

---

[135] N.I.D. and the Naval planners were quick to deduce from the two actions that 'under modern conditions' the normal result of an action between two unequal squadrons would be that the one with inferior speed and gun-power would be destroyed by the one which was faster and more powerfully armed, a conclusion which may now seem too obvious and simple to have been drawn in the forceful way it was.

[136] From April 1941 onwards, the Royal Navy had operational control of Coastal Command. The action of the Fleet Air Arm at Taranto had convinced Churchill of this. Events in both the Atlantic and Mediterranean were to show that closely integrated aviation was necessary to the Royal Navy if it was going to control the sea.

On this point of integrated sea and air power in Britain pre-1939 and during World War II, one distinguished American observer has written: "By establishing an independent air force, the British government removed from their battleships and cruisers the very officers who would have made their Navy air conscious, and denied the fleet what it needed most, close cooperation between surface and air, and a corps of aviators trained to fly over long ocean stretches and to work in harmony with the ships." Captain W.D. Puleston, U.S.N. The influence of Sea Power in World War II. p. 21.

The Battle of Taranto was the first successful employment of carrier-based torpedo planes against capital ships. Detailed accounts of the role of air reconnaissance during World War II in naval operations are given in three eminent books: Sir P. B. Joubert de

Admiral Cunningham was one of the first operational commanders in World War II to realise the value of air reconnaissance for accurate intelligence, though Beatty had certainly appreciated it in his day. In the New Year of 1942, there were little or no aircraft available for air reconnaissance in the eastern Mediterranean. At the time of the evacuation of Crete, the Admiralty had no idea of German intentions. Cunningham suggested remedies.

In *Sailor's Odessey*, he wrote: "I emphasised again what we needed was better air reconnaissance, which should allow us to keep our forces far enough away by day to avoid serious loss pending the moment when the enemy committed his convoys to their sea voyage, and we went in and destroyed them. I had not received the reinforcements of reconnaissance aircraft I had so correctly requested."[137]

The need to know, on a daily basis, the whereabouts and strengths of hostile units, Cunningham saw as the primary goal of operational intelligence. To this end, regular aerial reconnaissance, often providing photographic evidence, had a prime part to play. It was the sort of 'hard' intelligence from which could be deduced certain inalienable facts, and its efficacy increased as the range and endurance of aircraft increased, particularly in the filling of the mid-Atlantic gap,

---

la Ferte: The Third Service. The Story Behind the Royal Air Force; Sir J. Slessor: The Central Blue. Recollections and Reflections. (Both Joubert de la Ferte and Slessor were sometime A.O.C.-in-Cs, Coastal Command, Slessor succeeding Joubert de la Ferte in February 1943). W. S. Chalmers: Max Horton and the Western Approaches.

[137] Admiral of the Fleet Viscount A. B. Cunningham: A Sailor's Odessey. p. 375-376. Cunningham was highly critical of British Intelligence in general; referring to the Italian invasion of Albania and the criticism levelled at the Royal Navy for not being widely disposed throughout the Adriatic. Cunningham wrote: "Mr Churchill appears to have based his assumption that the Italian project was known to us beforehand on his belief, after twenty-five years' experience in peace and war, that the British Intelligence Service was the finest of its kind in the world...In 1939, our intelligence about anything inside Italy was sparse, almost non-existent." p. 201-202.

Cunningham, of Hyndhope, First Viscount, Admiral of the Fleet Andrew Browne: b. 1883; entered R.N. 1898; Rear-Admiral (D) Destroyer Flotillas, Mediterranean Fleet 1933-1936; Vice-Admiral Commanding Battle Cruiser Squadron and second in command Mediterranean, 1937-1938; D.C.N.S. 1938-1939; C.-in-C. Mediterranean 1939-1942; head of British naval delegation, Washington, 1942; Admiral 1941; C.-in-C. Mediterranean 1943; Admiral of the Fleet 1943; First Sea Lord 1943-1946.

an area which, because of its distance from Britain, was not patrolled by Coastal Command during the early years of the war.

Iceland was occupied in part to act as a vital refuelling and air reconnaissance base.[138] It was air reconnaissance, coupled with other data, particularly radio traffic, that enabled Captain Winn, R.N.V.R., to be so accurate in his predictions.

Cunningham, on returning to the Admiralty from his Mediterranean Command, made this observation of O.I.C.'s anti-U-boat activity: "The organisation for keeping track of the U-boats, analysing the intelligence and checking and cross checking all the information that came in, was centred in a large room under the Citadel…In charge of the organisation was Captain R. B. Winn, R.N.V.R., a barrister in private life, and his knowledge of U-boats, their commanders and almost what they were thinking about, was uncanny…every submarine leaving an enemy harbour was tracked and plotted, and at any moment Captain Winn could give the numbers, likely positions and movements of all the U-boats at sea.

"His prescience was amazing…the task of translating his knowledge into the appropriate counter-action on our part fell principally onto the broad shoulders of the C.-in-C., Western Approaches, Admiral Sir Max Horton, from his headquarters at Liverpool."[139] Winn had a direct link with H.Q. Coastal Command and he was provided with every piece of aerial intelligence as it came in. As a result, H.Q. Western Approaches were able to develop accurate plans for convoy compositions and routes.

Tactics were developed as a result of other sources revealing enemy methods, as well as being controlled of course by the anti-submarine weaponry available to the Royal Navy. Strategic plans for the Atlantic battle stemmed largely from reconnaissance and wireless intelligence, and from the tactical reports of commanders on the spot, when they had engaged or sighted the enemy. In this sense, tactical and strategic intelligence are inseparable, since it is the minute details of the former which help to build up an overall picture for the latter.

In the tactical situation, aerial intelligence was to prove invaluable, and in some cases, its absence was to prove disastrous. The loss of the Prince of Wales and Repulse off Malaya on 10 December 1941, attempting to attack invading

---

[138] The long-range reconnaissance aircraft were Sunderland and Catalina flying boats and by the end of 1941 Coastal Command were operating American Liberators.

[139] A. B. Cunningham: A Sailor's Odessey. p. 579. Horton succeeded Admiral Noble as C.-in-C., Western Approaches in November 1942.

Japanese transports, was partially due to Admiral Phillips not having air reconnaissance available, as well of course as 'air cover', to forewarn him of impending Japanese air strikes. Perhaps he did not wish to break radio silence, and consequently did not call for air support. We shall never know.[140]

Air intelligence provided the Admiralty with daily information as to whether the Scharnhorst, Gneisenau, and Prince Eugen were still in Brest in February 1942. Their escape shows how the absence of such intelligence could have completely confounded British attempts to locate the enemy and hence make effective plans, or take precautions, to counter him. In this particular instance it was not until 11:30 a.m. on 12 February, when the ships were actually off Bologne, that all British commands were made aware of their presence.[141]

Air intelligence was to be invaluable in giving tactical commanders on the spot, and Operations in the Admiralty, vital information in the Bismarck, and later in the Scharnhorst operations.[142] Throughout the Battle of the Atlantic, the Russian convoys, and the Mediterranean campaign, air intelligence was paramount in determining strategic planning and tactical procedure (details of which will be given later). For example, in early 1942, the Russian convoys were threatened by the Tirpitz, Scheer, Hipper, and Lutzow. Only continuous aerial reconnaissance of the Norwegian ports could tell Operations the location of the enemy, and whether there were signs of movement, or actual departures.[143]

It is appropriate to comment that in the war at sea in the Pacific, air and radio intelligence gave the Americans the tactical advantage, or, looked at from the other side, its absence in the Japanese fleet gave them a decided disadvantage. Within a few days of the Battle of the Coral Sea, 8 May 1942, intercepted radio messages indicated that the enemy's next thrust would be against Midway Island, 1,200 miles, W.N.W. of Pearl Harbour. Aerial reports confirmed this and

---

[140] The details of this are in Admiral Layton's article in the London Gazette, 26 February 1948.

[141] The official Report on the Escape of the Scharnhorst, Gneisenau, and Prinz Eugen from Brest to Germany. Cmd. 6775. 1946.

[142] Full details are contained in R. F. Jesel: The Bismarck Operation. The German Aspect. R.U.S.I. Lecture, 19 November 1952; Admiral Tovey; Sinking of the Bismarck, May 1941. London Gazette, 23 June 1948; Admiral Fraser. Sinking of the Scharnhorst, December 1943. London Gazette, 7 August 1947.

[143] I. M. R. Campbell gives details in his R.U.S.I. Lecture of 16 January 1946; Russian Convoys; 1941-1945, as does Air Vice-Marshall A. B. Ellwood in his: Coastal Command in the Victory of Europe, R.U.S.I. Lecture, 16 April 1947.

American carriers delivered their blows first and at a time when their opponents were most vulnerable.

Somewhat ironically, the Battle of the Philippine Sea, 19 June 1942, although an important victory, was not a pre-eminent victory because more could have been gained. Admiral Spruance played safe, and rightly so. He stood on the defensive, refusing to lay open the Saipon operations to a thrust from the southward, and the reason was his uncertainty about Japanese movements. His air reconnaissance was inadequate, having too few Catalinas at his disposal; additionally, he did not receive information that two U.S. submarines had sunk two major Japanese fleet carriers, Taiho and Shokaku.

With further knowledge, he may have, in consequence, advanced to the westward during part of the night of 18/19 June 1942, and so brought the enemy to action the next day. The Battle of the Philippine Sea would, in all probability, have ranked with the great naval battles of history.[144] Admiral Halsey was to face the same problem at the Battle of Leyte Guls, 24/25 October 1944—he had no adequate information on Japanese movements, or of what their attacking groups consisted. Even his general information about the number of ships fit for service was by no means precise.[145]

Whatever the shortcomings of British and American air reconnaissance, there is no doubt that the Germans fell far short of them in this field. Goering's maritime air policy was very much a secondary consideration to the main deployment of the Luftwaffe. The Kriegsmarine did have control of air reconnaissance over the sea, as well as tactical air operations during contact between naval forces, but it was never able to develop forces similar to Britain's Coastal Command, and Goering did his utmost to forestall aircraft being under direct naval control.

Admiral Ruge makes this comment in his book: "In December 1940, Donitz therefore made a further empathetic appeal to higher authority, arguing that whereas every other weapon of war was provided with its own reconnaissance, the U-boat's capacity for destroying shipping was being largely wasted for lack of air support, without which they could neither find nor concentrate on the

---

[144] See Admiral Spruance's own appraisal of the situation in his R.U.S.I. Lecture of The Victory in the Pacific. 30 October 1946.
[145] See C. Vann Woodward: The Battle for Leyte Gulf, p. 84 and J. A. Field's observations of the various moves and reasons in his: The Japanese at Leyte gulf. The Sho Operations.

worthwhile targets. And if, having contacted a convoy, a shadowing U-boat was driven off by the escorts, as frequently happened, then the problem of regaining contact would be much less difficult if aircraft were available for guiding it back to the target."[146]

Intelligence and German Naval Strategy in World War I

What analysis of World War I strategic thinking have revealed was the absence on the German side of pre-war appraisals similar to those made by the Committee of Imperial Defence. The German High Command certainly believed the war would be a short one, too short for any blockade by the Royal Navy to make itself felt. It was always assumed that the massive pre-1914 German naval re-armament program and their naval exercises were geared to a confrontation with the British fleet as soon as circumstances allowed, in the event of war. All British Naval planning and reorganisation had this in mind.[147]

Neither the N.I.D. nor the operational staff of the Royal Navy anticipated the somewhat inept use of the German naval resources, which in turn was a result of a lack of thorough German naval intelligence and planning. Somewhat ironically, though, this ineptitude did bring dividends, but not major ones. The High Seas Fleet was simply kept in being whilst the British fleets were harassed and their command disputed by every means of minor attack. This was opportunistic rather than the result of any long-range naval planning by the German High Command.

---

[146] Vice-Admiral Freidrich Ruge: Sea Warfare, 1939-1945. A German Viewpoint. p. 123.
[147] From October 1904 onwards, when Fisher became First Sea Lord, his major reforms were directed towards this goal. There was a wholesale scrapping of obsolete warships, radical reorganisation of the reserve fleet, a re-distribution of the fleets and squadrons to provide an interlocking system of reinforcement in any threatened area, and the new design of capital ships—the Dreadnoughts and battlecruisers, revolutionary ships which gave Britain a two-year start on other nations in the modernisation of her Navy.
He created an Atlantic Fleet, based on Gibraltar, which was to reinforce the Mediterranean and Channel fleets as required, though the principal aim was to make certain that the main concentration of sea power was always within easy steaming distance of the North Sea. The formation of the Home Fleet in 1907 was created as the prime weapon to face a possible German challenge. By 1910, when Fisher was force from office, the Royal Navy was already highly tuned and trained for battle. In 1914, Britain possessed twenty-nine Dreadnoughts and battle-cruisers, with twenty more on the stocks; Germany had twenty and seven respectively.

However, their successes were indeed significant, and the Germans were quick to realise that by enormously increasing their power of minor attack they could at least hope to reduce the Royal Navy's margin of superiority, perhaps so low as to eventually warrant the High Seas Fleet taking the offensive. The C.-in-C. Grand Fleet, Admiral Jellicoe, unable to pursue a policy of blockade,[148] was dedicated to a major fleet action, but one he was determined to restrict to the northern half of the North Sea, where the Germans could not rely on having submarines and minelayers to assist in a fleet action.

Thus, the variables which each side imposed on each other tended towards stalemate, rather than action, the very anti-thesis of the strategy the Naval Staff had so assiduously planned. Instead of steaming northwards to meet the Grand Fleet, the High Seas Fleet, or a considerable part of it, was occupied in covering the coastwise transport of troops and supplies to East Prussia. It was this great shift in the use of the German fleet from that which the N.I.D. and Naval Staff had anticipated that rendered not so much strategic naval intelligence in World War I obsolete rather than the limited uses to which Britain's major fleet units could be put.

Moreover, the N.I.D. could not have been expected to foresee something which was to have a major effect upon the British Naval effort, and indeed the outcome of the war, namely Germany's total disregard for solemn international agreements, such as the violation of the Hague Conference of 1907, regarding mine warfare, and their later policy of unrestricted submarine warfare.

It can be seen that what may appear to be the obvious naval intentions of an enemy do not always work out in practice. This was never more true than of the German High Seas Fleet. Although great emphasis was to be placed on the U-boat campaign, this was the result of war experience, and not of any pre-planned strategy. The Germans never intended to use the High Seas Fleet against British commerce, and, save for the earlier stages of the war, it could never have been employed as such even if the Germans had changed their minds.[149]

---

[148] This in itself was a major departure from traditional strategy, necessitated by the advent of mine and submarine warfare, and the fact that the amount of coal that could be carried for ships' coal-fired boilers restricted the time that ships could remain on blockade and patrol.

[149] Other units were used for attacking British commerce. For example, between 10 September-28 October 1914, the Emden, (Captain von Muller) sank twenty-three merchant vessels. The Emden was eventually caught by the light cruiser Sydney.

It is certainly true that Germany changed her naval strategy in the Nazi era, and the nature of her forces enabled N.I.D. and the J.I.C. to give more accurate predictions of how Raeder would use his major naval forces. Their forecasts were accurate—the major German fleet units were deployed to attack neutral and hostile merchantmen bringing essential foodstuffs and raw materials to Britain. In the event, the fate of the Graf Spee and the Bismarck were to prove the futility of commerce destroying alone as a means of winning a naval war. Both Raeder and Donitz appreciated this before 1939. In his memoirs, Grand Admiral Donitz bitterly complains that Hitler had not anticipated war with Great Britain and had neglected the Navy.[150]

The sudden emergence of a new method of conducting a war at sea, against accepted traditional codes and international law, temporarily threw the Naval Staff off balance in World War I, and Admiral Hall's men were equally unprepared. Intelligence was totally unknowledgeable of the new German minelaying policy and the Admiralty was stunned for some time, not having suitable methods of counter-attack immediately available.

Corbett describes the situation thus: "The loss of the Audacious in one of the great highways of the Atlantic trade naturally forced to the front the necessity of dealing firmly with the increasing disregard with which Germany was treating the accepted limitations of naval warfare. Regardless alike of civilian and neutral life, she was sowing mines broadcast and surreptitiously in the highways of the world—and sowing them, as was then believed, under neutral flags. Even without this last aggravation, so ruthless a stretch of legitimate belligerent action could not be met within the old canons of war; that was clear."[151]

To many senior British Naval officers, German methods were distasteful; to the N.I.D., it became clear that the niceties of the old naval code would have to be abandoned; to N.I.D., and Jellicoe concurred, the policy Germany was adopting was the proper one for a belligerent in her position, in order to weaken the British battleline before the main action was fought. However, this tended to restrict the activities of the Grand Fleet. Jellicoe said that his policy, as a result of German methods, would be to resist all temptation to activities which entailed undue risks to major units, and the Navy would devote itself to strangling enemy trade and destroying his submarines.

---

[150] See K. Donitz: Memoirs: Ten Years and Twenty Days; translated by R. H. Stevens in collaboration with David Woodward.
[151] Corbett: Naval Operations. Volume I. p. 246.

He went so far as to say: "If Germany uses fishing craft, let us do the same."[152] Although the anticipated battles did not come in the way Jellicoe had hoped, he did, nonetheless, achieve one of the primary objectives of British strategy—containing German naval power, except for the U-boats, by keeping it hemmed in the North Sea, and not allowing it to break through the Denmark Strait. It was an objective achieved in part through stalemate. Room 40 was constantly waiting for signs that this was changing.

It is a truism to say that in both wars, N.I.D.'s greatest operational successes were scored in the war against the U-boat, measured in terms of the consistency of effort employed, the magnitude of the problem and its significance—that in both wars the U-boats had to be defeated. N.I.D.'s fight against the U-boats was not encouraged or enhanced by any peculiar feature of the submarine or submarine warfare, which lent itself to intelligence work, though of course it is true to say that the whole range of N.I.D.'s intelligence facilities were required to fight the U-boats.

It was simply that in both wars, after early unsuccessful actions by large surface units, the German Navy soon realised it could best cripple Britain by U-boat attacks on merchant ships. In World War II, the higher echelons of the German Naval Staff appreciated this more than their predecessors had in World War I, when the full use and effects of unrestricted attacks on merchantmen was not realised until much later in the war. It was very much still an unknown quantity to the Germans in 1914. However, Donitz and his supporters had urged Hitler to build more U-boats long before 1939.

Intelligence and the Unpredictable

In 1939, N.I.D. was unable to predict how British Naval strategy should evolve; intelligence can account for some unpredictable variables by creating contingency models, using hypothetical situations, but it cannot look into a crystal ball. For example, in June 1940, three facts changed radically British Naval thinking: firstly, the fall of France, making the possibility of invasion greater.

Secondly, the availability of French Atlantic coast ports for German naval bases—the traditional role of Scapa Flow as a base for preventing a breakout into

---

[152] Jellicoe, in his 'The Crisis of the Naval War', records his thoughts at the time and his assessment in the light of the passage of time.

the Atlantic was now undermined, the Western Approaches were now severely threatened, and convoys in mid-Atlantic (out of range of anti-submarine patrols) were now in even greater danger from Donitz's wolf packs, aided by Focke-Wulfe aircraft from Bordeaux; thirdly, on 10 June, Italy entered the war, upsetting the balance of capital ships, and naval balance in the Mediterranean—routes were closed and shipping had to come via the Cape.

These factors could perhaps have been foreseen, but their timing and nature would make any intelligence appreciation for formulating strategy based on these assumptions so hypothetical as to render the valueless for the present, and it was perhaps far more valuable to rely upon other sources of enemy strengths and intentions for strategic planning rather than assumptions about what the enemy might achieve. Major enemy successes or failures will naturally modify strategic thinking, but only after the event can intelligence make sound appraisals.

This does not mean that N.I.D. did not work on certain assumptions at times, but rather that it placed greater emphasis on that which is, rather than that which might be.

The Dardanelles

As already emphasised, the taking of the initiative in any strategic enterprise gives considerable advantage. This was perhaps nowhere more apparent than in the great amphibious landings of World War II. In World War I, the Dardanelles Campaign illustrates well the application of strategic intelligence—using command of the sea to strike at a point with great military and political advantage, based on sound intelligence appraisals. The idea had full support of the N.I.D., and whatever the eventual failings of that campaign, one of which was the very poor collection of more detailed intelligence, the basic reasons for its inception were very sound, based as they were on wide-ranging intelligence, thorough and painstaking in their content.[153]

Admiral Hall's views were those which are now seen as the classic reasons for the Dardanelles and, in essence, few naval historians have questioned their validity. Hall saw that in one stroke Britain could remove all dangers to Egypt,

---

[153] The Dardanelles reveals tragic weaknesses in on-the-spot British intelligence work. For example, accurate knowledge of Turkish armament and defences was lacking, as was topographical intelligence. During the period 19-21 March 1915, following bombardment of the Turkish positions, little was known of any damage done, or the state of Turkish ammunition. See Adm. 137, 713 Public Record Office.

secure the Balkan states, win the wavering respect of the Arabs, put an end to the hesitation of Italy, and open the back door into Europe. Hall was advocating a move to surround the Central Powers with a ring of enemies and to cut them off, just as Napoleon had been cut off by British Naval and Combined Operations in the Mediterranean and prevented from spreading the war beyond the confines of Europe.

To Hall and his staff, Turkey was placed in an intolerable position on the main lateral line of communication between the Western Powers and Russia, and until that obstruction was removed, a real combined effort such as was needed to crush so great a military power as Germany was impossible. The Dardanelles illustrates how sound strategic intelligence fails if the minutiae of intelligence, the hard data necessary to carry out operations, is collected and or interpreted badly. Its consequence can be epochal—the breakdown of the second attempt to force the Turkish defences at Gallipoli constituted a definite landmark in World War I.

The hope of rapidly completing the investment of the Central Powers and opening up direct communications with Russia was at an end. This will be seen later when a marked contrast will be made with the rigorous intelligence operations that preceded the amphibious landings of World War II.

In the years preceding the outbreak of World War I, the C.I.D., together with N.I.D. and Naval Plans had considered the possible implications of a possible German invasion threat. As early as October 1913, the Admiralty had set up dispositions for the defence of the Channel. The N.I.D. worked on the assumption that Germany would be threatening British shores with all her naval power, and considered the various ways in which such a threat could be made. As the last days of peace ran out, the N.I.D. busied itself determining what exact naval movements Germany intended making and what signs there were of an invasion threat.[154]

---

[154] With Hall in office, the whole process of intelligence collection and assessment was intensified. He quickly obtained as much data as possible from Germany before war was declared. For example, in June 1914, a vast quantity of invaluable data was obtained in Kiel and went straight to N.I.D. for analysis. This is to be found in Adm. 137, 1013, Ps. 101-155, Public Record Office. N.I.D. set to work to make assessments of German intentions—see Adm. 137, 1013, p. 76-86, (assessment of German Naval Plans, 23 August-5 September 1914) and Adm. 137, 1013, p. 282-288 (German Plans for an attack

Intelligence showed that the Germans seemed to be more concerned with repelling a threat than actually making one—their destroyers and submarines were spread fifty miles north and south of the Elbe and entrances to their North Sea ports had been mined and lightships removed, whilst the High Seas Fleet hurried back to port from exercises. The night before war was declared, N.I.D.'s intelligence showed that the Germans meant to get a number of commerce destroyers to sea before the outbreak of war, and at 0400 on 4 August 1914, the Grand Fleet received orders to carry out a movement in force to intercept them.

British Naval forces were strategically deployed and ready for such contingencies, and 'hard' intelligence determined how such long-range plans would be implemented in the immediate tactical situations.

The overall need was to prevent invasion, and strategy was evolved to meet that need. The particular ways in which that need was met could only be decided in the light of events themselves. In this sense, long-range strategic intelligence is very general and decisions made in the light of it should be as flexible as possible so as to allow for changed circumstances. For example, pre-1914, the N.I.D. could not have predicted that the battle of Mons would occur and that its outcome might seriously affect naval plans.

Corbett records the effects of this particular battle on naval operations thus: "…Admiral Jellicoe was informed of the serious consequences which seemed to be developing out of the Battle of Mons, and warned to consider the possibility of having to fix a new position for the Grand Fleet should the Germans get control of Calais and the adjacent French coast—that is, in fact, if they succeeded in breaking into the Dover defile."[155]

However, this sort of strategic problem does not preclude specific actions; for example, as a result of what appeared in early October 1914 to be a deteriorating military position (due to extensive reinforcement reaching the German right), it was felt at the time that if the situation was to be saved, something had to be done to secure for the Army its indispensable sea communications. The spectre of invasion arose with the possible threat of German control of Allied ports. The decision was quickly taken to extensively

---

on the British Fleet, 23 September-8 October 1914). Technical intelligence was stepped up too.

For example, between 6 and 16 October 1914, a committee sat to analyse German naval gunnery capabilities, (Adm. 137, 1013, p. 309-325).

[155] Corbett: Naval Operations. Volume I. p. 94.

mine the entrances to the German ports as a further means to threaten movements of major German naval units.

Again, during World War II, the strategic plans for a blockade against Germany were rapidly put into operation.

The Norwegian Campaign

N.I.D. and J.I.C. had planned before war, for example, on a blockade against the iron ore supplies from Narvik to Germany, although initially there were difficulties since most of the iron ore's journey was through neutral territorial waters. This altered after 9 April 1940, with the German invasion of Norway. Any long-range strategic blockade requires an overall appraisal of the enemy's economy, raw material, and trade sources and routes. From such intelligence, operational plans can be evolved. In the event of war, more detailed intelligence will reveal precisely where the enemy can be hit hardest.

Norway illustrates this well—the growing need to capture Norway became more apparent as 1940 dawned, for strategic as well as economic reasons. It was realised a German occupation of Norway would increase the difficulty of maintaining supremacy over the northern exits to the Atlantic. Captain Warburton-Lee's attack on Narvik on 9 April and the eventual landings from assault ships on 28 May 1940, were aimed at securing the country, and more particularly the crucial ports.

The fall of Norway was to reveal, in part, weaknesses in intelligence appraisals, not least of all the prime question of the probably chances of success of severely weakened ground and air forces (caused by the crisis in France) and the effects that the lines of sea communication would have on the outcome of the Norwegian campaign (it is eight hundred miles from Scapa Flow to Narvik).[156] In the Pacific, war there was a similar recognition of the need to cut off the enemy's supply lines and hit his sources of raw materials at source.

After the formation of the British Pacific Fleet (Admiral Fraser) and British East Indies Fleet (Admiral Power), intelligence soon recommended intensive attacks on the Japanese supply line to Burma in the Malacca Straits, mainly by

---

[156] Although initially a disaster, Hitler was forced in January 1942 to send the Tirpitz, Scheer, Lutzow, Prinz Eugen, Hipper, Koln, and five destroyers to Norway for fear of an Allied invasion of northern Norway, thus using up valuable naval units at a time when the Allies had no such intention.

submarines, and air strikes against critical Japanese centres, particularly the great oil dumps. On 19 April 1944, air strikes from H.M.S. Illustrious and the U.S.S. Saratoga were made on the port of Sabang and on 17 May against Surabaya. On 21 June, Port Blair in the Andamans was attacked.

On 24 and 29 January 1945, the Fleet Air Arm launched its highly successful attack on the Japanese oil refineries at Palembang. These attacks were the result of highly successful Anglo-American intelligence cooperation, without which long-range Allied strategic planning would have been impossible. General Eisenhower made this comment on British intelligence revelations to the Americans whilst the early plans for an invasion of Europe were being made: "We gained access to all the British intelligence and learnt the exact strength and commitments of British land, sea and Air Force."[157]

Intelligence and Tactics, and Tactical Situations

In the tactical situation, intelligence is equally important. Before conflict, a detailed study of enemy ship capabilities and tactical procedures can facilitate tactical planning and preparations and exercises can take place along these lines.[158] Intelligence appraisals following actions, giving insight into possible future enemy moves and ones' own mistakes, gives more reliable guidelines, since they are based on what has occurred rather than what might occur. This was especially true in the post-Jutland period when assessment studies soon revealed the weaknesses of British tactical procedures (as well of course, of the chronic lack of cooperation between Room 40 and the War Room).

The classical tactical errors of Jutland are well-known and were already deeply rooted in the Grand Fleet before it went into action. Besides signalling errors, Jellicoe's understandable caution (he could have "lost all in an afternoon" as Churchill said) and fear of U-boat and torpedo attacks, and deficiencies in gunnery and ship and shell design, there were perhaps more important aspects of tactical errors that emerge. Jellicoe adapted the line-ahead broadside when he would have done well to have practiced 'divided' tactics. The Grand Fleet was under too much central control and written orders.

---

[157] Dwight D. Eisenhower: Crusade in Europe. p. 76.

[158] Throughout both World Wars, such appraisals were being continuously made. An example of this is Adm. 137, 1080, p. 27-30, N.I.D. report of 19 January 1915—a comparison of the Grand and High Seas Fleets.

Save for some destroyer captains, most captains were not given enough scope to display initiative. Moreover, when the time came, several captains failed to make enemy reports at critical times. The N.I.D. never attempted to tell Plans and Operations their business, and nor was it N.I.D.'s task to initiate tactical studies and analysis, and because of the often-delicate balance between the roles of the various departments of the Naval Staff, it never made great inroads in tactical intelligence studies as a matter of routine.

Where N.I.D. made its contribution was in providing Operations and therefore operational commanders with the vital information that enabled them to design or change tactical procedure. This was particularly true of convoy escort policy for Atlantic convoys during World War II, which was radically altered after the successful U-boat attacks of 1940. The N.I.D. gained a great deal for the service by the analysis of tactical errors or bad planning which, when analysed, provided valuable insights and data for future operations.

For example, the disastrous raid on Dieppe, 19 August 1942, gave valuable information to the N.I.D. (as well as to Combined Operations) on how an amphibious operation should be mounted, and more particularly for N.I.D., what intelligence data was required. In a memorandum of 7 November 1942, Admiral Godfrey was able to write: "I believe this is excellent now that intelligence and operations occupy adjacent tables in the O.I.D. with no wall in between."[159]

Tactical intelligence was vital for helping to determine or reinforce decisions made by commanders at sea. However, there arose occasions when the possession of intelligence gave the command ashore a better-informed picture than the man-on-the-spot, and consequently tighter operational command was exercised from ashore. In the event of action at sea, the commander still stood on his own, and it was his immediate decisions which determined the outcome of conflict, other than in highly detailed pre-planned operations, where to a lesser extent the need for instant decisions was demanded.

The constant updating of intelligence for ships at sea required a constant dialogue between N.I.D. and Operations. During World War II, this was not lacking. There were occasions, though, when Operations made decisions and gave orders to commanders at sea on the basis of insufficient intelligence. There was nothing N.I.D. could do to alter such decisions. Perhaps the most outstanding example of this was the loss of the ill-fated convoy, PQ17, which illustrates how scanty intelligence was misinterpreted, and formed the basis of a

---

[159] Godfrey Memoirs: Vol. 5 Part 2. p. 216.

decision to scatter, made from headquarters, instead of leaving the decision to the man-on-the-spot.

The convoy consisted of thirty-three merchant ships, three rescue ships and one tanker. The escort consisted of twenty-one vessels with a covering force of two battleships, one aircraft carrier, seven cruisers and some twenty destroyers. The intelligence report was that the Tirpitz and eight destroyers had put to sea.

Intelligence is vital in the area of weaponry—detecting the development of new enemy weapons and assessing the impact these might have on war at sea. Equally important is the need to assess the impact that one's own developments will have upon tactical procedures, and more especially what advantages this will give over the enemy. This was particularly true of the development of radar, which although only still in its infancy in the autumn of 1938,[160] would, according to J.I.C. and N.I.D. assessments, be vital.

It helped turn the tide in the Mediterranean especially as an air-raid warning device,[161] and in the Atlantic battle against the U-boats (although its detection capabilities were reduced by the German development of the 'schnorkel' technique, which in turn though reduced the speed of the U-boats), and was invaluable in other major naval actions—the sinking of the Scharnhorst was, for example, due in part to superior British radar. Throughout World War II, one of the Germans' main troubles was their inability to detect the radar transmissions of Allied ships and aircraft and their consequent vulnerability to surprise. The development of the British centimetric radar set gave the initiative to the Allies in all weather, day and night.

N.I.D. was able to keep Plans and Operations well-informed of the development and possible effects of weapon technology on both sides. From the early part of the twentieth century, the N.I.D. prepared technical intelligence reports on all manner of subjects, and this involved constant surveillance of other powers' weapon and ship design and operating techniques.

For example, after the Russo-Japanese war, the N.I.D. produced a series of reports on technical subjects relating to Russian and Japanese methods, such as the ways in which they maintained their ships' hulls, boilers, and machinery in the theatre of war without resort to dockyard facilities, their methods of raising and repairing sunken warships, and the effects of shot and shell, torpedo and

---

[160] Only two ships were then fitted with it, the Rodney and the Sheffield. Their trials with it were very successful.
[161] See Cunningham: A Sailor's Odessey. Ps. 272 and 369.

mine explosions upon hulls, boilers and machinery. These reports went hand-in-hand with operational analysis reports mentioned above. In the case of the Russo-Japanese war, an analysis was made of both sides' operational methods.

Later in World War II, it was realised many U-boats were escaping destruction from depth charge patterns when, in fact, it was felt they should have been destroyed. It was eventually deduced (and later confirmed by the capture of a U-boat) that U-boat design must have been improved so as to permit them to dive to a greater depth, in fact to a maximum of six hundred feet, hitherto considered impossible. To counter this, escorts were instructed to set depth charges to explode at greater depths and to release them in greatly increased numbers.

N.I.D. was quick to measure the effects of other enemy weapon developments and initiate appropriate action to counter these, such as the development of asdic decoys, improved magnetic torpedo pistols, acoustic and zig-zag running torpedoes and the high-calibre AA guns fitted to U-boats to counter surface attacks by Coastal Command aircraft.

To give the advantage of tactical surprise and to know possible enemy strengths and intentions are two of the prime roles of intelligence from the viewpoint of the operational planner or the commander. Prior to the D-Day landings, the joint Anglo-American intelligence staff executed a complex plan to deceive the Germans into thinking the landings would be in the Calais region. It is now known that the Germans gave extraordinary credence to these deceptions.[162] Before the Allied landings at Salerno, joint intelligence reported that the Italian garrison in the Salerno Bay area was being replaced by the best of the German troops available.

---

[162] See Field Marshal Montgomery: Normandy to the Baltic. Ps. 36 and 37. The decision to invade N.W. Europe was in fact made in the summer of 1942. In close conjunction with the intelligence departments, the Allied planners decided that the initial landings must be somewhere between Cherbourg and the mouth of the Seine. This area provided beaches sufficiently wide for the assault and suitable terrain for airfield construction and manoeuvring after the forces ashore had been built up to full strength. Furthermore, they were not too distant for fighter cover from England and not too bristling with coast and beach defences.

In the event, the Allies achieved tactical surprise. German air reconnaissance was bad and they had no usable radar. Even after the invasion, into July 1944, the Germans still thought a second landing in the Pas de Calais region was in the offing, and they retained strong forces in that area.

Intelligence further predicted a bitter battle in the beach-head culminating in a strong counter-attack somewhere between the fourth and sixth day after the landing.[163] These predictions were to be proven very accurate. Admiral Fraser was to be very grateful to the N.I.D. during 25 and 26 December 1943, when flying his flag in the new battleship Due of York, (10 14" guns) he was warned by the Admiralty that the Scharnhorst was at large.[164] At the Battle of Midway, Admiral Nimitz was to be equally grateful to radio intelligence, which had deduced from Japanese signals that their objective was Midway.

As a result of this intelligence, Nimitz, like Fraser, made a momentous decision—he accepted the challenge and prepared for actions, knowing the intention, and later the whereabouts too, of the enemy. At Midway, American flying boats made reconnaissance flights covering an area up to seven hundred miles around Midway, thus providing Admiral Nimitz with a timely picture of the enemy's positions. The Japanese carrier fleet neglected all reconnaissance.[165] Locating the enemy is in itself invaluable. Whatever the method it uses, as long as it is reliable, intelligence has a prime responsibility to locate the enemy.

The attack on the Tirpitz in Alten fiord by midget submarines on 22 September 1943, could not have been reliably planned but for continuous intelligence reports. As has already been shown, mining can be pointless unless one can be sure of enemy movements. Intelligence located the U-boat work-up areas in the Baltic for example. These were strewn with mines. This had the desired effect. In early 1944, Donitz reported that the mine situation was a cause of deep anxiety, and that the ore imports from Sweden were seriously threatened.[166]

In his *Sea Warfare, 1939-1945*, Captain J. Creswell, R.N., says this of the effects of British mining policy: "...some four hundred merchant ships and hundred minesweepers were sunk by British mines and many more were damaged. Most of them were sunk in the western Baltic and the southeastern North Sea in 1943 and 1944, and about 80% fell to mines laid by aircraft."

---

[163] See General Eisenhower's account of this in: Crusade in Europe. p. 205 and 206.
[164] Admiral Bey had transmitted a signal to the effect that the weather was unsuitable for destroyers. This signal was intercepted.
[165] See L. B. Kirkpatrick: Captains Without Eyes, and Midway, the Battle that doomed Japan, the Japanese Navy's story, by Mitsuo Fuchida and Masutake Okumiyu.
[166] See K. Donitz: Memoirs: Ten Years and Twenty Days.

Without intelligence of where mines could be most profitably sown, these totals would never have been achieved.

Politics and Strategy

Whatever the strength of strategic and tactical intelligence, both in peace and wartime, and the ability of naval forces to perform certain tasks, there can be no doubt that political rather than naval decision-making will, in the last resort, decide the fate of large-scale naval forces. This is a factor that will be dealt with in detail later, but it is appropriate to recognise this dichotomy at this stage between what often appeared as the obvious courses of action to N.I.D. and the planners on the one hand, and decisions different to their views made by politicians on the other hand.

This is apparent when reviewing the degree of influence strategic intelligence played in moulding grand strategy vis-à-vis the Royal Navy during the Great War.

Captain Sir Basil Liddell-Hart concluded in one of his last works, "History of the First World War," that Britain had shown "…tacit acceptance of acting as an appendix to the French left wing and away from her historic exploitation of the mobility given to her by sea power." He cites the landing of a naval division to reinforce the defence of Antwerp and of the Seventh Infantry and the Third Cavalry Divisions at Ostend and Zeebrugge[167] as "the first and last effort to make use of British amphibious power." The critical point is why was this so. Why was it that the grand strategic naval designs of the Committee of Imperial Defence fell on stony ground when war came?

Why was it that the official military historian of World War I, General Edmunds, was able to write of the Battle of the Marne, to choose but one example: "Had some of the 14 British Territorial Divisions and 14 Mounted Brigades, with the Sixth Division still in England, been landed at the Channel coast ports to fall on the German communications and rear, a decisive tactical result might have been obtained and the war finished?" Political-military decisions will be examined later, but the point remains here nonetheless that a divergence can

---

[167] This, in fact, was somewhat ironic, as it was done on Churchill's insistence, in fact a political decision forced against military and naval advice.

occur between carefully worked out war plans and strategic concepts, based on unrelenting intelligence reports, and the later execution of policy in war.[168]

However, it has already been recorded as a major principle of intelligence, that, if it is to retain its integrity and authority, it cannot cross the bridge linking the intelligence organisation and those who make plans and operational decision. The forcefulness with which intelligence is given, and indeed the standing of those who give it, is of course though another matter.

What World War I shows is not the complete collapse of C.I.D. and N.I.D. grand naval strategy, but the missing of crucial opportunities, and the conspicuous pursuit of inept campaigns on land, and nor was intelligence completely blameless for those campaigns which, though faulty in execution, were sound in conception. The Dardanelles must fall into this category. Britain did establish early command of the sea and did implement, for example, her design to seize German colonies which were invaluable assets to bargain with, and indeed Liddell-Hart reaches this conclusion in the Epilogue of his book.

"…if the historian…has to select one day as decisive for the outcome of the World War I, he will probably choose 2 August 1914…when Mr Winston Churchill, at 1.25 a.m. sent the order to mobilise the British Navy…For the Navy was the instrument of the blockade, and as the fog of war disperses in the clearer light of these post-war years that blockade is seen to assume larger and larger proportions, to be more and more clearly the decisive agency in the struggle…It was the stranglehold of the British Navy which…constrained Germany to carry out that felo de se offensive of 1918. She was dogged by the spectre of slow enfeeblement, ending in eventual collapse."

As Liddell-Hart says, Britain had exercised sea power in Mahan terms; that it was not extended and exploited in depth is another matter. The roots for this policy lay in the work of the C.I.D., the N.I.D., and the planners of the Naval Staff. Certainly by 1939, major lessons had been learnt, and fortunately too, since the threat of invasion was greater.

---

[168] The records of the Committee of Imperial Defence for before World War I, when compared with the war record revealed in the official histories and the more distinguished commentaries, show a disparity that would surely have been unbelievable to the pre-war D.N.I.s and their colleagues on the C.I.D. See the List of the Papers of the Committee of Imperial Defence to 1914, H.M.S.O. 1964, for the references, many of the ideas of which are discussed in N.H. Gibbs' book on pre-1914 strategic thinking: The Origins of Imperial Defence. O.U.P. 1955.

After the withdrawal from France, sea power was paramount, as the Allies were able to transport their armies to areas where they could land and engage the enemy at points most favourable to the development of their strategy, and before the great amphibious landings, it is quite clear that British sea power was the decisive influence on the outcome of the war in that critical year June 1940 to June 1941 when Britain obtained and maintained control of the sea, and control of the air over certain strategic areas, such as the Dover Straits, the English Channel, and the waters around Malta. In Mahan-like phrase domination of the sea was to bring domination of the land.

The Degree of Flexibility of Intelligence and Naval Policy

A military organisation is not as ideally flexible as perhaps one imagines it ought to be. Its sinews may be strong but its reflexes may not be as quick as desirable. This is apparent after a prolonged period of peace. Intelligence can always help to keep a service on its toes, provided it is given the wherewithal to operate effectively. Admiral Godfrey makes this cogent comment in his memoirs: "Intelligence deals with the enemy and the potential enemy. When there is no enemy, it languishes and its importance is forgotten. Its strategic functions are only vaguely appreciated by those and this includes the real talent of the Navy— who have no personal experience of intelligence in war."[169]

His comment applied to the inter-war period, and perhaps no one more than John Godfrey saw in the early and mid-1930s how low the N.I.D. had been run down. During his time as Deputy Director Plans, Godfrey witnessed the hardening of the Navy's arteries caused, in part, by a failure to assess naval requirements, coupled to other major factors, not least of all the move towards an arms run-down and the national anti-war feeling and the sense of false security engendered by Fascist and Nazi blandishments, a situation that has been well summarised by Admiral of the Fleet the Viscount Cunningham:[170]

"...there were still gaps in our armour after years of unenlightened popular belief in the efficacy of collective security under a League of Nations which did not include the United States, and unilateral disarmament which caused many of our still useful ships to be scrapped whilst permitting other nations to build. A

---

[169] Admiral J. H. Godfrey: typescript memoirs. Vol. V. Part I. p. 2. Copy used is in the Manuscript department of the National Maritime Museum, Greenwich.

[170] Cunningham: A Sailor's Odessey. p. 193.

succession of naval treaties which could only be considered disastrous in their effect had caused the Navy to be whittled to the bone, particularly in its building and replacement programmes and the number of its personnel."

Even before World War I, there were major errors made in assessing possible shifts in enemy policy caused by reasonably predictable wartime events. This was particularly true of German U-boat policy. Until March 1915, Britain continued to believe that Germany, like herself, would continue to use submarines solely for naval objectives, whereas it became clearer week by week, as further losses were reported, that the Germans were devoting their main energy to the development of their commercial blockade. N.I.D. had reported early in the war, on numerous occasions, how it saw German policy developing and that counter-measures should be developed quickly.

As Corbett recalls in the official history: "…intelligence indicated that in the near future it (German submarine warfare) would increase in intensity as it was increasing in barbarity."[171] In the last years of peace, 1912-1913, during the Jackson-Oliver tenureship of the D.N.I. appointment, N.I.D. had foretold that the Germans would not scruple to use the new weapon against merchant ships, both belligerent and neutral, but the general belief among many senior members of the Naval Staff and government was that the Germans were too sound strategists to risk raising fresh enemies against themselves by so flagrant a violation of the traditions of sea warfare.

Even in Germany, this ostensibly saner view was held by many, but under the pressure, and some Germans argued, provocation, of the severe British blockade, a more reckless submarine policy was needed. Hall's men in Room 40 were to dramatically prove how devastatingly wrong were some of the views of certain sections of the naval planning staff and political decision-makers.

There were many lessons learnt from World War I that were useful for World War II operations, but by 1939, there were new factors which were to revolutionise sea warfare, but several of these, even if appreciated, were not always acted upon, mainly for political reasons.

The role of the aircraft, as a substitute for the big gun, was to come into its own, and it was carrier-borne and not shore-based aircraft that were to prove themselves of prime importance, the unknown quantity, radar, revolutionised naval operations and the ability to replenish and refuel at sea, reaching its zenith in the great fleet trains of the Pacific fleets, changed the pattern of planning and

---

[171] Corbett: Vol. I. p. 288.

operations, as did the range and firepower of the submarines. Central to World War II maritime operations and ultimate victory, were the great amphibious assaults, preceded by a series of smaller Combined Operations and the development of a welter of amphibious craft.

These operations, especially in the Pacific, showed how sea power could be so overwhelmingly exerted at so great a distance from home bases. It is six thousand miles from Pearl Harbour to Singapore, and three thousand two hundred to Japan, and none of the other American Pacific bases were particularly satisfactory, Manila Bay and Subic Bay in the Philippines were poor bases, and Wake Island and Guam were untenable, being too near the Japanese Mariana islands and Iwo Jima.

It is a truism to say that the pace of weapon development, strategic and tactical practices, as well as the other host of naval business, recruitment, training, manpower deployment and so forth changes with the exigencies of war, and it is natural therefore to find Britain, in 1939, not in an ideal position as her policy was unaggressive and she was attempting to gain momentum for what seemed to be an inevitable war. For these reasons, N.I.D. could not have given accurate predictions for Naval Plans and Operations of how things would go.

During the late-30s, it competently collected most of the vital statistics about the German Navy, allowing for the absence of certain technical data. This is pertinent when compared with the Americans' position. The latter did not realise how the Japanese valued carrier-borne air power and how they were way behind Japan in attack techniques, especially in the use of torpedo and dive-bomb attacks, and the development of their long-range high explosive torpedo for their destroyers.[172]

Ironically, the Americans never examined the precursor to 7 December 1941, namely the surprise Japanese attack on the Russian Fleet in Port Arthur in 1904 (nor for that matter did Britain see Scapa Flow, pre-1939, in such a light). Politically, there were some major errors in Anglo-American Naval relations, the hallmark of which was uncooperativeness. Throughout the 1930s, the bitter

---

[172] As early as 1927, the N.I.D. began continuous studies for providing defence for ships and installations against air attacks and ways of obtaining intelligence to give such warnings. See Adm. 116, 2519. From 1936 until the war, the N.I.D. made intelligence appraisals for a naval air policy—no. of aircraft needed, type, weaponry and tactics. See Adm. 116, 4030.

feeling between the British and American navies increased and until 1937 this was skilfully utilised by Japan to strengthen her own fleet.

The Americans projection into the Formosa-Philippines-Singapore triangle was greatly reduced, leaving the western Pacific open. Later in the war, the Navy Department in Washington was to be against a British fleet going to the Pacific. They thought the United States should go it alone and would have done but for Admiral Chester W. Nimitz, C.-in-C. Pacific, who welcomed the idea of a British Pacific Fleet. Political factors such as these were beyond the scope of the N.I.D.[173]

Where the N.I.D. scored before the war was in very specific areas,[174] and in relating the German Navy's strength—numbers, weapons and endurances, to the Royal Navy's capability.[175] Moreover, the N.I.D. was able to sow what many members of the Naval Staff and certain politicians and sections of the public knew and feared, but not in detail—British Naval weaknesses and how these would probably show themselves in the first stages of a war with Germany.

It was known, for example, that there were nowhere enough cruisers to give protection to convoys against major surface attacks, particularly if the Germans waited until the Tirpitz was completed, and patrolled this, Bismarck, and the battlecruisers, together. This sort of fact, placed alongside the known German naval building plan, had alarming implications (Raeder's so-called Z-Plan of naval construction allowed in the long term for four aircraft carriers of forty thousand tons).

However, it should never be forgotten that the process was two-way—the Germans had no precise information as to the efficiency of British anti-submarine techniques and Hitler had a pathological fear of committing his major fleet units to a full action.

---

[173] It is chastening to note that Germany probably made a great diplomatic mistake by not persuading Japan to enter the war in 1940, without declaring war on the United States. This would have taxed British resources beyond their capabilities.

[174] N.I.D. had investigated, for example, the prospect of mining German river mouths from the air, in addition to submarines, destroyers and minelayers, and the Admiralty and the Air Ministry worked on this, producing eventually suitable mines for the task.

[175] See Appendix B for the type of information N.I.D. was able to present, giving the radius of action of some types of German warships, outward and homeward passage, allowing 20% reserve for fuel consumed in a battle. It was assumed pre-1939, before the later fall of France, that U-boats would pass south of Iceland. The occupation of the French Biscay ports was to give the boats a greater range of action.

As stressed earlier, there can never be any accurate prediction of what actual war will produce. Only intelligence in war itself will give the better picture, and in 1939-1945, the N.I.D. came into its own. Its assessments then had a life and death significance, and above all, it was to operate on a day-to-day, even hour-by-hour (and often for an organisation like Winn's, minute-by-minute) basis, feeding in the vital information. In wartime, pre-war hypotheses change, and a situation crystallises.

In 1939, the prospect of many surface raiders in the Atlantic seemed daunting. Who could have foreseen that Hitler would insist on withdrawing these from the west to help cover the Norwegian situation, and who could have decided in 1939 that by crippling a dock in St. Nazaire by an old destroyer in March 1942, the Nazis would be deprived of the only major repair facility for the Tirpitz and Bismarck on the French Atlantic coast?

Similarly with implementing generally accepted war principles: for example, to conduct a blockade across the entrance to the Bay of Biscay (a large area to be patrolled and with only small forces available), there was a primary need for intelligence of forthcoming movements of enemy merchant ships, obtained by submarines and air reconnaissance agents' reports and by studying convoy cycles. In wartime, the jigsaw process of fitting together a mass of apparently disconnected evidence begins in earnest.

The critical value of air power rapidly became apparent to N.I.D. The Norwegian campaign soon showed that in any amphibious operation air cover was essential; Taranto, Cape Matapan and the Crete campaign proved this point very quickly in the Mediterranean. The Germans knew this too—nothing could be achieved in the Mediterranean without overwhelming strength in the air.[176] However, not all issues were as clear-cut as this to the N.I.D., and several had to wait for post-war analysis to unravel.

For example, N.I.D. never deduced that forces employed on area searches sank fewer submarines, (proportionate to the effort involved) than did similar forces on escort and close support operations.

---

[176] Hence, their desire to push their airfields even further forward, hoping that they might diminish the area in which British ships could operate, and eventually gain domination of the Mediterranean. When in July 1941, the Malta convoys were less harassed by German air power, because of the all-out German efforts in the invasion of Russia, the tide began to turn in Britain's favour.

Chapter Four
A Survey and Critical Analysis of the Relationship between Selected Naval Operations During the Period and Intelligence

The Beginnings of Operational Intelligence in World War I

The acid test for any intelligence organisation must be the demands which war makes, and it is during wartime that the operational planners and commanders place a premium on intelligence. This is not to devalue the importance of intelligence in peacetime, far from it. Intelligence in itself may enable those who make major military decisions, both politicians and senior officers, to prevent those situations developing which lead to war. The records of the Committee of Imperial Defence are testimony to the extent to which the British government went in order to prepare for war contingencies.

However, the most detailed plans and well-accumulated intelligence data have often proved inadequate once conflict has started. There can be no precise prediction of the intentions of an enemy.

The Great War confronted the N.I.D. with its first major challenge since its inception. Pre-1914, it had a hand in limited operations, such as the trouble with the Mahdi in the Sudan and the expeditions to relieve Khartoum and rescue General Gordon. In 1914, the Naval Staff, despite the preparations of the C.I.D. and the copious N.I.D. reports, were worried about many aspects of a war with Germany. The C.-in-C. Grand Fleet was very concerned about torpedo attacks by German destroyers, as well as meeting the High Seas Fleet in a night action—

N.I.D. knew the Germans had made a special study of this and had trained accordingly.

The Germans had better starshells and searchlights, and they had trained to use them. The British had yet to develop means to recognise friend from foe at night. On the technical side, the Royal Navy had shells of poor design—they were not armour-piercing. Similarly with British warships' armour plating—it was woefully lacking. To be totally effective, it should have been laid on the decks as well as the sides to forestall the effects of long-range shells falling vertically.

There was a conspicuous failure by Britain to check the technical efficiency of its ships. For example, the Royal Navy remained ignorant of a serious defect in the turret design of all its Dreadnoughts. The Germans were more observant. After the Dogger Bank action, when the Germans nearly lost the Seyditz through poor turret design, they were quick to make improvements.

On the tactical side, the Naval Staff were worried as to how the Germans might use their submarines, and no real thought was given to the need for air reconnaissance. During the Battle of Jutland, only one air reconnaissance aircraft flew.[177] However, the N.I.D. responded immediately, once war seemed imminent and had begun to gain information about German intentions and how, and where, and when they would deploy their forces.[178] The N.I.D. was quick to make recommendations based on pre-war plans.

For example, U-boat indicator nets were laid across the Dover Straits. These were initially successful. U-boats were ordered not to use the Dover Straits, thus lengthening their journey to and from the Irish Sea by fourteen hundred miles and cutting their time on patrol by seven days. However, as Professor Marder has shown, U-boats were eventually able to find safe ways through the Dover barrage.

---

[177] The records speak of the very limited use made of naval air reconnaissance throughout World War I. The following contain surviving evidence of what naval reconnaissance was done from the air: Adm. 137: 146, 150, 157, 287, 290, 291, 292, 302, 333, 334, Public Record Office.

[178] See Adm. 137, HS 1013 in the N.I.D. records in the Public Record Office. Between August and September, the N.I.D. made accurate assessments of German naval plans (see p. 76-86), and the way they would probably attack the British fleet (see p. 282-288). In June and July 1914, N.I.D. busied itself collecting and assessing information about the German units' seaworthiness based at Kiel (see p. 101-155).

He writes: "Dover remained a difficult problem, as the Flanders U-boats continued to pass the Straits with ease and impunity, the mobile patrols and explosive mine-net barrage notwithstanding. In the latter part of the year (1917), the U-boats were sinking about twenty ships in the Channel every month. The D.N.I. informed Keyes, then Director of the Plans Division, in October that over thirty submarines were passing through the Straits monthly. The statement came from a German report on the passage of the mine-net barrage salved from UC-44 (blown up on her own minefield off Waterford in October 1917).

"It showed that hundred and ninety passages had been made between 23 December 1916 and 6 June 1917, chiefly at night and on the surface. There were only eight reports of U-boats touching a net and eight reports of their being forced to dive to avoid patrols. Clearly, the barrage was absolutely ineffective in denying the passage of the Straits to the U-boats."[179] Similarly, the N.I.D. was quick to assess German mining policy[180] and the use the Germans might make of Zeppelins and the extent to which they were being built.[181]

Many things left undone in peacetime have to be rapidly done in wartime. In some cases, though no amount of improvisation, however quickly done, can make up for precious time lost—this is particularly true of an organisation needed to continuously monitor the location (either at sea or in harbour) and deduce the possible intentions of enemy units. In this vital area, the N.I.D. was not found wanting in 1914. Room 40 was to play an increasingly important role in determining the outcome of operations.

Radio Intelligence in World War I

The key to this role lay in possessing, or being able to crack, enemy codes.[182] From very early on, the N.I.D. was able to decipher enough German radio signals to give the Admiralty warning of future German plans. It was learnt in December 1914, that a further raid on the east coast of Britain had been ordered for 16

---

[179] Arthur J. Marder: From the Dreadnought to Scapa Flow. Vol. 4. p. 316.
[180] Adm. 137, HS1013, p. 329-331 gives details of German mining policy in Danish and Swedish channels.
[181] Adm. 137, HS1013, p. 38-382, gives details of how between 17 October and 8 November 1914, N.I.D. obtained details, and reported on Zeppelin construction and policy.
[182] The N.I.D. was greatly aided in this when copies of the German Navy's Codes salvaged from the wrecked cruiser Magdeburg, tell into its hands.

December (though it was not known that this raid was to be supported by the whole German High Seas Fleet).[183] Throughout the whole of the war, the N.I.D. never ceased its vigil for enemy radio traffic.

On 22 April 1918, the High Seas Fleet, unknown to N.I.D., sortied from the Jade as far north as Stavanger. Admiral Scheer lost the convoy he sought and foolishly broke radio silence. The N.I.D. tracking organisation picked this up and Beatty was ordered to sea. Unfortunately, Scheer reached port safely. Throughout the war, N.I.D. had given Operations timely warnings of the High Seas Fleet's movements. On 23 January 1915, Hipper left the Jade to raid the British Dogger Bank patrol. N.I.D. gave the Admiralty enough warning to send Beatty southwards from Rosyth.

Regrettably, a major chance for a British victory was missed, in part due to faulty signalling and fear of running into a submarine trap. The intelligence had been first class. N.I.D. radio intelligence was critical at Jutland. It could have turned the odds completely in favour of the Royal Navy if it had been used properly.

In retrospect, accurate intelligence was the only way the two fleets could have met on the open seas, other than by chance, and perhaps by mammoth round the clock sea and air searches, which were well beyond the capabilities of the Royal Navy. Such methods also tend to reduce the capability to concentrate force in one point very quickly. Britain began to rely heavily on radio intercepts, and the Germans on submarine and Zeppelin reconnaissance. Jellicoe and Beatty would never have known where the enemy was.

On 14 December 1914, the Admiralty, using N.I.D. intelligence, were able to signal Jellicoe at 2130 that the Germans had sortied from the Jade. The First Sea Lord decided the strength of the force to carry out this operation but left its disposition to the Commander-in-Chief. Again, on 23 January 1915, when Beatty and Tyrwhitt sailed from the south to intercept Hipper, they did so with the

---

[183] Beatty's four battlecruisers and Admiral Warrender's eight Dreadnoughts were in position and waiting to spring a trap on Hipper's force. An unfortunate signal by the Lion, Beatty's flagship, misled Goodenough into losing touch with the enemy.

Footnote: Captain S. W. Roskill showed the author a letter he had received dated 2 May 1963 from Sir Eugen Millington-Drake, who was present in September 1914, in the British Embassy in St. Petersburg. Millington-Drake describes the furious activity as the Magdeburg's code was copied out, ready for dispatch to London.

advantage of the N.I.D.'s radio intelligence. Hipper, unsupported by the High Seas Fleet, believed all British heavy ships were in harbour.[184]

On 30 May 1916, the Admiralty received sufficient warning of Hipper's sorties to Norway from intercepted radio messages to send the Grand Fleet to sea. That the Operations Division in Admiralty misinterpreted intelligence to the extent of informing Jellicoe and Beatty that Scheer was still in the Jade when he was in fact at sea may seem incredible now.[185] During the night of 31 May/1 June, the Germans were able to break through behind Jellicoe's formations and head for their bases.

None of those British ships which actually engaged the German heavy ships reported to Jellicoe that the enemy fleet was breaking through. Even more extraordinary, some of the battleships in the rear of Jellicoe's night formation, and notably the fifth battle squadron, sighted German battleships, yet failed to report them to the C.-in-C. and took no action towards engaging them. The Operations Division further contributed to the chaos by failing to pass crucial signals to Jellicoe. During the night, three vital signals from Scheer were deciphered, each of them indicating beyond doubt that the High Seas Fleet was making for the Horns Reef.

Jellicoe held his course to the southward; had he received even one of them, he could have altered course and brought Scheer to action in the early morning of 1 June 1916. At 0400 on that day, Jellicoe received, somewhat ironically, a signal from the Admiralty, which said that Scheer was safe within the swept channel beyond the Horns Reef. Any knowledge of the crucial N.I.D. signals at Jutland is entirely due to W. F. Clarke, who worked in Ewing's team in Room 40. He made and kept copies of all the vital signals. He passed these to Captain S. W. Roskill, who kindly allowed the author to see these.

Captain Roskill also showed them to Professor Arthur Marder, who used and quoted them in his *From Dreadnought to Scapa Flow*. Clarke's letters to Captain Roskill substantiate statements made on the basis of other sources: in a letter

---

[184] The Life and Letters of David, Earl Beatty. Ed. W. S. Chalmers. p. 165.

[185] It is interesting to record on the question of the location of the German C.-in-C.'s signal code at Jutland that in a letter to Captain S. W. Roskill the late Donald McLachlan says how he had met Captain zur See Kupfer, who was the head of the German B Dienst in both World Wars. Kupfer told McLachlan that as well as transferring the C.-in-C.'s signal code ashore when he put to sea, in order to deceive the enemy, they also transferred his radio operator, so that his signalling touch would not be detected at sea.

dated 8 February 1959 titled, 'Retrospect, 1916-1945', Clarke says that the Operations Division never used N.I.D. signal intelligence to full advantage. He puts this down in part to lack of camaraderie between the two divisions; in a letter of 28 August 1951, he describes the reforms made after Jutland, especially the establishment of the daily intelligence summaries for the C.-in-C. Grand Fleet.

These reports were based almost entirely on wireless intelligence, and in order to maintain security (and in particular to guard the fact that the British possessed the German codes) only the First and Second Sea Lords, the D.N.I., Room 40's cryptanalysts, A.J. Balfour, and the C.-in-C. and his senior staff ever knew of these reports or saw their content. In his letter of 8 February 1959, Clarke graphically describes having dinner with Beatty on board the Queen Elizabeth after Jutland. Beatty was interested in Room 40 and Clarke explained to him the nature of its activities.

Beatty then felt he should show Clarke the C.-in-C.'s signal pack for the Battle of Jutland; Clarke was astonished to find that the Operations Division had obviously never passed vital signals at all, or had sent them in part, or too late to be of use. After talking to Beatty, it became obvious to Clarke that there had not been any analysis made of N.I.D.'s and the Operations Division's relationship before and during Jutland. In other words, it had not occurred to anyone that this was vital to the understanding of the outcome of the battle and the role intelligence can play if used properly.

It was not until 1922, with the Naval Staff Appreciation of Jutland (CB 0938) that this was done. Captain Roskill allowed the author to examine this document. Despite Clarke's very valid criticisms, the point nonetheless remains that wireless intelligence was the main source in World War I and without it, there would have been no Dogger Bank or Jutland. In an undated letter to Captain Roskill, Admiral Sir William James emphasises these points. In W. S. Chalmers' edited Life and Letters of David Earl Beatty, this comment by Beatty emphasises N.I.D.'s significance at Jutland:

"It is creditable to Admiralty intelligence that their information should have been in time to enable the Grand Fleet to get well into the North Sea before the High Seas Fleet had left harbour, and it also speaks well for the vigilance of British coast patrols that only two of a large number of enemy submarines were able to sight units of the British Fleet." He goes on to say: "Admiralty intelligence, however, was silent during the morning of 31. Scheer, on the other hand, had received reports from the two submarines already mentioned, misleading him to believe that only detached units of the British Fleet were at sea, which would have suited his plans admirably."[186]

Several aspects of Jutland intelligence are quite clear—it was accurate, so accurate that it enabled the Grand Fleet to beat Scheer to his destination. The latter's U-boat trap could not be sprung and, whatever the validity of Jellicoe's battle plan, the fact nonetheless remains that he was given ample time to formulate one and to engage on his own terms. Jellicoe and his fleet may not have made the most of their advantage, but at least Scheer was denied the advantage of tactical surprise.

The Battles of Coronel and the Falkland Islands

This is in marked contrast with the earlier battle of Coronel when the Admiralty had no precise information regarding the nature and location of the enemy. After Craddock's defeat, the Admiralty responded by sending strong reinforcements to every area to which von Spee might go. Once Sturdee deduced von Spee was in the Falkland Islands, he was able to obtain more precise information from local sources. Without this, Sturdee had intended to go through the Magellan Straits in search of von Spee off the Chilean coast. In other words, he was going to rely on chance patrolling to locate von Spee.

Without intelligence Sturdee would never have brought von Spee to action at the Battle of the Falklands. Let us look at this more closely. Between 4 and 13 November 1914, there was no sound intelligence from the South Atlantic, save for some indefinite consuls' reports. Then, on 13 November, the N.I.D. received definite news that the Dresden and the Leipzig had arrived at Valparaiso and would not be allowed to coal. They sailed at 0100 on 14, and this was reported, along with the news that the German squadron was waiting for them outside. The N.I.D. now knew that a fortnight after Coronel von Spee was still off the Chilean coast and this information was passed to Sturdee.

More intelligence came into the N.I.D., from the consul at Coronel on 19 November, and the Consul-General at Valparaiso on 21 November. When Sturdee arrived at Abrolhos Rocks on 26 November, he was sent a full intelligence report from the N.I.D., and he received further intelligence reports from the naval intelligence officers at Montevideo via the Port Stanley W/T

---

[186] See Chalmers. p. 223.

station on 7 December. The N.I.D. had been able to furnish Sturdee with as much data as possible on the location, nature and possible intentions of von Spee's force. The final action was left to the commander on the spot.[187]

After 1916, an attempt was made to remedy the inconclusiveness of naval action by an acceptance and heavy reliance on intelligence, unfortunately to no avail in terms of an overwhelming British victory. In the autumn of 1917, naval intelligence reported that Scheer intended in future to use battleships to cover minesweeping activities in the Heligoland Bight (mainly because the Harwich force had successfully damaged German destroyer escorts). On 16 November 1917, with plenty of warning, and fully prepared, Beatty put to sea to combat this force. Once again, the British were to be hamstrung.

An inconclusive struggle followed. The Germans could not be drawn from the protection of their minefields. The naval war continued in this vein until the end, each side ineffectively trying to draw the other in advantageous circumstances (Beatty hoping, for example, to tempt the Germans by the Dreadnought protection given to the Lerwick-Bergen convoys). It was a little unfortunate that Room 40 failed to detect the last German sortie of the war. The duty Officer in Room 40 misread the word 'Spannkraft' (full force). He thought this was a word from an incomplete signal.

Zeebrugge; the Baltic (1919)

From an intelligence point of view, the Zeebrugge Raid was not a great success, although at the time Room 40 thought it was. The objective of the raid was to block the entrances to Zeebrugge at all states of the tide, thus prohibiting its use as a submarine base. In a letter of 16 May 1958, W. F. Clarke, who was working in Room 40 at the time, told Captain S. W. Roskill how they had all drawn the wrong conclusions from the available evidence. In fact, the entrances were blocked at low water only. This was later confirmed in volume seven of the official German Naval History of the War at Sea, 1914-1918.

By the end of the Great War, Hall's N.I.D. was consulted about every major operation. This became very evident in the Kronstadt Raid.[188] Captain Augustus

---

[187] Naval Staff Monographs for World War I. Vol. 1.

[188] A flotilla of Coastal Motor Boats, commanded by Lieutenant Augustus Agar, V.C., D.S.O., Royal Navy, carried out an attack on the Russian submarine and warship base in Kronstadt harbour on 19 August 1919, supported by an aerial attack by the RAF. Agar's

Agar, V.C., D.S.O., R.N., gives a full account of this operation in his book, Baltic Episode.[189] Agar was involved in further clandestine activity in the Baltic. Through Commander Goff of the N.I.D., the British Secret Service briefed Agar to carry out the escape of the famous British agent ST25 (Sir Paul Dukes) from Russia. Dukes held valuable information, and his return in Britain was blocked when the Bolsheviks suddenly arrested the British-paid couriers.

Agar landed fresh agents destined for Petrograd, and made contact with British agents in Sweden, Finland, Russia, and the Baltic States.[190] The Kronstadt Raid and Agar's espionage successes are testimony to the system Admiral Sir Reginald Hall created.[191]

In general, Britain failed to learn many lessons from World War I. To implement necessary changes in the political and socio-economic climate of the 1920s and 1930s indeed would have been difficult. However, the recognition of a need to innovate in crucial areas, even if impossible in practical terms, was lacking, and the record of the N.I.D. in pressing for such innovations is undistinguished. Major reforms which were made seem to have originated from other sources. N.I.D. sowed few seeds compared with the dynamic eras of Hall in World War I or Godfrey in World War II.

C.M.B.s sank two Russian battleships, one destroyer, and seriously damaged one cruiser. The C.-in-C. Baltic, Admiral Sir Walter Cowan, planned the attack, called operation RK after Admiral Sir Roger Keyes of Zeebrugge fame. Cowan did not want a repetition of the Dardanelles when the Turks knew in advance that the British were coming. Complete surprise was achieved.

[189] Hodder and Stoughton, 1963, Agar won his V.C. for destroying the Bolshevik cruiser Oleg on 17 June 1919, in C.M.B. 4.

[190] Details of Agar's activities and N.I.D. intelligence penetration in the Baltic, and particularly at Kronstadt, can be seen in Adm. 137, 3060, 2060, Public Record Office.

[191] As are the intelligence packs pertaining to the Grand Fleet, 1914-1918, Adm. 137, 174-203, a vast collection of N.I.D. data revealing how well Hall's men fed the C.-in-C. with every available piece of intelligence they had acquired and digested, especially after the clarification of N.I.D.'s role in the post-Jutland period.

The Intelligence Position 1939-1940

N.I.D. maintained its normal channels of information, yet did not use them to either naval or political effect.[192] Hamstrung by lack of funds and a policy of non-rearmament on a large scale the Admiralty's position was difficult. N.I.D. was able to provide most of the necessary figures, and its assessments of German intentions in general were sound, in retrospect, but where N.I.D. failed was in not digesting the results of World War I—the failure of the big gun and the effects of extensive, unrestricted U-boat warfare.[193]

There was a blithe overconfidence in asdic and at no time does anybody within N.I.D. appear to record and stress to the appropriate authorities that the greatest U-boat damage was done at night, on the surface, when the U-boat presented a low silhouette, almost invisible to the eye, and undetectable by asdic.[194] A similar vacuum existed with regard to the torpedo, particularly the aerial torpedo. No real survey was made of the use of maritime air power—the use of the torpedo bomb, and aerial patrols to counter U-boat attacks.

The R.A.F. resisted the return of the Naval Air Service, resulting in the non-emergence of a strategic and tactical doctrine of naval flying. When the Fleet Air Arm did return, it had an urgent need for its own naval aircraft weapons. Only one carrier was fully operational in September 1939, flying Gladiators,

---

[192] Despite the restrictions placed on Germany by the Treaty of Versailles, secret German naval re-armament went on, especially research and training in U-boat warfare. Eventually, Britain was forced to recognise this, in the 1935 Anglo-German Naval Agreement, before political capital could be made of it. At the time, it seemed to many a satisfactory agreement for Britain, in terms of the overall balance of European naval power, though it contained no mutual inspection clause. Each country agreed to declare to the other the size and armament of all new naval building. In the event, both in battleships and cruisers, Germany built much larger and more heavily armed ships than she actually declared.

[193] Most of the large fleet manoeuvres and exercises of the 1920s and 1930s were still centred round the large fleet battle and the gun as the primary weapon, not protecting trade and anti-submarine warfare.

[194] Very early in World War II, the U-boats were to show their paces, with the sinking of the Royal Oak in Scapa Flow, the carrier Courageous in the Western Approaches, and the damaging of the battleship Barham.

Swordfish, Flycatchers and Skuas, no match for the German aircraft.[195] It was in the general area of strategic and tactical appreciations of possible future conflict at sea that the N.I.D. fell down badly in the inter-war period.

Most service organisations and government quickly adapted themselves to the problems of war in 1939. N.I.D. did not fail here.[196] However, N.I.D. could not make up overnight for twenty years of lassitude in other major areas.[197] Even in specific areas, British intelligence was heavily criticised for its poor quality in 1940, and it was not until 1942 that it can be said that the British gained the upper hand over the Germans. For example, N.I.D. was able to help a lot in the re-routing of convoys (to avoid U-boats and raiders) though this was impossible at certain points, such as the entrance to the Straits of Dover, and the Straits of Gibraltar.

However, unknown to the N.I.D., the Germans, when they captured the French Navy's signal school at Brest in 1940, and were able to study the records of British convoy diversion orders (based on the fixes of U-boats' positions),

---

[195] It is true that in 1939, Britain possessed superior surface forces to Germany—the U-boat menace was a different matter. On 3 September 1939, Germany only had two pocket battleships, Graf Spee and the Deutschland, and five light cruisers, operational. Britain was quickly able to deploy seven battleships, three battlecruisers, four aircraft carriers, and thirty-five cruisers.

[196] For example, in 1939 and 1940, it was crucial to prevent the enemy from becoming aware of the strength of British forces, and to conceal troop movements, especially those moving overseas, to places such as the Middle East. N.I.D. was quickly able to adapt here and prevent the Nazis knowing too much, a task not made easier by the vast number of refugees and persons of all nationalities who collected in Britain.

[197] N.I.D.'s greatest faux pas must remain its failure to detect Admiral Donitz's techniques, practiced extensively before the war—the wolf pack, on the surface, at night. The effect could have been, and nearly was, calamitous. By 1942, British shipping losses were indeed gloomy. Unless the battle of the Atlantic was won, Hitler could not be defeated in Europe. Before 1939, the Admiralty never thought Germany would again wage unrestricted U-boat warfare, in case it drew the U.S.A. into a war. Few seemed to have remembered or studied Admiral Hall's experiences. June-October 1940, was a disastrous time for British shipping, even though Donitz had only sixty operational U-boats, with no more than eight actually attacking the Atlantic convoys at any one time. In 1939, convoy escorts were poor. It was not until 1942, when anti-submarine frigates joined the anti-submarine corvettes that convoys had any real surface protection. In April 1942, when R.A.F. Coastal Command was put under Admiralty operational control, it still had no long-range strike aircraft.

they were able to assess the techniques and accuracy of British Naval intelligence methods very early on, in stark comparison with the great success of British intelligence at the time of D-Day, when the Germans were deceived into thinking Calais, not Normandy, was the main landing area, a point well-commented on by General Strong:

"Whatever mistakes Allied intelligence may have made in the war none can possibly equal this unparalleled blunder by the Germans and their failure to realise it."[198][199][200]

Faulty Intelligence

Throughout 1939 and 1940, there were several cases of faulty operational intelligence leading to increased tension in a very anxious period. Poor intelligence could easily lead to the misdirection and therefore, the misuse of vital forces. Between 8-10 October 1939, the German cruisers Gneisenau and Koln, with nine destroyers, sortied. Intelligence was slow and inaccurate. Admiral Forbes'[201] Home Fleet put to sea (in case the Germans made a break for the Atlantic). No damage was done to the enemy (which had been operating off the southern coast of Norway, hoping to entice the Home Fleet towards the Skagerrak for U-boat and aerial attacks).

Between 21-27 November 1939, the Scharnhorst and Gneisenau sortied (sinking H.M.S. Rawalpindi), escaping Forbes' Home Fleet and on 23 November

---

[198] Strong: Intelligence at the Top. p. 141.

[199] The Fall of France had cost Britain dearly—she had given, for example, many of her electronic secrets to her French allies. When France was overrun, instead of blowing up their radar installations, the French handed them over to the Germans—a disaster of the first order. Britain still managed to keep ahead. For example, in June 1942, the Germans installed radar search receivers in their U-boats to pick up the radar waves of R.A.F. Coastal Command aircraft. These failed as the wavelengths of British radar sets were simply reduced.

[200] In Vol. 8 of his Memoirs, Admiral Godfrey, when discussing the value of the French as allies, wrote: "If you give or lend them weapons it is wise to assume that they may let them fall into the hands of the enemy as they did our asdics, etc., in 1940. They had plenty of time to destroy the equipment." p. 125.

[201] Forbes, Sir Charles Morton, Admiral of the Fleet: 1880-1960; entered R.N. 1894; Commander 1912; Captain 1917; Director of naval ordnance 1925-1928; Rear-Admiral 1928; Vice-Admiral 1933; Admiral 1938; C.-in-C. Home Fleet, April 1938 (flagship H.M.S. Nelson); Admiral of the Fleet, 1940; C.-in-C. Portsmouth, 1941; retired 1943.

were in the Faroes-Iceland Channel.[202] British intelligence, regarding the movement of major enemy warships, was gravely weak on this occasion, especially the deficiency in the capability of patrolling aircraft. The official historian, Captain S. W. Roskill writes:

"Lack of regular visual and photographic reconnaissance of the enemy's main bases handicapped our forces from the start, too sanguine pre-war estimates of the effectiveness of our North Sea air patrols greatly extended this handicap and finally, the use by the Home Fleet of temporary bases several hundred additional miles from the 'cutting off position' in the North Sea all helped towards successful evasion by the enemy." As will be seen later, the Norwegian campaign emphasised poor intelligence.

The lack of reconnaissance at the time of Rear-Admiral Vivian's evacuation from Narvik led Admiral Forbes to write to the Admiralty on 15 June 1940: "The quite unexpected appearance of enemy forces. …In the far north on 8 June, which led to the sinking of the Glorious, two destroyers and a liner…shows that it is absolutely essential that our scheme of air reconnaissance should be overhauled…The enemy reconnoitre Scapa daily if they consider it necessary. Our reconnaissance of the enemy's main bases are few and far between…It is most galling that the enemy should know just where our ships always are, whereas we generally learn where his major forces are when they sink one or more of our ships."[203]

There were bound to be intelligence errors, some less forgivable than others, forgiveness perhaps being contingent upon the magnitude of the effect such error might have. For example, on 19 April 1940, a false intelligence report came in that the Bismarck had passed the Skaw, steering to the N.W. Cruiser patrols were strengthened and the Hood diverted in support. On 22 April 1940, false aerial reconnaissance firmly identified one heavy and two light cruisers in Narvik. They were, in fact, transport and patrol vessels.

Throughout June and July 1940, No. 18 Group, Coastal Command, made several highly faulty reconnaissance missions of German ships in Trondheim.

---

[202] The sinking of the Rawalpindi was initially attributed to the Deutschland.

[203] The Germans, by contrast, were being effective. The closely guarded secret of the use of Loch Ewe as a temporary base for the Home Fleet was known to them. Raeder recalls the effectiveness of his intelligence in those early days in his 'Struggle for the Sea', a point supported by Roskill who, when examining Raeder's reports to Hitler on the 1939 and 1940 operations, noted their intelligence accuracy.

None of these affected the outcome of the war. However, on 11 and 12 November 1940, accurate and timely long-range air intelligence helped swing the balance in the Mediterranean—Glen Martin aircraft from Malta took photographs of the Italian fleet at Taranto—these were flown to H.M.S. Illustrious, a strike carrier, from which aerial torpedo attacks were launched against the Italian fleet in Taranto harbour—the new battleship Littorio and two older ones were sunk.

Successful Intelligence

It would be entirely false to paint a picture of continuous intelligence errors during the first two years of war. This would be far from true. However, it is accurate to say that N.I.D. was improving its techniques and contributions to operations at sea throughout the war, and it is the intention throughout the remainder of this chapter to develop this theme. Where tragedy occurred to British Naval forces, they were usually way beyond the scope of the N.I.D., and this was not peculiar to the earlier period of the war.

Indeed, one can see where judicious intelligence work swayed the balance in 1939, yet, in late 1941, was unable to have any effect in the Far East theatre for instance, because of factors way beyond its control. On 30 September 1939, the Graf Spee (Captain Langsdorf) sank the SS Clement off Pernambuco. A signal from the stricken merchantman alerted the Admiralty, and Commodore Harewood, and the latter went in pursuit. The Admiralty formed eight hunting groups and, with advice from Britain, Harewood correctly deduced that the Graf Spee would run for Montevideo.

On 15 December 1939, the Battle of the River Plate took place. Later, in Montevideo, Langsdorf was to be fed false intelligence from British sources. On 17 December, he scuttled his ship and, on 20 December, committed suicide. A timely piece of information, well used by the Admiralty and a force commander at sea, brought about a notable and vital British victory, and very early on in the war. By way of contrast, the tragedy of the Prince of Wales and Repulse, attacked and destroyed by Japanese torpedo bombers off Singapore in December 1941, was equally caused by a lack of air support and reconnaissance and an absence of sound intelligence; as was the battle of the Java Sea a few months later on 27 February 1942.

The question remains, of course, should such forces venture forth at all, possessing no knowledge of enemy strengths and intentions, in an already desperate situation (Singapore had fallen to the Japanese on 15 February 1942)?

Furthermore, it may seem somewhat incredible, in retrospect, that Britain had not learnt a very quick and salutary lesson from Japanese maritime air tactics at Pearl Harbour (7 December 1941).

On the question of the sinking of the Prince of Wales and Repulse, the recently released War Cabinet papers for World War I (New Year 1972) substantiate what Richard Hough had already said on the basis of other sources in his The Hunting of Force Z, namely that: "He (Churchill) and he alone had been finally responsible for sending the battlefleet to Singapore at this dangerous time and against the strong pleas of those whose task it was to manage Britain's maritime affairs. He selected the ships and even the Commander-in-Chief (Tom Phillips). If direct blame for the catastrophe has to be attached to one man, then Winston Churchill must accept it."[204]

This does omit one salient point, which certainly does not emerge in the documents—the weakness, and failing health, of the First Sea Lord, Admiral Sir Dudley Pound. In his memoirs, John Godfrey is very critical of Pound, mainly for his inability to control some of Churchill's madcap ideas. He graphically describes the weekly meetings of the three service intelligence chiefs with the Chiefs of Staff and how, invariably, Admiral Pound was dozing (as a result of the terminal brain tumour from which he was ailing).

Godfrey writes: "What does all this boil down to. That for the last two years of the greatest war in history, the Head of the Navy was a sick man and should have stepped aside, or been relieved not later than the end of 1941."[205]

The Role of Technical Intelligence

Before investigating specific naval operations, it is imperative to remember the continuous process of technical intelligence that went on throughout the war, an area that was a crucial backup facility for all operations at sea. This covered devising counter-measures for known enemy techniques as well as developing new, improved offensive and defensive techniques independent of enemy actions.

On the latter point, for example, the Admiralty developed 'plastic' armour to prevent armour-piercing machine gun and cannon bullets killing merchant ships'

---

[204] The Hunting of Force Z, p. 238.

[205] Godfrey Memoirs: Vol. 5. Part 2. p. 311. Godfrey is equally critical of Pound for concurring with Churchill's figures, and not the N.I.D.'s on the number of U-boats in existence, in building, and destroyed in 1939-1940. p. 268-269.

crews, and Dr Alwyn Crow, working at the rocket research station, Aberporth, developed rockets for use by landing craft, and the rocket bomb, designed to penetrate shelters with thick, reinforced concrete protection, which the R.A.F. 'Tallboy' bombs had failed to destroy. N.I.D. selected targets for the rocket bombs—the U- and E-boat pens at Bergen, Narvik, and Trondheim in Norway, Hamburg, Kiel and Heligoland in Germany, and Brest, Lorient, St. Nazaire, Bordeaux and La Pallice in France.[206]

Radar was undoubtedly the greatest technical development of the war, with its multi-purpose roles—aircraft and U-boat warning and detection, in all weather, day and night, from the sea or air, and as a vital aid to gunnery (for examples, radar directed gunnery greatly contributed to British successes at Cape Matapan in 1941, and in the sinking of the Scharnhorst in 1944).[207] German scientists did not think that Britain had overcome the difficulties of centimetric radar.

The 'snowflake' was developed to counter U-boat pack tactics, as were better depth charges (more deeply set, and with greater explosive power), developed to counter the deep-diving U-boats.[208] In September 1943, the Germans used the acoustic honing torpedo for the first time. The 'foxer' was developed as the antidote—a noise-making device towed aft of ships (it attracted the torpedo to it, instead of to the ship's propellers). By February 1944, a better 'foxer' was in use, which did not slow the ship down (the first development did), or affect its asdic.

It was fortunate that the German schnorkel device came into use after D-Day[209] for it might well have upset dramatically the pattern and success rate of allied anti-submarine techniques.[210]

One aspect of technical development which perpetually concerned the Admiralty was the integrity of British cyphers. By early 1942, the Germans were

---

[206] See Captain Edward Terrell's book, Admiralty Brief, Harrap 1958, for a very full account of Admiralty activity in this area, and N.I.D.'s involvement.

[207] Pending the arrival of a more efficient radar receiver, able to detect transmissions from British centimetric sets, Donitz's U-boats were forced to rely on a radar decoy device.

[208] See Herbert A. Werner's book, Iron Coffin, for a full account of British technical developments in World War II to counter the U-Boat.

[209] It enabled a U-boat to travel underwater on its diesel engines, instead of batteries, and thus greatly increased its speed to some eighteen knots beneath the surface.

[210] The Admiralty quickly made thorough plans for possible attacks against British Coastal routes by U-boats fitted with the new device.

still able to read cyphered convoy control signals (even though they had been changed in August 1940), and it was not until the end of 1942 that British counter-measures took place, and not until May 1943 that the German cypher-breakers were finally defeated.[211] For example, the German cypher experts, via their wireless intelligence service, were able to tell Naval H.Q. of the intentions of convoy PQ18—where the outward and homeward convoys would cross and the escort would change over.

The Germans sent U-boats and destroyers to wait, and an auxiliary minelayer to saturate with mines the entrance to the White Sea and the waters of Novaya Zemla. Fortunately, only one Russian tanker was sunk.[212] By 12 November 1943, a memorandum of Donitz's staff read: "The enemy knows all our secrets, and we know none of theirs," eloquent testimony to British intelligence. This remained true, in general, throughout the rest of the war.[213]

The Invasion Threat, 1940

One of the greatest problems facing the Admiralty, the Prime Minister and the Chiefs of Staff Committee in 1940 was the degree of preparedness and state of readiness necessary for a German invasion. A great deal hinged on sound intelligence. The Navy was to provide information about sea movements—the strength and timing of a potential assault, and the Army and R.A.F. built up their pictures too.[214] Air intelligence was critical, and the losses of aircraft and crew were heavy, but it had to go on.

The Admiralty had to have warning so that escorts could be withdrawn from convoys, and so that forces could be moved from Scapa, the Forth and Clyde, in time. Admiral Forbes' Home Fleet had to be ready to deter invasion at a moment's notice. Many said at the time, and since, that the Admiralty and Prime Minister were overcautious in keeping extensive forces on the ready in the south and did not show enough confidence in the intelligence service's ability to give

---

[211] See Captain S. W. Roskill "The War at Sea." Vol. II. p. 112, 207, 208, 364.

[212] Ibid. p. 279, and see also p. 266.

[213] For example, the German use of the one-man, electrically-driven torpedo, the 'marder', in April 1944, off Anzio, was known to Allied intelligence very early on

[214] A special invasion warning committee was set up under the chairmanship of Commander Colpoys, assisted by Lt. Cdr. N.E. Denning (who was to become D.N.I. in 1960). They ordered twice-daily air reconnaissance, which provided excellent photographs of the ports from which the Germans might invade.

adequate warning, which would enable an invasion force to be defeated on passage.

The criticism stemmed mainly from the heavy shipping losses resulting from escorts of the Home and Western Approaches Commands being taken away. Two things are certain—Prime Minister Churchill was not prepared to take any chances, and the intelligence he was given was first class.

The Norwegian Campaign

This was in marked contrast with intelligence during the Norwegian campaign. Furthermore, the Admiralty was slow to act on the information it did receive. On 7 April 1940, Sir Dudley Pound, the First Sea Lord and Chief of the Naval Staff, failed to act on the suggestion that the Home Fleet should be deployed in the central North Sea (so as to be ready for a German move towards Norway). The First Sea Lord regarded this as a diversion from the Royal Navy's main role at that time, of protecting Atlantic shipping and preventing a breakout into the Atlantic.

The N.I.D. ended its intelligence report that day with the conclusion: "All the reports are of doubtful value, and may well be only a further move in the war of nerves."[215] In the event the British were too slow—Bomber Command struck the German force off the entrance to the Skagerrak, steering N.W. at 1:25 p.m. They had no success. At 5:27 p.m., Forbes slipped and proceeded to intercept. He was too late—there had been a complete failure to realise the significance of the available intelligence and to take all the necessary counter-action.

The only bold action taken was by British submarines—they did some damage, but not enough,[216] and the heroic ramming of the Hipper by H.M.S. Glow-Worm. By 9 April, the Germans had taken all the major Norwegian ports. However, it should be said that the Home Fleet could have done little without air support. Forbes needed fleet carriers.

---

[215] The N.I.D., and Godfrey more than anyone else, were in a very difficult position—he could only recommend action when he was absolutely sure, and if he took a risk, and recommended a course of action based on insufficient evidence, though perhaps sound reasoning and intuitive knowledge, he might seriously jeopardise the whole British operational position, and compromise his own and N.I.D.'s professional integrity.

[216] H.M.S. Truant sank the Karlsruhe, H.M.S. Spearfish put Lutzow out of action for twelve months, and several transports were sunk. The British lost two submarines.

The value of air power was shown on 10 April when two squadrons of Skua dive bombers based on the Orknies attacked Bergen, sinking the cruiser Kőnigsberg, and, in a negative sense, when the Scharnhorst, Gneisenau and Hipper were able to return to Wilhelmshaven without hindrance because of the absence of British air reconnaissance (just as Captain Warburton-Lee's attack on Narvik was overshadowed by the surprise his force received when they found ten destroyers, not the six expected, lying in the fiord).

The absence of adequate air support was to characterise the later amphibious landings on 17 and 18 April 1940, and subsequent evacuation on 27 April, and the second attack on Narvik on 28 May. The coup de grace was delivered when the carrier Glorious was sunk, unwarned and unprepared, on 8 June, returning home, by the Scharnhorst and Gneisenau.

Other Naval Operations and Intelligence in World War II

1940 taught the N.I.D. and the other intelligence services many lessons, especially regarding the accuracy of intelligence and the speed with which it should be disseminated. The Dakar campaign in August 1940,[217] showed how delays in receiving intelligence could affect operations—accurate intelligence regarding the state of French feeling in Senegal and of the defences of Dakar reached London too late. The security of 'Operation Menace' was poor too—the Vichy French knew it was about to happen. As a result, the surprise was lost.

1941 and 1942 saw a radical change in the situation. On 23 January 1941, the Scharnhorst and Gneisenau sailed from Kiel—intelligence soon knew that they had passed the Great Belt, and Admiral Tovey went in pursuit. For the first time, accurate intelligence had enabled the Home Fleet to take up a favourable position in good time.[218] The Bismarck operation showed how much N.I.D.'s efficiency had improved—as soon as the Bismarck slipped from Korsfiord on 22 May 1942, Godfrey's men knew.

Tovey was soon in pursuit. When on 25 May, Lutjens lost Tovey, the N.I.D. detected the fatal radio signal which enabled the Admiralty to fix her position. At 10:30, 26 May, R.A.F. reconnaissance aircraft picked her up.

---

[217] The aim was to install the Free French in the West African port to prevent it being used by enemy ships and aircraft, thus threatening the convoy routes. Although it failed as a combined operation, the Germans never did use Dakar as a base.

[218] Admiral Tovey appreciated the value of air reconnaissance. He called for continuous air reconnaissance of the Skagerrak and its approaches.

On 10 June 1941, Coastal Command reported that the Lutzow with two light cruisers, the Emden and Leipzig, had left the Baltic. The Lutzow was attacked by Coastal Command torpedoes and sufficiently damaged to keep her in dock until January 1942.[219] This pattern continued (despite the unfortunate circumstances which surrounded the escape of the Scharnhorst, Gneisenau and Prinz Eugen from Brest).

The Tirpitz's sortie to the Arctic in March 1942 was monitored by the N.I.D., and her position relayed to Admiral Tovey, without which he would have been operating in a vacuum, indicating too the reliability now placed on intelligence—the Admiralty felt it could give orders to a C.-in-C. afloat about the conduct of operations.[220] By the end of 1943, British intelligence was far superior to that of the Germans. The movement of the Lutzow from Norway to the Baltic between 23-26 September 1943, illustrates this well. N.I.D. worked quickly—sources showed that enemy fighters had been sent to Bodo, and the stationing of others near Bergen implied the run might be to the Baltic.

A tanker was also known to have arrived at Altenfiord from Kiel. On 23 September, Lutzow left Altenfiord. Between 24 and 26, she was at anchor near Narvik. On 26, she sailed for Gdynia, confirmed first by a British agent's report

---

[219] The German account of this attack shows great concern at the speed and accuracy with which British intelligence had worked.

[220] As already mentioned, this was carried to tragic extremes in the case of convoy PQ17 to Russia, but not solely because precise intelligence was unavailable. The decision to scatter was based on limited intelligence, but that which was available was thoroughly reliable. It was a case of a very bad decision, and on the part of the First Sea Lord himself. Donald McLachlan gives a full account of what happened in the Citadel in the Admiralty on that day: "When Clayton (head of the Operational Intelligence Centre) returned downstairs (to the Citadel) and told his officers of the decision, Denning was amazed and angry that his assurances that any move of the Tirpitz would be known had not been accepted. He begged Clayton to go back to Pound's room and stressed the strongly-held intelligence view that the German big ships were not yet at sea." Room 39. p. 288.
The signal had gone. It was too late in any case for Pound to change his mind. The First Sea Lord had totally disregarded Denning's assurances that the Tirpitz had not left Altenfiord. In mitigation for Pound, McLachlan writes: "It seems fair to say…that Pound's worries about the general situation at sea made him incapable of understanding the caution of the Germans, of recalling, for example, how the Tirpitz had recently had a narrow escape in a surprise attack by the torpedo bombers of the Victorious." Room 39. p. 283.

and verified by Coastal Command reconnaissance. The end of 1943 saw a great catch for the N.I.D.—the Scharnhorst. At 7 p.m. on Christmas Day 1943, she slipped. At 3:30 a.m. on 26 December, the Admiralty were able to signal Admiral Fraser that she was at sea, giving details. The N.I.D. had worked fast and accurately.

The expertise of the N.I.D. is nowhere more apparent than in the raid on St. Nazaire on 18 March 1942.[221] The idea originated in N.I.D.'s French section (headed by Lt. Cdr. George Gonin, R.N.). From aerial photographs, a model was made in conjunction with Combined Operations. The O.I.C. of N.I.D. gave Admiral Mountbatten's staff valuable data for the raid—details of swept channels and German naval movements. The really priceless piece of information N.I.D. secured was the identification signal for the destroyer Camperdown, with which she was able to answer the German shore batteries when challenged. In the event, this gained vital time before the Germans opened fire.

St. Nazaire, along with other similar raids, such as Dieppe and the capture of Madagascar,[222] gave N.I.D. and Combined Operations the experience in planning for the great amphibious landings which came later in North Africa, Sicily, Salerno, Anzio, Normandy and the south of France.[223] The two bodies became involved in assessing every conceivable piece of data for these operations—details of beaches, water depths, defences, how to secure surprise, what the enemy expected, deceptions to keep the enemy guessing as to the time and place of the landings and so on.

The German Operational Naval Intelligence Position 1943-1944

The efficacy of British Naval intelligence in World War II is in marked contrast with that of the Germans, who never ceased to marvel at British accuracy. This was true not just of naval intelligence, but equally so of British military

---

[221] The aim of the raid was to destroy its large dry dock, to prevent the Tirpitz using it, and therefore reducing the possibility of successful Atlantic sorties from a French port.
[222] On 5 May 1942, Madagascar was seized in case the Japanese threatened it, thus dramatically affecting the Cape route to North Africa, and the British Army there.
[223] After Dunkirk, a Combined Operations H.Q. was set up in London to study the problems of amphibious operations and assault from the sea.

intelligence.[224] By early 1943, the German naval high command was so disturbed by the N.I.D.'s obvious successes that a full investigation was ordered of the sources from which it was presumed to derive its intelligence regarding U-boat movements and dispositions. It was concluded that there was no internal treachery and that cyphers were still secure.

British success was put down to radar and constant air patrols. At the end of May 1943, the British introduced new cyphers and thereafter (save for a short period at the end of the year) the Germans were deprived of what had been their most valuable source of intelligence. This, together with the German failure to detect Allied use of centimetric radar, rendered German naval intelligence inept. At the end of August 1943, Donitz thought the U-boats were being detected by emissions from his boats' search receivers, and not from the development of centimetric radar.

It was not until the beginning of 1944 that the Germans found that the British were working on the ten-centimetre wave band. Certainly, the Germans gained a good deal from wireless traffic, especially regarding convoy movements,[225] and some information from aerial reconnaissance and agents' reports.[226]

Without accurate intelligence, the Royal Navy could not possibly have improved its position so strongly and consistently as it did throughout the war. It was, indeed, one of the Trinity, as Captain Roskill has written, which led to the British victory at sea.

---

[224] See Decisive Battles of World War II, edited by H. A. Jacobson and J. Rohwer, ps. 35, 115, 117-119, 224, for illustrations of where German military intelligence blundered incredibly badly.

[225] U-boats often carried specialists to listen in and interpret such messages. The Germans were further led astray by a captured Coastal Command pilot who told his German captors that the British 'homed' on the German search receivers. He was believed, and the Germans concentrated on trying to reduce the radiation from their search receivers instead of seeking the wave lengths of the new Allied radar sets.

[226] This was notably true in Iceland. For example, a convoy J.W. 56A, on passage to Russia from Loch Ewe, and diverted to Iceland because of bad weather, lost three ships on 12 January 1944, as a result of an agent's report.

Chapter Five
The Methodology and Techniques of Naval Intelligence

Basic Method and Sources

The growth of the N.I.D., and its impact upon naval policy-making, both long and short-term, was dependent upon successful techniques for gathering, analysing and interpreting data. Without extensive and continuous raw data, the lifeblood of an intelligence organisation, the N.I.D. could not have had any legitimate impact upon naval affairs.

The techniques which it came to employ were naturally closely related to the development of the numerous sources of intelligence, each of which in themselves demanded highly specialised interpretive skills, and it was towards the 'mosaic' or 'jigsaw' concept of intelligence that the N.I.D. gravitated—the collection of data from as many sources as possible and assembling this to give an accurate and coherent picture within the constraints which circumstances might from time to time impose.

From this stemmed the watchwords of the N.I.D.—reliability and accuracy, that is the source of information, be it human or mechanical, and the content, should be reliably collected, and then accurately interpreted by N.I.D. staff.[227] There was always a strong subjective element within N.I.D.'s work—the intelligence worker was forced to make value judgments, especially the initial grading of intelligence material. Hence the need for, and reliance upon, as many different sources of information as possible when a picture was being built up,

---

[227] Admiral Godfrey developed a classification system, on a scale A1 to D5, the initial indicating source reliability, and the number the probable reliability of the source's information.

thus lessening the degree of subjectivity which tended to accompany limited, and initial, information.

Unless absolutely A1, no single piece of information could, for instance, be satisfactorily used. To pass on to planners and those who conduct operations, either ashore or afloat, scanty, inconclusive intelligence is the beginning of the end for an intelligence organisation. It was imperative, therefore, that the N.I.D. should never give way to the pressure of events, and release low-quality intelligence. The O.I.C. (Operational Intelligence Centre) in World War II never sent A1 intelligence regarding enemy intentions in its raw form to H.M. ships at sea. This might be picked up by the enemy, who would then deduce that their codes had been broken, as well as giving away the fact that such knowledge was now possessed.

During the chase of the Bismarck, when it was to become known to the O.I.C. that she was running for Brest (O.I.C. had intercepted Athens-Berlin diplomatic signals which had been deciphered, giving the vital information), the O.I.C. advised the Admiralty to signal Tovey, "act on the assumption Bismarck will proceed to Brest," thus giving Tovey his orders (based on A1 intelligence) but not revealing to the Germans in the event of that signal being picked up and deciphered, anything more or less than what might appear as good British Naval logic, and possibly a certain amount of luck. The Battle of Jutland and Convoy PQ17 illustrate the chronic misuse of A1 intelligence, as will be seen shortly.[228]

Technological and World Political Changes

N.I.D.'s methods were contingent upon many factors, not merely the apparent demands of the service, or what those who directed N.I.D.'s work thought it ought to be doing. Technological change, notably in communications, affected the whole pattern of intelligence collection and distribution to those who needed it. World change places constraints upon intelligence collection. Pre-1945 Europe, for example, was still 'open', certainly when compared with the contemporary world, when it is clearly divided.

This has affected the West's intelligence capability and its reliance upon different methods of collection, in keeping with technological developments. In World War I, Holland, Denmark and Norway were neutral and they provided a

---

[228] These facts and points emerged during a discussion with Captain S. W. Roskill on 7 July 1971.

no-man's land between the belligerents. Others, though not formally aligned, had allegiances: Sweden with strong commercial ties with Germany, tended to be pro-German; the South American republics were not unsympathetic towards Germany, until the German declaration of unrestricted U-boat warfare, and Spain, although neutral, was quite amenable to giving assistance to U-boats in Spanish ports.

Political sympathies, whether ostensibly neutral or otherwise, were to have a major effect upon the pattern of intelligence collection.

Intelligence in Peace and War

The scope and range of intelligence techniques varied a great deal between peace and wartime. In the inter-war period, one sees a drastic reduction in intelligence activity. In peacetime, intelligence should be one of the main bases for planning (operational and technical, tactical and strategic) and training. No exercise in peacetime can be thoroughly useful unless it is set against the known or estimated capabilities and techniques of potential enemies. The commander in peacetime must have a clear idea of how his future enemy might behave, and this is dependent upon a judiciously well-balanced intelligence picture, which neither exaggerates or under-estimates.

For this reason, peacetime intelligence is more demanding, as well as equally vital. General Strong recalls an incident when it was inferred intelligence had overstated the case: "Admiral Sir Andrew Cunningham said to me in North Africa on some occasion when I suggested that the Germans would act rather more rapidly than he thought: 'the trouble with you fellows is that when you come to speak of the Germans, all the roads to Berlin are uphill and all the roads from Berlin are downhill'."[229]

In peacetime, the fears of Cunningham about intelligence's credibility are equally great. In wartime, the strengths, weapon capabilities, endurances, location, tactics and general policy of enemy naval forces assume greater urgency. Peacetime intelligence cannot predict specific enemy wartime operations, and its work embraces much more the world of probability and imponderables. To acquire technical information, observe enemy exercises, compute enemy ranges and hitting power, how long he can stay at sea, how he might deploy himself, and so on, is the duty of intelligence in peacetime, so that

---

[229] Strong: Intelligence at the Top. p. 78.

should war start, at least the odds are well known, even though they may not be favourable.

In peacetime too, of course, certain information is easily available which is not so of wartime.[230] The dynamic of war produces rapid change, and intelligence must intensify its vigil to detect enemy changes—it is given a fillip to its role, and the whole rationality of naval policy, and ultimately the successful conclusion of war, may depend on several cogent intelligence reports.[231] Techniques and the overall methodology of collection, analysis and interpretation then become critical.

A close examination of the techniques of intelligence will reveal how N.I.D.'s early struggles to gain standing within the hierarchy of the Naval Staff was greatly dependent upon its ability to give accurate and timely intelligence to those who often least demanded it, though needed it most. The perfecting of successful techniques brought with it increasing dependence upon the work of the N.I.D., and an acceptance of it that reflected both the quality of its work and expertise of its staff.

Radio Intelligence and Cryptanalysis

This becomes nowhere more apparent than in the development of wireless intelligence. In the pre-wireless era, the enemy had ambushed dispatch carriers. With the advent of wireless, the enemy's wireless traffic could be ambushed— since signals could be intercepted, there developed a need for cyphers. For this reason, radio and cypher intelligence are very much inter-related. In both World Wars, intercepted enemy signals were the major source of intelligence, measured

---

[230] Between 1936-1939, Britain regularly supplied to Germany forecasts of British naval strengths, under the terms of the Anglo-German Naval Agreement, 1935. See Adm. 116, 3929, in marked contrast with the strength comparisons belligerents made of one another in wartime, such as that made by the N.I.D., dated 19 January 1915—comparison of Grand and High Seas Fleet. Adm. 137, 1080. p. 27-30, N.I.D. 010071.

[231] For example, N.I.D., throughout the latter part of 1915, was constantly looking for a possible change in German submarine policy. See Adm. 137, 1100, p. 170-173, for such a report.

in terms of their effects upon operations at sea.[232] The main reason was that it constituted, usually, A1 information.

A plain language or cyphered signal, or a fix derived from HF/DF intercepts gave conclusive evidence, with one qualification—a signal can be deliberately sent to give a wrong impression. In some cases, the possession of the enemy's cypher was not even necessary to deduce certain valuable facts—a rapid increase in radio traffic from a ship, force or shore command, might give, for example, indications of impending movements.[233]

In wartime, radio was the only means by which quick communications could be made.[234] In so doing, the enemy gave away his location, nature, intentions and so forth; a picture of enemy dispositions could be built up. The stricken merchantman, sending his last, desperate signal, might give away the presence of a U-boat or surface raider.

In both World Wars, the tracking rooms were to become the heart of the N.I.D.—information coming into the Admiralty from directional wireless stations, signals being assessed, and information being fed to the command organisations (the liaison which the N.I.D. developed in World War II with HQ Western Approaches in Liverpool must surely stand as the classic illustration of the degree to which intelligence and operations can fruitfully operate if roles and responsibilities are clearly defined).

Like every technique N.I.D. developed, radio intelligence and associated cryptanalysis had their teething troubles. Ewing's ID25 (based in Room 40 of the Old Admiralty Building) failed to decipher one of the early and highly critical messages—at 0135 on 4 August 1914, the German naval high command transmitted to the C.-in-C. Mediterranean: "Alliance with Turkey concluded 3

---

[232] In World War I, during Hall's era, naval radio intelligence was to play a major political role, as was revealed in 1925, with the release of all the political intercepts, to assist American lawyers acting for the companies whose property had been destroyed by German saboteurs before America entered the war.

[233] The only way to avoid a radio fix was to maintain radio silence. The identification of a ship's radio call-sign, or the recognition of a radio-operator's 'fist', or characteristic way of sending morse code could give a ship away.

[234] In the Great War, on 5 August 1914, Germany's transatlantic cables were cut by the British cableship 'Telconia'. Thus, to communicate outside of Europe, Germany had to use radio or cables controlled by her enemies, via neutrals. Hence the urgent need which Rear-Admiral H.F. Oliver (D.N.I. 1913-1914) saw for the establishment of a cypher department, to be headed, initially, by the then DNEDS, Sir Alfred Ewing.

August. Proceed at once to Constantinople." The Royal Navy assumed the Germans would proceed westwards to break through the Straits of Gibraltar.

In fact, they steamed into the Dardanelles, the Göben bombing the Russian Black Sea ports. The cryptanalysts soon became experts. At 1025 on 23 January 1915, Ewing's men were able to issue the following decoded German signal: "Signal to Rear-Admiral Franz von Hipper. First and second scouting groups, senior officer of destroyers, and two flotillas to be selected by the senior officer scouting forces are to reconnoitre the Dogger Bank. They are to leave harbour this evening after dark and to return tomorrow evening after dark." Beatty intercepted and the Battle of the Dogger Bank ensued. David Kahn estimates that between October 1914 and February 1919, Room 40 intercepted and solved fifteen thousand German secret communications.[235]

To possess an enemy code was the greatest catch ever for the N.I.D. Hall never released to anyone (including Britain's French allies) except for those who worked in Room 40, or who were closely attached, the details of the 'Magdeburg's' codes. With such information and power, Hall was able to switch Room 40's emphasis from the tactical to the strategic, and furthermore to international decryptments.[236] On 17 January 1917, the Rev. William Montgomery and Nigel de Gray presented Admiral Hall with a cryptogram, consisting of thousand numerical codegroups, dated Berlin, 16 January 1917; it was from the German Foreign Minister Arthur Zimmerman, to the German ambassador in Washington, von Bernstorff.[237]

---

[235] David Kahn: The Codebreakers. p. 274. Kahn gives extensive biographical details of all the main cryptanalysts in Room 40.

[236] Hall's men read the Berlin-Madrid diplomatic messages, in both the Spanish and German codes. Room 40 intercepted the German naval Attaché's in Madrid signals asking for funds and instructions for agent H21—this was Mata Hari, who was to be caught and executed by the French.

Footnote: In World War I, the Royal Navy had a series of D/F stations sited in key locations throughout the world—the main ones were at the Cape, Freetown, Gibraltar, Newfoundland, and the Orkneys. D/F fixing was greatly augmented by America's entry into the war, her stations thus becoming available.

[237] Room 40 found the Zimmerman Telegram in an American Cable. It had been delivered to the American Embassy at 1500 on 16 January 1917, and the Americans dispatched it via Copenhagen and London. Von Bernstorff had persuaded President Wilson that American-German relations could be improved if he could communicate more directly with Berlin. Wilson agreed to let the Germans use the American cable.

Not only was this symptomatic of Room 40's excellence, it also revealed Hall's consummate skill in using such intelligence for both naval and non-naval purposes, and his brilliance in maintaining N.I.D.'s security and integrity.[238] At the same time, no other single piece of cryptanalysis has ever had such enormous consequences—all turned upon the solution of a simple message.

As 1918 dawned, Room 40's efficacy decreased. German W/T signalling was noticeably decreasing, and they were also changing their signal book more frequently. It was quite obvious that the Germans had become suspicious of British activity. The N.I.D. did not dishearten at this. It felt itself more than fortunate that it had been able to acquire so much radio intelligence surreptitiously since 1914. In 1918, N.I.D. began to rely on other sources for monitoring German naval movements. British submarines, fitted with new and powerful transmitters, began long patrols off the Heligoland Bight.

It should be remembered too that other overt signs of possible German moves—such as mine sweeping or Zeppelin reconnaissance, had been observed throughout the war. It was, indeed, unfortunate that Room 40 missed the last major sortie of the High Seas Fleet on 24/25 April 1918, because one signal (and in fact one word, Spannkraft—full force) was misinterpreted amongst a welter of general signal traffic. Somewhat unfairly, both Beatty and Wemyss became disillusioned with Room 40's value after the April 1918 incident. Professor Marder quotes from the Wemyss manuscript on this topic.[239]

After World War I, the N.I.D.'s cypher organisation was run down, and in 1922, received the coup de grace when responsibility for cypher matters was passed from N.I.D. to civilian control. This led to a slackening of security matters, such that by the early '30s, when Europe witnessed the first signs of a threat to the Versailles order, there was a chronic need for the Navy, and what should

---

[238] Hall realised that if he released the telegram, or the British government revealed N.I.D. as its source, the Germans would know the N.I.D. had their codes, the Americans and others would know the British were monitoring neutral telegrams, and the telegram itself might lose credibility if it was known a D.N.I. had issued it to the world. One of Hall's agents in Mexico City obtained from the Mexico City telegraph office a copy of the message which Bernstorff had sent to Eckhardt, the German ambassador in Mexico, via Western Union. The American ambassador in London was to be given the telegram and a series of half-truths—the Americans might have begun to wonder whether Britain was reading their coded messages as well.

[239] Arthur J. Marder: From the Dreadnought to Scapa Flow. Vol. 5. p. 168. (He quotes Wemyss to Beatty, letter dated 15 August 1918, Wemyss MSS).

have been N.I.D.'s preserve, to re-establish a cryptanalysis organisation, to check the Fleet's signal security and educate naval personnel in the ways of enemy tracking organisations.

Unknown to the N.I.D., the B Dienst of the German Naval Intelligence Division possessed British cyphers and codes, and as early as the Abyssinian crisis. They were able to monitor the activities of the British Mediterranean Fleet, which itself was attempting to monitor the activity of the Italians prior to and during the invasion of Abyssinia. No real progress was made in the '30s with cryptanalytic technology. Louis Mountbatten urged for research and experimentation. The only trials done were with cypher machines and these were dropped.[240]

It was not until the summer of 1943 that this incredible disadvantage was overcome. From its H.Q. in Berlin, the B Dienst had tracked British Naval operations. In 1940, the Germans knew virtually every move made, or about to be made, by the British in Norway. Canaris' men were able to locate all the major units of the Home Fleet, and although in August 1940, the Royal Navy changed its administrative code and operational cypher, the Germans were able to crack these. In June 1943, the Admiralty had, at last, an unbreakable cypher. Somewhat ironically, the B Dienst were able to observe what the O.I.C. in the N.I.D. was thinking of Donitz's Submarine Command.

This is not to say that the Germans were deciphering every British signal. In November 1942, Operation Torch succeeded without cyphering problems and when the Scharnhorst was sunk in December 1943, the Germans were not able to penetrate the British cyphers, and therefore be aware of British intentions.

The combined tracking and deciphering skills of N.I.D. in World War II were a major reason for the eventual defeat of the U-boats. They intercepted, tracked and read the wireless signals passed between U-boat H.Q. and the boats at sea, and the homing signals a shadowing U-boat would send to call her comrades to a convoy. The Germans were employing the same technique—listening to wireless signals sent by the C.-in-C. Western Approaches to divert convoys from danger zones. They were therefore able to deploy the boats accordingly.[241]

---

[240] There was no joint service cryptanalysis research done, or even signs of cooperation in the area. The problem was never really recognised until war.

[241] The passage of convoy SC42 well illustrates both sides of the story. It left Sydney, Cape Breton Island, on 30 August 1940, passing the southern tip of Greenland. The

The Foreign Office and Naval Attaches

Continuous and efficient sources of intelligence, in both peace and war, were British diplomatic and Foreign Office channels, and the Royal Navy's own system of naval attaches, the former feeding information either to the latter, or direct to the N.I.D. in London via the Foreign Office. The relationship between the two was not easy, since a Naval Attaché was expected to serve two masters, the ambassador on whose staff he served, and also the D.N.I. in London. In a time of disagreement this could, and was, fraught with difficulties, as will be seen in the next chapter.[242]

Naval Attaches' tasks involved maintaining regular contact with the forces of the country to which they were appointed, obtaining information from every available source,[243] such as the public press, observing exercises and manoeuvres, the state of training and methods, the character and qualities of commanders (a Navy will train in peace as it will act in war), analysing the economic state of a country (and in relation to its defence policy), financial commitments to naval resources, general naval policy, capabilities, technical developments and so on.

A Naval Attaché must be very well versed in a multitude of naval subjects, and be able to produce clear, concise, analytical reports, as well as probably having to be a competent linguist. He must be a good public relations man and be able to make worthwhile, reliable contacts, such as correspondents from the British and American learned press, and news agencies such as the B.B.C. and the C.B.S. (people who are often allowed to travel wherever they wish). Illustrations from World War I will show how N.I.D. gained a wealth of information from Foreign Office sources, and this pattern persisted in World War II.

---

direction-finding stations tracked a pack of U-boats gathering about the convoy. Alternative orders were given. At the same time, the U-boat Command knew of British penetration and counter-action. In all, seventeen U-boats were called in for the attack.

[242] For example, all of the British military attaches in Berlin in the late thirties were at loggerheads with the policy of the British embassy, under Sir Neville Henderson, whose reports seemed at total variance with the military information they had available. On receiving such information, the D.N.I. was faced with a major political, let alone naval, problem.

[243] Naval Attaches were not allowed to deal in espionage. Much material, inevitably, came from the Chancellery and commercial departments of an embassy restriction or observation).

On 31 December 1914, the British Consul at Bergen gained information from two Norwegians (who had just returned from a visit to Hamburg) of an intended German attack on the east coast of Britain. By 2 January 1915, the Foreign Office had submitted a full report to the D.N.I.[244] On 17 January 1915, the Foreign Office submitted a report to N.I.D. on German Zeppelin airships. The source was H.M. Ambassador in Rome.[245] On 20 December 1916, the Foreign Office produced an invaluable report for N.I.D., on the particulars of German submarines—how many, what type, where they were, seaworthiness, state of operational readiness and so on, and on the 23 December, a report on the submarine blockade of the United Kingdom.[246]

In January 1917, the British Embassy in neutral Berne acquired information about future plans for the German submarine campaign. The source was an influential neutral who had been in conversation with high-ranking Germans.[247] On 2 June 1918, a report on German submarine construction was passed on to the N.I.D. The source was the British legation in Copenhagen, which had obtained its information from a German deserter.[248] These are but a few selected examples of several hundred major Foreign Office reports which reveal the significance of this throughout this period.

The naval attaches sent in their reports in much the same way. On 11 May 1915, for example, the Naval Attaché in Petrograd reported on German naval losses in the Baltic,[249] and in early 1917, the Naval Attaché in Norway, acting on information received from a neutral source who had visited Germany, reported in detail on increased German submarine activity.[250] Diplomatic and attaches' reports were invaluable because they called upon a great variety of sources. In peace or war, the neutral or non-aligned countries were the centres of greatest activity, where enemy and ally met.

In World War II, Stockholm was undoubtedly the best centre with its proximity to occupied Norway and Denmark, and the Baltic region in general,

---

[244] Adm. 137, 1080, p. 9-10.

[245] N.I.D. 011246, Adm. 137, 1629, p. 179-182.

[246] N.I.D. 011351, Adm. 137, 1629.

[247] N.I.D. 61164, Adm. 137, 1629. p. 210-214. Headed, Foreign Office Report, dated 27 January 1917.

[248] N.I.D. 31248, Adm. 137, 1630, p. 223-231.

[249] N.I.D. 769. Adm. 137, 1080, p. 272-276.

[250] N.I.D. 010162, Adm. 137, 1629, p. 153-155.

and Madrid, Ankara, and Istanbul coming close behind, the former acting as an observation post for Gibraltar, the western Mediterranean and North Africa. All were centres of gossip and a certain amount of intrigue, just as Rome, Berlin and Tokyo were pre-1939. Paris was virtually useless during World War II as a source for naval intelligence. Stockholm became the most effective centre—money flowed in for Captain Henry Denham's use, the brilliant Naval Attaché.[251]

In Madrid in World War II, the attaché, Commander Hillgarth, was mainly engaged in counter-espionage activities.[252] Hillgarth occupied a central role in the deceptions played before the 'Torch' landing in North Africa.[253] His behaviour was to convince the Germans that the body they found washed up carrying important plans was in fact genuine Operations 'Torch' went through with complete surprise. The German ambassador in Madrid, Dr Stohrer, was recalled in disgrace. On each side of the Straits of Gibraltar, the Germans set up observation posts, maintaining radio contact with Berlin and Madrid.

In March 1942, the N.I.D. detected German plans for a radar station to be built on Spanish soil near Gibraltar. Via the D.N.I., then the J.I.C., the Admiralty, the Chiefs of Staff Committee, the problem reached the War Cabinet, who directed the British Ambassador in Madrid to see General Franco. Within a month, Franco had interviewed Canaris and told him to remove his agents and

---

[251] It was a message from Stockholm on 20 May 1941, which started the hunt for the Bismarck, and the British government's protest to the Swedish government of 15 February 1943, stemmed from the Denham report to the N.I.D. But not all of his information was listened to—Norwegian agents informed him of anti-torpedo nets in Altenfiord protecting the Tirpitz. N.I.D. never got to know of this—on 22/23 September 1943, one of the X-craft in the midget submarine attack on the Tirpitz was to become entangled in a net. However, N.I.D. did receive Denham's report of 16 February 1943, indicating that smoke-making apparatus surrounded the Tirpitz in Trondheim. In the R.A.F. Bomber Command raid of April 1942, seven aircraft were to be lost, the leader later claiming that it was due to effective AA fire, due in turn to his squadron's unawareness of a smoke screen possibly being set up.

[252] Mainly persuading the Spaniards that they should not allow the Germans to abuse their neutrality.

[253] See Ewen Montagu's book: The Man Who Never Was. Evans Brothers, 1953.

end his plans for a radar station. This is a good example of how effectively intelligence and diplomacy could work together.[254]

The value attached to Commander Hillgarth is shown by Godfrey's comments in Volume 8 of his memoirs: "Hillgarth was rather a super-attaché for several reasons: (a) I encourage him, during his periodic visits to London, to report direct to the Prime Minister after seeing me. (b) I had an A1 source in Spain whom I kept in contact with, through him and Gomez Beare. (c) Hillgarth was uniquely the coordinating authority in Spain for S.S. and S.O.E., as well as N.I.D. (d) Hillgarth was the only member of the Embassy staff who knew Spain and had many contacts in high places, political and social. Don Gomez Beare linked up with commerce and could go anywhere as he looked like a Spaniard (actually a Gibraltarian)."[255]

It is not the intention of this chapter to discuss the degree of influence exerted by naval attaches on the outcome of naval and political events, and the influence their reports had in particular on naval and general defence policy-making. In a period of relative international tranquillity or disarmament, they often provided the only constant and reliable source of intelligence. In the '20s and early '30s, with the run-down of the N.I.D. as a whole, attaches provided the continuity which ensured the survival of a fully professional British Naval intelligence organisation.

In the '30s, with the advent of Nazi, Fascist and Japanese aggression, attaches' reports read, in retrospect, like alarm bells which, with other conclusive sources, should have awakened the slumbers of successive British governments. Reference to a few of these will illustrate the point. The Naval Attaché in Berlin, Captain Densch, forwarded reports to the N.I.D. and the Foreign Office on 9, 10

---

[254] The D.N.I. was also responsible for liaising with foreign naval attaches both in London and those dealing with his own attaches abroad. His greatest problem here was security, and somewhat ironically, what information could be safely given to friendly or allied powers. Donald McLachlan summarises the position thus:
"One problem that was never far from the front of the D.N.I.'s mind was the possibility that a friendly foreign naval attaché, to whom he had given important information, might pass it to his government in a cypher or code which would be read by unfriendly governments. There were cases in which the D.N.I. knew that the communications of the government in question were insecure. He would then have to find ways of either delicately drawing his attention to the fact or of suggesting that a cable or letter would be safer, or even that British communications might be used." Room 39. p. 403.
[255] Godfrey Memoirs. Vol. 8. p. 123.

and 11 April 1934 and 6 and 7 May 1934, in which he gave the first official indications of a deliberate re-awakening in the German public mind by the Nazi government of the need for an expanded German Navy, and especially of the submarine service.

Densch commented on his conversations with Raeder, which had been dominated by a discussion on Germany's need for increased naval forces to provide security in the Baltic. Somewhat naively, Densch tried to explain away the increased German naval estimates for 1934/1935 by the urgent work that was needed to maintain, repair and refit German warships.[256]

Later that year, on 2 November 1934, the British Naval attaché in Paris, reported that he had received an inconclusive report from the French Deuxieme Bureau that the Germans had five submarines building at Krupps yard at Kiel.[257] This crucial report made the Admiralty become dissatisfied with the reliability of information being sent to them regarding new constructions, especially the dates on which ships were laid down. The Berlin attaché was immediately instructed to investigate and report.

On 7, 14 and 22 January 1935, the Berlin attaché sent his reports to the D.N.I. and to the Foreign Office. He made it quite clear that the Nazis were deliberately hiding from the public the fact that the last two Deutschland class ships (to become the Scharnhorst and the Gneisenau) had been laid down in October and December 1934. The attaché surmised, quite accurately, that they must be over the treaty limits.[258]

Following the Anglo-German Naval Agreement of 1935, the Berlin attaché's duties intensified. He became one of the main link-men in Anglo-German affairs. On 12 April 1935, for example, Captain Muirhead-Gould, the attaché, was asked to attend the Marineleitung, to be given information about the German building programme for 1935 (this comprised recommencement of work on ships D and E, and the building of two new cruisers, sixteen destroyers, but no submarines).

He was expected by the D.N.I. to keep his ear to the ground so as to pick up any signs that might affect Britain's naval policy or position. On 11 July 1935,

---

[256] Cabinet Papers 29/148. Naval attaché, Berlin, correspondence with N.I.D. and F.O. April/May 1934.
[257] Foreign Office Papers 371/177765 (C4727/2134/18). Naval attaché, Paris, correspondence with N.I.D. and F.O. November, 1934.
[258] Foreign Office Papers 371/18860. Naval attaché, Berlin, correspondence with the N.I.D. and F.O. January 1935.

Muirhead-Gould reported from Berlin that, following the signing of the Anglo-German Naval Agreement, opinion in Latvia and Lithuania strongly condemned it, as it was thought to encourage a naval race between Germany and Russia.[259]

British Naval attaches' reports often formed the main, and sometimes the only basis for N.I.D. reports (which were then channelled through the J.I.C., the C.O.S. and the C.I.D. to the Cabinet itself if need be). For example, the N.I.D. report of 15 October 1934,[260] dealing with the high scale of naval preparations being undertaken by Japan (modernisation of capital ships, increase in personnel, development of the Air Arm, the increased import of raw materials, and an increase in naval estimates) was based solely on the attaché's reports.

The D.N.I. and his staff were always able to obtain substantial and generally very reliable information from foreign naval attaches credited to embassies in London, whether they were friendly or regarded as being a potential foe. In 1935, for example, the D.N.I. was anxious to know what the German reaction would be and what the German naval building program would be like in the event of the Anglo-German Naval Agreement falling through. The German attaché, Captain Erwin Wassner, visited the N.I.D. to discuss these problems with Commander C. M. R. Schwerdt.

The talks endorsed what the N.I.D. thought already—that by 1942, the Germans would probably attain a 35% ratio in any case (assuming that their yards worked at full pressure).[261] This particular document heightens the point that relations with successive German naval attaches in London between the wars were good, symptomatic of the cordial relations that existed in general between the British and German navies. This was not true of the Luftwaffe and the R.A.F. German air attaches in London had a very different reception.[262]

---

[259] Foreign Office Papers 371/18738 (A6432/22/45).
[260] Foreign Office Papers 371/17600 (A8313/1938/45).
[261] Documents on German Foreign Policy, Series C, Volume 3, No. 541.
[262] See Von Schweppenburg: The Critical Years. Wingate, 1952. He was himself a German air attaché on the staff of the embassy in London.

Capturing and Salvaging Enemy Ships

The capturing of enemy ships, both warships and merchantmen, often revealed to N.I.D. a wealth of data. When U450 was sunk off the Durham coast in 1918, and later salvaged, her wreck disgorged a valuable log book, signal codes, charts and orders. N.I.D. dried and chemically treated these. They were cyphered and revealed the effects of British anti-submarine tactics and details of newly planted German minefields, nets and the like. U450 had drawings of the silhouettes of the whole German fleet. Copies were made and circulated to ships of the Royal Navy. Above all else, the submarine revealed the tracks used by the other U-boats to enable them to proceed safely to the Atlantic.

N.I.D. passed this on to operations. Within an eleven-week period, five U-boats were destroyed in the areas shown by the documentation from the wrecked U450. In addition, the Germans had revealed their thinking procedures and complete technical details of a U-boat.[263] In World War II, the Royal Navy captured two valuable prizes relatively early in the war, U110 on 9 May 1941 and U570 on 27 August 1941, south of Iceland. The latter was to be commissioned as H.M.S./m. Graph. In 1941, Britain was still ignorant of the technical details of German U-boats—basic factors such as speeds on the surface and submerged, turning capacity under water, endurance, and the design of the pressure hull (whether they had riveted plates or a welded hull).

Such information was vital for determining successful anti-submarine tactics. Pressure hull design would, for example, determine the area in which British depth charges would prove lethal and would also indicate the maximum depth to which a U-boat could dive.[264]

As a result of the information, N.I.D. was able to obtain and deduce from the U570, Captain Edward Terrell R.N.V.R. and Vice-Admiral Usborne (a former D.N.I., 1930-1932, and now personal assistant to the First Sea Lord, Sir Dudley Pound) were able to design a course for British convoy commanding officers in anti-submarine warfare, run by Captain J. H. Roberts, R.N. What U570 gave to the British too was the German cypher machine, standard equipment on all U-boats.

---

[263] See R. M. Grant: U-boat Intelligence, 1914-1918. Hampden, Connecticut, 1969.

[264] At one stage, the Director of Naval Construction in Bath staunchly maintained that an all-welded pressure hull was impossible to produce. The capture of U570 proved how wrong he was. See Captain Edward Terrell: Admiralty Brief. p. 139.

Many merchant ships were captured by both sides during the two World Wars, and they revealed Merchant Navy codes, Admiralty instructions to merchant ships, dispositions, convoy procedures, rendezvous points for escorts and refuelling, and so on.

Prisoners of War, Deserters, Refugees, Resistance Groups, Friendly or Neutral Observers

In each World War, a collective group embracing prisoners of war, deserters, refugees, resistance groups, and friendly or neutral observers, supplied the N.I.D. with vital intelligence. To deal with most of these, the N.I.D. had its own group of trained interrogators. To be optimally effective, an interrogator has to be fully briefed with background details so that he can put his interrogation in the right context. As a single source, interrogation material was never taken as A1 in its own right. As a result, a valuable piece of data might not be acted on,[265] but it was a risk considered worth taking when offset against the wild goose chases which might have ensued.

Selected illustrations will show the scope and nature of N.I.D.'s activity in this area. Deserters were always fairly forthcoming—in 1916, the N.I.D. was given details of minefields laid by the Germans in Heligoland—the exact location, the types of mines used,[266] and later in that year, a deserter gave extensive technical details of German destroyers, torpedoes, submarines, and the latest German losses.[267] P.O.W.s/survivors proved a valuable source too—in 1918, the Belgian Army General Staff H.Q. handed over to the N.I.D. a German prisoner who was able to give valuable information on the state of the German fleet.[268]

---

[265] The Naval Staff in World War II, for example, would not accept the results of N.I.D.'s interrogators regarding the maximum depth to which U-boats could dive. Interrogation had established six hundred feet as the maximum. It was not until after the capture of U570 that this was proven true. Dr D. B. Welbourne of Cambridge University was one of N.I.D.'s main interrogators of U-boat P.O.W.'s. As well as being an engineer, he had a good command of German. (N.I.D.'s chief U-boat P.O.W. interrogator was Captain Trench, Royal Marines, who, it will be remembered, was captured and tried in 1911 by the Germans for spying on their Frisian defences. See page 43).
[266] Adm. 137, 1629, N.I.D. 5346, p. 113-116.
[267] Adm. 137, 1629, N.I.D. 016600, p. 156-167.
[268] Adm. 137, 1630, N.I.D. x/11955/1918. p. 204-223.

U-boat survivors were particularly vulnerable to sound interrogation as the N.I.D. records show.[269] In World War II, interrogation of U-boat survivors provided the N.I.D. with detailed knowledge of the 'Pillenwerfer', a gadget designed to produce a submarine bubble target, and above all else, of the search receiver specially designed to give U-boat warning of radar contact by aircraft or ships. After D-Day, the N.I.D. set up a Forward Intelligence Unit which advanced with the van of the Allied forces as they advanced across Europe. Under Lt. Cdr. R. Izzard, R.N.V.R., one of its prime tasks was to interrogate P.O.W.s in the ports.

Friendly observers gave N.I.D. sound data in both wars. From very early on in World War I, data poured into the N.I.D. from a variety of sources day after day. Let us take 26 August 1914 as one such day. At 1244, the N.I.D. received a signal from the naval intelligence officer at Grimsby. The master of the trawler 'Elmira' had reported seeing two German destroyers at 1533, 25 August, hundred and twenty miles N.E.N. of Spurn Head, one destroyer coming alongside and questioning him, but left again suddenly towards flashes on the horizon, which events revealed as two large men-of-war, apparently German steamers, W.N.W., and last seen at 1700.

At 1940, a signal was received by N.I.D. from the Consul-General in Rotterdam. He had learnt from a reliable source that a Norwegian vessel just arrived in Rotterdam had been stopped 95' N.W. of Heligoland by five German cruisers and eight small craft, either torpedo boats or torpedo boat destroyers, at 1830 on 24 August. This volume and quality of data continued throughout the war.[270] On 29 July 1915, the N.I.D. issued a report based on the information received from the master of the SS Llama on U-boat design. This friendly merchantman, who had made contact with U58, sent his data to the N.I.D. in London via the Admiralty port officer at Kirkwall.[271]

In like manner, the captain and crew of a Dutch steam trawler provided the N.I.D. with certain information about the position of German defensive

---

[269] Adm. 137, 1100, N.I.D. 10591, 18 September 1915. p. 208-217 for details of the information secured from the survivors of U6, Adm. 137, 3060, contains further details of interrogation of survivors from captured or sunk German U-boats.

[270] Naval Staff Monographs for World War I. Vol. 1. Appendix A. Intercepted Signals and Reports.

[271] Adm. 137, 1100, Ps. 120-123.

minefields.[272] In World War II, refugees and resistance workers were able to give information about such things as the fighting shape of ships in the dockyards, morale amongst sailors and logistical data such as the maintenance and repair facilities, fuel supplies and damage done to dockyards and ships by R.A.F. bombing. Most of this type of information came to the N.I.D. second hand from other intelligence bodies.

For example, M119 screened and interrogated all refugees arriving in Britain in World War II. Such data was obviously of equal value to the Ministry of Economic Warfare and the Special Operations executive (especially for training agents—it was essential to have the latest details of German daily life, communications and so forth).

Clandestine Intelligence

In wartime, the agent or spy assumed greater significance, and could be employed more legitimately than in peacetime when detection or capture often exacerbated relations.[273] Where reconnaissance proved difficult or impossible, the N.I.D. depended on agents' reports for details of the location and strengths of enemy forces. Communication presented the greatest problem—relaying information accurately and quickly without detection. In World War I, even though British cryptanalysts had deciphered the German signal codes, only the agent could send details of the progress of German naval building, repair work in hand in the dockyards and the state of morale.[274]

---

[272] Adm. 137, 1629, N.I.D. 32055, Ps. 127-131.

[273] On 7 December 1911, there began in Leipzig the trial of five alleged British agents. All were found guilty and sentenced to penal servitude for various numbers of years. The information they were supposed to have secured was virtually useless, their cases being deliberately magnified out of all proportion to the offences committed.

[274] After the Battle of Jutland, a British paid agent in Wilhelmshaven gave the N.I.D. full and accurate reports of the damage received by practically every ship in the dockyard there. The Germans tended to be less well organised, as has already been discussed. On 18 October 1918, U116 tried to enter Scapa Flow. This U-boat had not been informed that the Grand Fleet had been moved to the Firth of Forth. Similarly, the Germans were not aware of Scapa's detection installations—U116 was sunk by mines. By 1939, the German naval intelligence organisation had learnt certain lessons. In October 1939, H.M.S. Royal Oak was sunk by a U-boat in Scapa Flow. A German spy in Kirkwall in the Orkneys had done his work well.

The N.I.D. in the inter-war period and during World War II never controlled agents. This was the responsibility of the British Secret Service. The D.N.I. maintained close contact and N.I.D. briefed many agents, but never controlled their movements. Peacetime espionage and wartime sabotage were never the briefs of the N.I.D. The agents of the S.O.E. mainly committed to sabotage operations and organising resistance, were seldom used for intelligence collection. Different skills were required. As with the N.I.D. interrogators, agents had to have a good idea of what was already known in the N.I.D. so that he could be selective in his collection.[275]

The British Secret Service took two years to recover from the effects of the Nazi's overrunning Europe in 1940 and re-establish agent organisations. The greatest problem was solving communication problems in occupied countries. It is generally acknowledged in all reliable narratives that alternative forms of intelligence gave equally valuable results. However, in several major instances, agents' reports were critical, such as the reports about German ships in Norwegian and other European ports such as Brest.[276]

Aerial Reconnaissance and Aerial Photography

The development of the technique of aerial reconnaissance and aerial photography led to precision in plotting enemy locations, movements, and concentrations, thus helping in analysing tactical and strategic situations, and selecting targets for sea and air attacks. It had certain limitations—although regular photographic reconnaissance of the enemy's bases conferred inestimable advantages, it often led to the exaggeration of the importance of any movement by a major warship. It could not, therefore, eliminate the need for intelligence about the enemy's intentions derived from other sources.

A photograph will show numbers and condition (damage, seaworthiness, state of readiness, etc.) of major units and give away information such as petrol barges, minesweepers and tankers—the support units for a major force.

---

[275] See, for example, Adm. 137, 1629, N.I.D. 011064, an agent's report which came via the Foreign Office on 15 December 1916, giving details of ship-building at Kiel and Wilhelmshaven.

[276] A Norwegian agent in Altenfiord gave the N.I.D., and thence the Fleet Air Arm invaluable information in February 1944, for the attack on the Tirpitz, such as details of German radar installations, high tension cable and flak. Just before the raid took place, he provided intelligence, including two-hourly weather reports.

Photographic reconnaissance did not come into its own until World War II, and indeed it was as late as 1942 that the operational intelligence centre in the N.I.D. began to receive high quality pictures. However, on 4 November 1939, the first full aerial reconnaissance photographs of the Tirpitz revealed for the first time Tirpitz's dimensions and how the Germans had obviously cheated.[277] The Germans were particularly lacking in this area. Regular photographic reconnaissance of the major British ports alone would have rendered impossible the surprise element in the Allied invasion of Normandy in June 1944.

Visual sightings from the air proved equally valuable. It was a Coastal Command aircraft which detected that the Bismarck and Prinz Eugen had slipped from their Norwegian lair, and later on, it was a Catalina reconnaissance flying boat which sighted the Bismarck after she had given her pursuers the slip.[278] In the Mediterranean in 1941, it was a Fleet Air Arm reconnaissance pilot who sighted the Vittorio Veneto. This example illustrates well that a pilot had to be trained to recognise ships' silhouettes and assess types, especially in bad weather or when being shot at.

A false sighting might prove disastrous, as indeed it did to the Germans when the Scharnhorst was sunk. A German reconnaissance pilot mistook British ships for German escort destroyers. It was too late by the time German naval intelligence realised their error.

Commanding Officers' Reports and De-briefing

Any form of eye-witness report had to be carefully handled by the N.I.D. Survivors, and especially masters of merchantmen who had lost their ships might give such details as the date, position, and nature of the enemy (armament, appearance, tactics). Interviewing had to be carefully done so that distorted impressions were not given. This was equally true of interrogation of Royal Navy commanding officers and crews. They often had valuable tactical feedback to give, and also technical information, which was then fed to the scientists.

For example, the reports of the U-boat pack tactics made it clear that the U-boats must be seen somehow at night and be deterred from surfacing. A new

---

[277] This emerged in conversation with Vice-Admiral Sir N. E. Denning on 11 January 1972.

[278] The Germans, on the contrary, were without eyes in the air—German intelligence, and certainly Admiral Lutjens, had no idea that Admiral Tovey was bringing the Hood, Prince of Wales, King George V, the carrier Victorious, and Force H to bear.

illumination was invented—the 'snowflake', which exploded at thousand feet, illuminating a wide area for several minutes, thus revealing any surfaced U-boats, within striking distance of a convoy.

In war and peace, the press and radio may be used to collect intelligence, to deceive, or for propaganda purposes. To illustrate the first of these, an article appeared in the 'Dresdener Anzeiger', on 20 May 1915, *First Three Months of the Submarine Campaign*, by Vice-Admiral Kirckhoff, which was passed to the N.I.D. and translated. It provided an invaluable insight into how a very senior German naval officer saw the impact of the submarine campaign on the Allies.[279]

In peacetime, the press may reveal a wealth of information about governments' policies, strengths, deployment, morale, as well as, in many journals, even sufficient technical data from which reasonably accurate scientific deductions may be made. In wartime, press statements have to be carefully released. The Admiralty took special pains in both World Wars when it released news of losses, damage and successes.

They may deliberately deceive too: In a special edition of the *Daily Mail* of 12 September 1916, Admiral Hall had the Northcliffe Press (where he had many friends and contacts) give the impression that a British expedition was shortly to be landed on the Belgian coast, the aim being to relieve pressure on the Belgian flank. It worked. The Germans moved troops to the Belgian coast.

The Press and Radio

In the totalitarian states, the press and radio distorted information. In Germany, Goebbels' Propaganda Ministry deceived the Germans more than the British, and from propaganda broadcasts (such as the interviews with U-boat commanders and crews), the N.I.D. deduced a great deal about German morale. In both democratic and non-democratic societies, mail censorship was rigorously employed in both wars.

World War II witnessed, as was seen in Chapter Three, a good deal of inter-service cooperation and integration. The R.A.F.'s intelligence service, for example, kept the N.I.D. informed of all significant Luftwaffe movements which might affect the Royal Navy (i.e., those from which it might be deduced that enemy naval movements were afoot). Likewise, R.A.F. mining operations, for example, depended on N.I.D. information about swept channels and convoy

---

[279] Adm. 137, 1080, p. 210-214.

routes. In the field of intelligence techniques, inter-service cooperation reached its zenith with joint service topographical intelligence.

Topographical Intelligence and the I.S.T.D.

After the disaster in Norway (and indeed Gallipoli too, where landings were launched without any topographical intelligence whatsoever), it was soon realised by the Admiralty that detailed topographical intelligence was going to be vital for the forthcoming amphibious assaults. The N.I.D. led the way. Admiral Godfrey virtually took over the Geography Department at Oxford. The leader in this field was Mr A. F. Wells, the Oxford Classics Don, who collected experts and sources from all over the world to work for him. He organised a working relationship between the Photographic Reconnaissance Unit and the I.S.T.D. and visited R.A.F. Medmenham and R.A.F. Benson once or twice a week.[280]

The topographical intelligence given by the N.I.D. to the planners was excellent. An operation on a much smaller scale but one nonetheless where topographical intelligence was essential, will suffice to illustrate the excellent quality of N.I.D.'s topographical intelligence service—for the attack on the Tirpitz in Altenfiord by midget submarines to be successful details of the fiord's terrain was vital.

The topographical experts provided the attack's planners and the X-craft commanders with exact and detailed information, such as that relating to the numerous small islands in the approaches to the fiord, which would provide cover, thus enabling the X-craft to surface in order to re-charge their batteries. N.I.D.'s men also briefed the crews on their best escape route into neutral Sweden after they had scuttled their craft.

During peacetime, the role of the N.I.D. was very much different from its role in both World Wars, when a premium was naturally placed on operational intelligence. The limits placed on N.I.D.'s activities after 1918, and the political and economic problems of the '20s and '30s, in a period when the ideas of re-armament and defence planning were anathema to many, combined to minimise the part which the N.I.D. could, and ought, to have played in the inter-war period. In peacetime, the emphasis of intelligence tends to shift towards assessment, with

---

[280] Godfrey Memoirs: Vol. 8. p. 131.

a view to long-range planning, rather than the day-to-day operational crises which is the essence of any wartime intelligence organisation.

From 1919 until the beginning of the more blatant and overt acts of Nazi, Fascist and Japanese aggression, the N.I.D. contributed little to the composition and deployment of the fleet and the tactical and strategic factors involved in naval policy-making. The reasons for this will bear analysis in Chapter Six. Within the Naval Staff hierarchy, the N.I.D. lost its prime place, and one sees evolving very quickly after Versailles, and through to 1936, a system of planning, policy-making and operational control and evaluation based upon the triumvirate of the other Naval Staff departments (mainly Plans and Operations) the Admiralty Board and the Committee of Imperial Defence.[281]

The C.I.D. had direct links with the Cabinet. The N.I.D. played a minor role in the great controversies and decisions of the period. The decline of naval intelligence was symptomatic of the lack of direction in several areas of British defence thinking from 1919 to 1939. This situation, therefore, had a direct effect upon the techniques which N.I.D. had so assiduously developed and the organisation which supported them. When Admiral Godfrey took over in 1939, he was faced with a major task of reconstruction (as if time had stood still since Admiral Hall had left the N.I.D.) and revitalisation.

The Inter-War N.I.D. and Peacetime Intelligence

Where the N.I.D. should have shone during the inter-war period was as the main adviser to the Naval Staff, and through them to the Board, the C.I.D., and thence the government of the day, since in theory it was the only repository of data and the independent and objective commentator, and if need be, critic of and for naval policy. This was not to be. Hence, many of the decisions made at all these levels were often based on little or no sound data, untested hypotheses, and inaccurately analysed findings of past naval actions, some of which were irrelevant to the present, and certainly the future, in any case (Jutland was still hanging over Naval thinking twenty years later).

Moreover, there was nobody staffed with the sort of personnel Hall had recruited in World War I and Godfrey recruited in World War II to cope with the material N.I.D. should have been collecting if policy had been different, that is

---

[281] From February 1921, until the outbreak of World War II, the C.I.D. resumes its original function as the principal adviser to the government on all matters of defence.

the intensification on a wide-ranging scale of the collection and analysis functions. In mitigation, it is true to say that it was considered by many, sufficient for a body such as the C.I.D. to deal with the sort of information N.I.D. could have provided. However, it is also true that the C.I.D. was, administratively speaking, incapable of dealing with the minutiae of data which an efficient intelligence body needs for its work to be worthwhile.

As a result, C.I.D. tended to dismiss crucial facts with the sweep of the pen, which no intelligence body would have so blatantly written off as irrelevant.[282] The Royal Navy tended not to help itself during the inter-war period too, and often the real issues at stake became entangled with political and misconceived strategic issues which had no real bearing on actual problems. This was nowhere more true than in the naval aviation controversy. N.I.D. evidence and analysis might have provided scientific evidence and analysis might have provided scientific evidence to decide the issue.[283]

Without a clear directive to become involved, the professional expertise of the N.I.D. waned. The methodology of intelligence, the hard-won techniques which it had accumulated, were run down, and defence thinking in the twenty years of peace moved at worst into the realms of misguided fantasy and, at best,

---

[282] For example, as early as October 1921, the C.I.D. received a warning from the Control Commission that para-military organisations were forming in certain parts of Germany. The C.I.D. dismissed the idea. In December 1926, Britain and France disbanded the Control Commission.

[283] Admiral Beatty said himself, somewhat precipitously, to the Naval Ship-building Sub-Committee of the C.I.D.—the Bonar Law Committee, 7 December 1920, instituted to investigate the question of 'naval strength': "…the Admiralty are of the opinion that there is nothing in the present offensive qualities of aircraft which render them a menace to the capital ship." Beatty had no real evidence for this statement. The N.I.D. was not consulted. This is even more poignant in the light of the communication of the Director of the gunnery Division to the Board, dated 24 June 1922: "As time goes on, it becomes more and more evident that the greatest menace H.M. ships have to fear…is attack by low-flying planes attacking with torpedoes, poison gas, machine guns and close bombs." Adm. 1/8646-207/23.

into the realms of informed and well-intentioned opinion.[284] Within the Naval Staff itself, the N.I.D. was no longer in the front-line.[285]

One of the overriding pieces of evidence against the N.I.D.'s efficacy, and therefore against those who demoted intelligence, and should have insisted on a high-powered intelligence body to provide high-grade and timely intelligence, must be the total failure by British Naval intelligence, and the other British intelligence organisations, to detect German's secret plans in the 1920s to revive its Navy (and particularly the U-boat service), in violation of the Treaty of Versailles and the spirit of Locarno. This was not discovered until the German naval archives became available on Germany's defeat in 1945.[286]

In the field of defence appreciation, the N.I.D. lost out to the C.I.D. In the great political battle for Trenchard's 'unified air' concept on the one hand, and the survival and growth of the Fleet Air Arm on the other, intelligence was never invited to have a real say in the deliberations.[287] There were the Royal Navy's firm protagonists, men like Admiral Dreyer, a great Vice-Chief of Naval Staff, and the R.A.F. had theirs too—the prolonged dispute was based on anything but sound evidence, rather, inter-service rivalry, and a certain amount of jealousy. It almost led to disaster.

Captain Roskill writes: "In dive-bombing, the U.S. Navy achieved an early and marked ascendancy over both the Royal Navy and the Royal Air Force,"[288] and, "a curious feature of the British and American attitude towards the Japanese that they were rather inferior copyists. That false judgment was only eliminated

---

[284] One of the few signs of hope was to be found in the report of Mr Churchill's Committee of 1922, which sowed the seeds of starting a Joint-Panning and a Joint-Intelligence Sub-Committee of the Chiefs-of-Staff Committee. This report was the genesis too of the Imperial Defence College, which started its first course in January 1927, with Admiral Sir Herbert Richmond as its Commandant.

[285] In May 1923, the Naval Staff discussed the factors involved in the defence of the Singapore Base. The ideas emerging were not those of the clinical, objective intelligence organisation whose judgments should have been in the forefront. Adm. 116, 2416.

[286] See S. W. Roskill: Naval Policy Between the Wars. Vol. I. p. 440-441, The War at Sea, Vol. I. p. 51-52; Erich Eyck: A History of the Weimar Republic. Vol. II. p. 397-400; Alan Bullock: Hitler, A Study in Tyranny. p. 185-214.

[287] See Lord Chatfield: It Might Happen Again. p. 102-110, for a description of the victory of the 'unified air' doctrine, and the failure of the navy to win the day.

[288] S. W. Roskill: Naval Policy Between the Wars. Vol. I. p. 525.

in Pearl Harbour and by the quick and efficient dispatch of the Prince of Wales and Repulse."[289]

In the development of strategic and tactical thought (based on exercise reports in large measure), the N.I.D. played but a minor role, when in fact, it should have been paramount—relating enemy capability, and possible intentions, to the British side (developing doctrine, and helping in the formation of plans and exercises and assessment of these).[290] There is no direct evidence for a causal relationship between the decline of the N.I.D. in the 1920s and the sterility of tactical thinking.

However, this does not negate the argument that a high-powered N.I.D. might have more adequately performed some of the functions of the Staff College and the Tactical School.[291] Little or no attention was paid in the 1920s to the tactical and strategic role of naval air power, and tragically, between 1919 and 1939, the Royal Navy did not conduct one extensive exercise in the protection of a convoy against air and submarine attacks, allowing for all the experiences of World War I, and the extreme contingencies a future war might bring.[292]

---

[289] Ibid. p. 531.

[290] The official records of the Royal Navy's strategic and tactical exercises between 1919 and 1937, lodged in the R.N. Staff College Library at Greenwich, were destroyed by enemy bombing in World War II.

Footnote: Besides the unfortunate loss of the exercise reports mentioned above, another sad blow to the researcher was the destruction of the 1924 Fighting Instructions, and associated documents. These were the first issued in the post-war period, by Admirals Oliver and Brock.

[291] [**Footnote cont.**]: No evidence survives of any N.I.D. involvement in the tactical re-appraisals after World War I.

Both of these bodies analysed World War I policy and operations, especially Jutland. The Grand Fleet Battle Orders were examined and certain changes introduced. The Naval Staff came down against the night action idea, the value of destroyers for both night and day attacks was enhanced, and 'divided' tactics were introduced. However, the main concept remained—that a major victory at sea could only be gained by two great fleets shelling each other at long range on parallel tracks. In a private letter to Captain S. W. Roskill of 4 July 1964, Admiral Troup wrote: "As late as 1935, great effort was given to extracting the utmost guidance from Jutland."

[292] There were no joint exercises with the Submarine Service. The Naval Staff considered that asdic developments had minimised the capability of submarines. Ironically too,

The situation did improve slightly in the 1930s with the Chatfield-Fisher era in the Mediterranean Command when they realised the value of air strikes.[293] In 1933, when Hitler came to power, carrier-borne strike forces had been finally recognised as invaluable by the Admiralty.[294] What it did not recognise, until war came, was that the greatest threat to trade would come not from surface raiders, but from submarines. British fleet exercises were geared to the former contingency.

What N.I.D. could have done, and indeed ought to have done, are purely speculative questions, but the point must hold good that, in retrospect, there was throughout the inter-war period a continuous need for a separate and influential body, well-organised and thoroughly professional, to properly assess those far-reaching questions with which neither the Naval Staff, nor the C.I.D. were well-equipped to deal.

Pre-1914 N.I.D. Work

We have seen that in peacetime an intelligence body must deal with hypotheses, testing these against hard facts, and creating models, and trying these out in exercises, and analysing the results, in close conjunction with the Plans and Operations Divisions. One sees this system operating on a limited scale in the pre-1914 era, from the time Admiral Custance became the D.N.I. 1899-1902) through to Halls time (1914-1919) followed by the decline of the N.I.D., some aspects of which have been indicated above. An examination of selected aspects

---

those exercises carried out in the Mediterranean, simulating Japanese attacks on Singapore, minimised the role of air power.

[293] 1929 had been the turning point for the U.S. Navy when the carriers Lexington and Saratoga played dominant roles in their Fleet exercises. See A. D. Turnbull and C. L. Lord: History of U.S. Naval Aviation. p. 270-283.

[294] However, the Royal Navy's position seems less acceptable when compared with American advances. Roskill has made this summation: "…the U.S. Navy was far ahead in the application of carrier-borne air power, in the defence of slow convoy against submarine attack, and in the problems involved in supplying a fleet which had to operate far from any fixed base. In the practice of combined operations, there was not much to choose between the two services." Naval Policy Between the Wars. p. 543. On the latter point, the Royal Navy conducted no exercises in amphibious warfare pre-1939, although it had been a subject of much discussion at the Staff College. In April 1939, Britain's first landing craft were ordered.

of N.I.D.'s work during this fifteen-year period will show the general methodology of a peacetime intelligence organisation at its best, in ironic contrast with the inter-war period.

Two levels will be investigated—the involvement of the N.I.D. in the secondary contingencies of a possible war and the more immediate aspects of general naval policy, and then the higher-level issues of long-range strategic naval planning, and the relationship of this to British political policy.

One thing is certain about the N.I.D.'s work in this particular period, (irrespective of any action following from it)—it was of a very high quality. A thorough examination of the records shows this.[295]

From June 1898, the British government became acutely aware of the effects war might have on the supply of food and raw materials, so much that a Royal Commission was set up (In 1898, Britain was thinking in terms of a possible war against France and Russia). The N.I.D. became intimately involved in the work of this commission, especially concerning the means by which an enemy might deny food to Britain in time of war, and the means by which the Royal Navy might counter these.

The N.I.D. investigated every aspect of the problem, issuing several interim reports. In a preliminary to such a report, dated 15 July 1901, Custance, the D.N.I., stated: "The question of whether the food supply of this country can be relied upon in time of war with France and Russia depends on:

1. The sources from which it comes.
2. The protection which can be afforded by the Navy.
3. The attitude of neutral nations."

N.I.D. findings and proposals were then given in detail. Prince Louis of Battenburg (D.N.I. 1902-1905) continued the good work.[296]

In 1904, the C.I.D. asked the Admiralty Board to comment on the scheme for making the Tyne a major naval base. The Board immediately consulted the

---

[295] The major source for the above contention is the Baddeley Papers, Adm. 1, 7734, presented to the Public Record Office in August 1935 by Sir Vincent Baddeley.

[296] See Louis Battenburg's report dated 31 October 1904, Baddeley Papers; also, the letter from Selborne to Balfour dated 2 November 1904 congratulating the N.I.D. and Battenburg on their work. Appendix A to these papers contains the correspondence of the Admiralty Board on this question and shows how influential N.I.D.'s work was.

N.I.D. and the Hydrographer, and called for reports. On the basis of N.I.D.'s report, the Naval Staff rejected this idea.

In an appended letter dated 4 August 1904, the D.N.I., Battenburg, added: "It may not be amiss to point out to the Tyne Improvement commissioners that the mere deepening of the Channel will not (as stated on page 3) turn the Tye into an important naval base. The Hydrographer clearly shows its limitations as regards water space, besides which a port requires a good deal more than a dry dock and machine shop before it can be called a naval base. The establishment of a real naval base at Rosyth will largely discount the value of the Tyne as regards strategic placement."

These papers show the extent to which the N.I.D. was involved in general naval policy, and how it was able to generate its own lines of investigation. Throughout, there is a cool, detached, analytical approach with an obvious desire to retain independent action and its own professional integrity.[297]

At the higher level, the N.I.D.'s work was critical to British defence policy-making.[298] N.I.D.'s work in this area was never again, before 1945, to be

---

[297] See the Baddeley Papers—N.I.D.'s involvement with the work of the Admiralty's Machinery Design Committee, Minutes and Journals of Proceedings, June 1904-January 1906. One of the many problems N.I.D. tries to solve was, for example, the loss of water in H.M. ships caused by condenser failure. See Adm. 116,886B for many more instances of N.I.D.'s activities and quality of work, revealing the analytical method. As examples, it was concerned with: Australian Naval questions, especially an 'Australian Naval Agreement'—see the correspondence between the Colonial Office and the N.I.D., May-July 1897, particularly the D.N.I.'s letter (Beaumont) of 1 July 1897; the Conference of Colonial Premiers, 1897; establishment of a Colonial R.N.R.; and even rates of pay to Colonial Contingents in South Africa, 1899-1902.

[298] The main sources for this contention are: The Slade Papers, lodged at the National Maritime Museum, Greenwich, a series of letters, memoranda and Slade's diary, which he was encouraged to keep by Corbett himself; D. M. Schurman: The Education of a Navy: The Development of British naval strategic thought, 1867-1914; A. J. Marder: The Anatomy of British Sea Power, a History of British Naval Policy in Pre-Dreadnought Era, 1880-1905, London, 196; Adm. 116,866B, Naval Staff Memoranda, 1889-1914; P. K. Kemp: The Papers of Admiral Sir John Fisher, Vol. II, Navy Records Society, London 196; and an unpublished London University PhD thesis (1970), N. W. Summerton, Department of War Studies, King's College: The Development of British Military Planning for a war against Germany, 1904-1914.

surpassed.[299] As early as July 1904, the N.I.D. was planning for a war against Germany.[300] In 1905, Fisher asked Ottley (D.N.I. 1905-1907) for his department's views on the readiness of the fleet for a war against Germany. D.N.I. gave a full report, concurring in general with his predecessor, Prince Louis of Battenburg; in addition to the latter's plan to close the German North Sea ports, he envisaged penetrating the Baltic and blockading the coastline.[301]

Marder shows how Ottley was against the idea of Combined Operations[302]— he foresaw administrative and organisational difficulties involved in amphibious assaults,[303] and the N.I.D. also calculated that the extensive navigational difficulties and fortifications would inhibit such landings[304] However, the N.I.D. did not rule out the concept of a highly mobile expeditionary force, able to threaten German weak points to advantage. Via the Board, the C.I.D., and thence the Cabinet, the N.I.D., through a ruthlessly methodological approach to strategic planning, was to influence the future course of the Great War.

Summerton makes this incisive comment about N.I.D.'s influence on the C.I.D., and more particularly the Army's thinking, over military planning: "…the General Staff rejected the idea of conducting a war against Germany in the manner previously envisaged for a war against France and Russia, by maritime warfare and the capture of overseas naval bases and colonies. By the autumn of 1905, the General Staff were strongly attracted to the idea of concentrating an expeditionary force in the main theatre of a Franco-German war."[305]

---

[299] Save for when its views were solicited, in a very limited way, over such issues as the amendments of the Covenant of the League of Nations.

[300] Marder, p. 479-481.

[301] Marder, p. 502-503.

[302] Marder, p. 550-568.

[303] See also Ottley's memos., Adm. 116, 866B, referring to combined military operations in war, with notes by Sir George Clarke, Secretary of the C.I.D., dated July 1905.

[304] Summerton's thesis, p. 36-39. He quotes a memo of the D.D.N.I., Captain Ballard to the Army's Director of Operations, dated 2 August 1905, in which he states that the only contingency worth considering was that of a war in alliance with France against Germany. He postulated that Britain, single-handedly, could not attempt any operations against the German seaboard.

[305] Summerton thesis. p. 49. See also p. 51 for his comments on Army-Navy politics.

The power and influence of the D.N.I. and the N.I.D. in general is shown by Slade's term of office (1907-1909).[306] Above all, it shows how the N.I.D. methodology was sufficiently flexible, totally uninhibited, and free from external pressures. Slade was courageous enough to reverse the Ottley theses; he also became very friendly towards the Army—N.I.D.'s relationship with D.M.O. (Director of Military Operations) became free, frank, and worthwhile. It was also cordial. Some have claimed Slade was dismissed by Fisher because of his overfriendliness with the military.

The idea of 'combined ops' against Germany returned. Moreover, he thought the Baltic was vital, and therefore Denmark, connecting the entrances to the sea, was fundamental to his hypothesis. N.I.D. and D.M.O. saw Combined Operations as part of a general naval offensive in the Baltic. Slade argued the case with Fisher.[307] His arguments reflect the precision of N.I.D. thinking.

A crucial diary entry of Slade's must surely be: "Sir John Fisher agreed that the best form of defence would be to send an Army to sea. It would paralyse all German initiative and tie up a large portion of their forces on the sea coast."[308] Slade furthered N.I.D.'s cause by having the R.N. War College and the Foreign Office study the implications of his amphibious strategy. The N.I.D. and the War College drew up detailed plans.

Dr Summerton's thesis gives a detailed account of the relationship between N.I.D., the Admiralty Board, the C.I.D., and the Cabinet, and the inter-service relationship. He throws great light on the politics of defence planning. It is sufficient to say here that N.I.D.'s work was regarded as invaluable. With regard to the war plans, the N.I.D. drew up he makes this comment: "…they were

---

[306] <u>Slade, Admiral Sir Edmond John Warre</u>: 1859-1928; entered R.N. 1872; Commander 1894; Captain 1899; served in H.M.S. Hecla during the Egyptian war 1882; May 1904 Director of Senior Officers War Course; R.N.C., Greenwich; <u>D.N.I. Nov. 1907-March 1909</u>; C.-in-C. East Indies 1909-1912; retired 1917; Director of the Anglo-Persian Oil Company.

[307] See the Slade MSS, the file headed, 'Summary of the Papers written by Admiral Slade for submission to the First Lord or First Sea Lord between November 1907 and March 1908' for details of this.

[308] Ibid. Diary entry, dated 25 January, 1908.

probably the only plans which existed and, if war had threatened, the Admiralty would have pressed for their adoption."[309]

Whatever the eventual outcome of the Great War, the point must surely stand that the N.I.D. had exerted for many years the dominant influence from within the Naval Staff on naval war planning. Its influence was felt throughout the upper echelons of British defence policy-making. That the Slade-Ballard school did not, in the event, win the day, and, instead of an amphibious attack on the German right flank, Britain moved from 1911-1914 towards a European orientation in foreign policy and defence planning, committing itself to a N.W. Europe land war, backed by colonial troops, remains a political-military issue which it is not within the scope of this chapter to examine.

The Corbett-Jellicoe concept of drawing the High Seas Fleet out so as to expose itself to being struck by the Grand Fleet in waters unfavourable to itself in a great set-piece battle in the classical tradition won the day.

The pre-1914 era in the N.I.D. was marked by a growing professionalism, and initiative, originality, and a dedication to naval war planning which was based on a departmental strength which was to be found so patently wanting during the high years of appeasement. Its heart was a rigorous methodology.

---

[309] Summerton. p. 264. His views are substantiated throughout the sources. See P. K. Kemp. p. 318-468, details of the formation of the Ballard Committee in 1906, set up by Fisher, to investigate the provision of naval war plans.

Chapter Six
Aspects of Naval Intelligence and Political Decision-Making

The British System of Politico-Military Decision-Making and its Relationship with Naval Intelligence

Before we can begin a thorough examination of its relationship between naval intelligence and political decision-making in this period, it is important to establish two bases. Firstly, the rationale behind the system of politico-military decision-making which underlined the contribution which intelligence could make to this side of British defence must be made clear, and secondly, indication must be made of the politico-military structure within which N.I.D. developed and operated at the several levels.

Throughout this period, one sees emerging a logical approach to defence planning, characterised above all else by the work of the Committee of Imperial Defence, which with and through the Cabinet and the Chiefs of Staff Committee, came to review defence in terms of how the national interests could be best secured, requiring reviews and analyses of the forces required to achieve this, and how much it would all cost. On the latter point, government began to clinically weigh the costs against the value of the interests to the country as a whole.

Any reduction in expenditure invariably meant a reduction in military capability, and herein lay the dichotomy, and stumbling block for many governments (especially during the depression)—can a government legitimately make such reductions without parallel reductions in political defence commitments?[310] Even at a time of relatively prolonged world stability, military run-down may have the attendant dangers of losing-out in the technological and personnel training fields to those who are less inclined to diminish manpower and military hardware.

The naval strength of one's potential adversaries, whatever the world and internal politico-economic situations is, therefore, paramount. Constant review of their capabilities, as well as their possible intentions, must be an essential role of an intelligence organisation. Comparisons of relative strengths is as critical as a review of defence commitments, and the two are by nature closely inter-related.

At both the political and the military level, intelligence can be the arbiter, not an infallible one, but one at least based upon a reasoned exposition of well-ascertained facts—Parliament rightly demands to know why and how money is being spent on defence and whether or not the defence organisation is satisfactory,[311] and the services must have a basis for their strategic policies, and more particularly for when they cannot agree. Without accurate data, defence can become a willy-nilly process of expediency, and the worst consequences of which might be what George Canning described thus in 1803:

"We might have been strong with advantage, and were then cowardly that our enemies became pre-emptory; and the coming of war was owing, therefore, to our weakness and not to our strength and courage."

It is possible to soundly hypothesise that without intelligence, this logical approach to defence planning and organisation may well malfunction—if one starts from the premise that defence policy is basically a two-way arrangement, with the political leadership on the one side laying down objectives, and the military on the other preparing plans and proposals with costs (with the Cabinet making final decisions on what can be afforded politically and diplomatically, in terms of the greatest value for the least expenditure), then it is absolutely necessary for the Naval Staff to have all the necessary factual information at their disposal if they are to draw up plans for any contingency given in government directives.

From the immediate viewpoint of conducting naval warfare, both at the tactical and strategic levels, the absence of such data can have a deadening effect upon naval planning and training to such an extent that when hostilities occur,

---

[310] See Mr Denis Healy's R.U.S.I. lecture of 22 October 1969, in which he discusses these problems when he was Secretary of State for Defence.

[311] As early as 1889, such questions in the House led to the Harrington Commission.

the Royal Navy may either fail to apply its resources in the correct manner, or, at worst, be in a total quandary as to what should be best done.[312]

On the level of the conduct of naval operations, the Navy may be in a dominating position relative to the political arm, by sheer weight of professional competence and involvement, but on the level of political decision-making, where senior naval officers might well be as equally well-versed in the totality of factors embracing any particular defence posture, the role of naval intelligence bears careful examination.

It is certainly true that many senior naval staffs in the last fifty years have witnessed either several major run-downs or the maintenance of equilibrium within the Royal Navy when potential aggressors have been building up, and this poses the question of how far naval intelligence, as a factor within the Navy as a single unit, and within the politico-military structure as a whole, has interacted with the other major factors, particularly economic, to influence the development of policy. The dilemma, and indeed paradox, which, at all costs, should be avoided in this position.

Allen Dulles thus described when discussing World War I: "The Great Powers of Europe entered World War I with intelligence services which in no way were commensurate with the might of their armed forces or equipped to cope with the complexity of the conflict to come."[313]

In the contemporary context, despite any marginal advantage which technological superiority in warning systems might give, government must surely depend on intelligence to provide some long-range warning that a strategic attack is possible. The present consequences of a politico-military decision-making breakdown are, therefore, much more costly in theory. Hence the need for the right data and those who can satisfactorily handle it. However, in a democracy, those best able to use military information through their knowledge and experience do not necessarily hold the right political seats.

Good intelligence in the wrong hands might either be wasted or misused. There is no better illustration of this than the appointment, on 9 March 1936, of Sir Thomas Inskip as Minister for the Coordination of Defence.[314] Churchill

---

[312] Allen Dulles: The Craft of Intelligence. p. 32.

[313] Allen Dulles: The Craft of Intelligence. p. 32.

[314] <u>Inskip, Thomas, Viscount Caldecote</u>: 1876-1947; born in Bristol, son of a solicitor; ed. Clifton, King's Cambridge. Called to the bar, practiced on the western circuit. KC

himself probably describes better than anyone else the feeling this engendered in certain quarters of the politico-military leadership in and out of office: "On 9, Mr Baldwin selected Sir Thomas Inskip, an able lawyer, who had the advantages of being little known himself and knowing nothing about military subjects. The Prime Minister's choice was received with astonishment by Press and Public. To me, this definite, and as it seemed final exclusion from all share in our preparations for defence, was a heavy blow."

[315] Caustic, and a little sarcastic, but Churchill's words echo a fundamental point—decisions can only be as good as those who are in a position to make them, not the data upon which such decisions might be based.

Let us now look at the structure of defence within which N.I.D. developed. Before the first committee on colonial defence at the end of the nineteenth century, there was no regular central machinery for defence policy-making and planning. The Board of Admiralty provided some form of centralisation (and became a model for the reform of the War Office recommended by several bodies between 1890 and 1904) but there was no organisation especially for strategic thought.

The emergent Naval Staff responded well to the material, hardware problems of the service, but not to the tactical and strategic problems of war. Professor Arthur Marder quotes Lord Selborne, First Lord in 1903,[316] thus: "We have been shamefully unenthusiastic in the way we have treated questions of national defence."[317] In the previous year, 1902, a breakthrough had come, following the colonial conference, with the founding by Balfour of the Committee of Imperial Defence.

As an informal committee of the Prime Minister's, it acted solely in an advisory capacity, and membership was by invitation. Even by 1914, the C.I.D.'s position was still equivocal, both on grounds of its professional usefulness and its political desirability. However, what is significant is that at its first meeting,

---

1914; MP (Con.) 1918-1939; Solicitor-General 1922; Minister for the Co-ordination of Defence, 1936. On the outbreak of war, he received a peerage and became Lord Chancellor. May 1940, Minister for the Dominions. October, 1940, Lord Chief Justice.

[315] W. S. Churchill: The Second World War: Volume I. p. 156.

[316] <u>Selborne, William, Second Earl</u>: 1859-1942; MP (Lib.) 1885; Lib. Unionist from 1886; succeeded to title 1895; Under-Secretary for the Colonies 1895-1900; First Lord of the Admiralty 1900-1905.

[317] Arthur Marder: British Naval Policy. 1880-1905. p. 417.

on 18 December 1902, there were present Balfour, the Lord President (Devonshire), the First Sea Lord, the C.-in-C. of the Army, the Director of Military Intelligence and Prince Louis of Battenburg, the then Director of Naval Intelligence.[318]

The D.N.I. was invited because the Prime Minister desired his presence and advice. Pre-1914, during the high summer of the Fisher era, the N.I.D. played a major role in the formulation of naval war plans (as was seen in Chapter Five)—regrettably though some of those plans were never given the review by the C.I.D. or the Cabinet they deserved because of Fisher's unwarranted wish to maintain his own and the Naval Staff's autonomy. In 1906, when the C.I.D. asked the First Sea Lord for his plans, he actually refused to reveal them.

At the same time, he said the Royal Navy could not guarantee the passage of an expeditionary force across the Channel. Since the Prime Minister did not intervene, the C.I.D., with no statutory authority, could not challenge Fisher. In 1907, Haldane eventually persuaded Campbell-Bannerman to demand that he produce the Admiralty's war plans. This he did, but it was only a technical victory for the C.I.D., since there was no attempt to integrate these plans with those of the Army or assurances given that the Admiralty would be more cooperative.

The critical point is that whatever the value of N.I.D.'s role and the quality of its work, which was high at this stage, the higher politico-military relationships prevented the production of integrated war plans, which would have to stand the test of combined scrutiny from the Admiralty and Army Boards and the C.I.D. In this sense, it is not unjust to say that Fisher did the service and the country immeasurable harm, both upwards and downwards[319] in the Navy, and when the time came for serious commitments to a given strategy, the naval

---

[318] The forerunner to the C.I.D. was the Colonial Defence Committee, of which the D.N.I. was a member. The Committee offered suggestions on broad imperial defence problems, leaving local authorities to provide details of planning and execution. This committee had no staff for research or planning. Between 1885 and 1892, it had 58 meetings, dealing with 478 agenda items, from which it drew up 61 colonial defence plans and made 151 detailed recommendations.

[319] In 1908, the Secretary of the C.I.D., Captain Ottley, who had been the D.N.I. 1907-1907, wrote, "not one naval officer out of fifty has any knowledge what a British fleet will have to do in war, or how it will do it."

concepts lost the day to a large military presence in N.W. Europe. N.I.D. had produced ideas and plans which countered this policy.

The blue-water school of the N.I.D. never had chance to fight its case. Fisher's attitudes are nowhere more obvious than in his reluctance to form, and expand (as the C.I.D. were always encouraging him to do) a Naval Staff. The heart, and senior echelon of this staff, was the N.I.D.

The price was indeed paid in World War I. Despite an expanded Naval Staff, disagreement at the top, the seeds of which had been sown before 1914, prohibited joint staff work and the provision of informed staff thought for the Cabinet on high matters of strategy.[320] Fisher's idea of the Army as 'a projectile to be fired by the Navy'[321] was lost in the mud of Flanders and he could blame no one more than himself.[322] Fisher had just not used the C.I.D. the way he should—N.I.D. and the M.I.D. forwarded data to the C.I.D. Secretariat, and it was this body which tended to interpret and explain such data to ministers.

Through his D.N.I. and the C.I.D., Fisher could have exerted more influence than, in effect, he did.[323] However, it is important to remember the climate in which these events occurred, which has been described by Lord Hankey himself: "Given the circumstances of the day—a hundred years without a great war, the inexperience of statesmen and soldiers alike of war on the grand scale, a government busy on a great programme of social reform, a policy directed above

---

[320] One example will suffice to illustrate the consequences of such an organisation: pre-war both the N.I.D. and the M.I.D. had produced reports for the C.I.D. on the effects 16-inch naval guns and Army howitzers had on shore defences, especially heavily protected gun emplacements—they hardly made a mark. These reports were fed through the staff channels to the C.I.D., and were filed for future reference. When the Dardanelles committee laid down initial plans for that campaign, these reports were totally ignored.

[321] Lord Fisher: Memoirs p. 171.

[322] The C.I.D.'s early work was very Navy-oriented. It centred on the reliance of British sea power defence against invasion and the defence of India. It was the perfect vehicle for the D.N.I. to express his staff's ideas, as well as an arena for developing a unified strategy for the Dominions.

[323] There seems to be no doubt among scholars that the C.I.D. was the most influential body on government policy—pre-1914. Its Secretariat, whose functions were defined in Balfour's Treasury Minute of 4 May 1904, became very powerful—Parliament never questioned its working, or the state of British preparedness.

all to the maintenance of peace—given all this, our defensive arrangements were not ineffective."[324]

The C.I.D. went into abeyance during World War I, to be revived after the war was an absolute necessity to ensure that the Cabinet's organisation functioned effectively. In 1923, a sub-committee was set up under Lord Salisbury to review the central defence machinery. It proposed a Chiefs of Staff Committee, to be chaired by the Prime Minister or his deputy—"with an individual and collective responsibility for advising on defence policy as a whole."[325]

The C.O.S. (Chiefs of Staff) was born (1923). Together with the C.I.D., the C.O.S. organisation became the Cabinet's strategic authority. In 1928, Baldwin told the House of Commons: "…the C.I.D. now receive collective advice on all General Staff questions instead of receiving, as in the past, separate and even contradictory advice from three different quarters." Chamberlain made very similar remarks in 1938.

The D.N.I. was not a member of the post-war C.I.D. Nothing is more indicative of the deliberate policy to reduce the power of the D.N.I. and the scope of the work of the N.I.D. after the Hall era. In its subordinate role, it was to lose the pace and involvement so assiduously nurtured by Hall, such that by the mid-30s, it was indeed in the doldrums.[326] The D.N.I. made his representations through the First Sea Lord to the C.O.S. and the C.I.D. and thence the Cabinet. Further indication of the malaise into which defence intelligence slipped as a

---

[324] Lord Hankey: Diplomacy by Conference. p. 54.

[325] Cmd. 2029. p. 18.

[326] In his 'My Naval Life, 1906-1929', Stephen King-Hall gives some graphic accounts of his work in the N.I.D. in the mid-20s. In 1925, before joining the staff of the C.-in-C. Mediterranean, as principal intelligence officer, King-Hall was briefed in the N.I.D. He writes: "I spent some weeks at the Admiralty attached to the Naval Intelligence Department and formed a very poor opinion of the organisation as it was. It may be better now (1951). I hope so. At this time, all the officers in the N.I.D. were on their way out, that is to say they had been passed over for promotion, and had no prospects. They were soldiering on for a pension and most of them were dead from the neck up." p. 215.

King-Hall writes that no useful intelligence at all emerged from the Mediterranean Fleet during 1925-1926. p. 223. (At this time, the N.I.D.'s main source in the Mediterranean consisted of the ports' consuls and the ships' intelligence officers usually Royal Marines, filling in N.I.D. questionnaires, and usually with data quite easily available in major public sources).

whole is shown by the fact that the Joint Intelligence Committee (J.I.C., consisting of the three service directors of intelligence or their deputies) was not established until as late as 30 January 1936.

It was chaired by a representative from the Foreign Office, and was attended by a member of the Department of Overseas Trade, and other departments as necessary. It is significant that the C.O.S. had established their own Joint Planning Sub-Committee as early as 1926, but no regard was paid to intelligence.

From 1926, the C.O.S. prepared for the C.I.D. their own annual strategic report, relying upon, to a large extent, the Foreign Office annual surveys of the international situation, including 'threats to peace', and to a lesser extent, the intelligence reports of the three service intelligence departments. Both the C.O.S. and the C.I.D. were dynamic in themselves. In 1932, the C.O.S. pressed and succeeded in ending the Ten-Year Rule, and in November 1934, the C.I.D. told the defence planners to plan on the assumption of a possible war with Germany within five years.[327]

In World War II, Churchill formed a War Cabinet, the C.I.D. went into temporary abeyance again, and the C.O.S.'s position was strengthened. The three service ministers were not members of the War Cabinet or the C.O.S. (only as invited by the Prime Minister). This is significant—these ministers had access to Churchill, and were kept informed as members of the Defence Committee, but they did not guide military operations or participate in formulating strategy, though they were responsible for the organisation and the administration of each service.

With the establishment of the Combined Chiefs of Staff (Britain and American), responsible for overall Allied military planning and operations for overall Allied military planning and operations, four Confined C. S. sub-committees were established, this was the Intelligence Sub-Committee.

The Politico-Military Environment Within Which N.I.D. Operated

The traditionally highly structured, hierarchical nature of NID personnel relationships and deployment exhibits certain characteristics which could not be

---

[327] Unlike C.O.S., the C.I.D. was not at all Services dominated—only one out of more than fifty sub-committees of the C.I.D. was confined to representatives of the Services alone.

described as democratic, yet it has to function, and be seen to function, in a democratic system of government. If this factor is coupled to the world events which determine the role and composition of the Royal Navy (and this is just as true in the contemporary world, with increasingly more destructive weapons available, and the threat of strategic nuclear attack), particularly those which are patently antithetical to the British way of life and interests, one sees circumstances calling for responses which the principles of British democratic government do not necessarily always permit.

The alternatives may be total inertia, or inaction, or limited, ineffective action, or the use of military force in such a way or with such consequences, as to be contrary to public opinion. Is there a means for reconciling these divergent factors? It is one of the hypotheses of this study that a body, such as the N.I.D. (and on higher levels, the Committee of Imperial Defence and the Chiefs of Staff Committee), was able to fulfil, admittedly with varying degrees of intensity and success, the vital functions of providing both necessary professional intelligence and was, in itself, an objective basis for politico-military decision-making, and all that this entailed, in terms of the legitimate use of British Naval power.

Naval intelligence as such, as a microcosmic part of the overall British intelligence commitment in this period, fulfilled, therefore, a role within the state that went beyond the scope that any superficial analysis might reveal. It is now one of the objectives of this chapter to examine this standpoint in depth.

The Varying Emphasis Placed on N.I.D.'s Work Throughout the Period

The value attached to intelligence in peace and war during this period has varied as much through administrative and internal political changes as through what might be considered to be the more important controlling factors—such as the world situation, its stability or otherwise, the state of knowledge of the military capabilities and intentions of other powers, and the relationship of Britain's own naval resources and their strengths and capabilities to the latter point. As has already been demonstrated naval intelligence did not grow in a logical way.

Before the Great War, the D.N.I., as principal assistant to the First Sea Lord, and the kingpin of the Naval Staff, held sway. Whatever the state of the intelligence art, in terms of methods, and it was pretty primitive at times,[328] the fact remains that the N.I.D. played the dominant part in the creation and the evaluation of Naval strategic and tactical policy, and, to a large extent, was intimately concerned with the day-to-day running of the Royal Navy.[329][330] By the time Slade became D.N.I. in 1907, the early hopes of those who had been primarily involved in the creation of the Foreign Intelligence Committee and the later N.I.D. were realised.[331] The Papers of Admiral Slade reveal the incredible scope of the N.I.D. in its early period.[332]

In the Great War, with the rapid shift from static to operational intelligence, N.I.D. improved the whole range and quality of its intelligence activity,

---

[328] See Admiral Sir Barry Domvile's book: By and Large. Hutchinson, 1936. As a newly promoted Commander Domvile joined the N.I.D. in 1909. He wrote this about his work there: "Naval intelligence was in the early stages of development and our work consisted largely of scanning the Foreign Press, and snipping and pasting in its literary yield into various scrap books." p. 39. In 1927, Domvile was promoted to Flag rank and made D.N.I. (1927-1930).

[329] In Fisher's Naval Necessities of 1905/1906, this revealing comment is made: "In the report of the Special Committee presided over by the late Director of Naval Intelligence (Prince Louis of Battenburg), it was recommended that England should maintain a superiority in battleships of at least 10% and 2:1 in armoured cruisers, over each of the two combinations, viz: (a) Germany and Russia, (b) France and Russia." The Papers of Admiral Sir John Fisher, Vol. 2, ed. by P. K. Kemp. p. 60-69. Nothing illustrates better the position, responsibility and influence of the D.N.I. in the early period.

[330] See Mark Kerr: Prince Louis of Battenburg. Longmans. 1934. Kerr quotes a letter from Battenburg to Admiral Sir John Fisher, dated 11 February 1902: "Since the present D.N.I. Captain Custance (D.N.I. 1899-1902) assumed office, it has made great strides; with irresistible, yet hardly perceptible force, it has backed up the Naval Lords; invaded every department of the Admiralty, and it is no exaggeration to say now—that no question of any greater importance than the say, change of an article of uniform, is decided upon without the N.I.D. having had its say." p. 165. Battenburg was D.N.I. 1902-1905. Supported by Lord Selborne, the First Lord, and his D.D.N.I., Captain Inglefield.

[331] As we have seen, some of the main moves for the creation of an intelligence department had come from the R.U.S.I., and particularly J.C.R. Colornb, who had led a group in the early '80s which advocated the creation of an N.I.D., where relevant strategic assessments could be made so war plans could be 'realistically drawn up'. See J. R. C. Colornb: Naval Intelligence and Protection of Commerce in War. R.U.S.I. Journal (1881). p. 553-78.

[332] Slade Mss., National Maritime Museum, Greenwich.

especially its methods. From 1919 until 1936, there came near disaster for the N.I.D. with the wholesale axing of its functions. D.N.I. was a shadow of his former self. As will be seen later, the Chiefs of Staff Joint Planning Sub-Committee tended to fulfil those functions which should rightfully have been performed by the service's professional intelligence department—the N.I.D.

The golden age of the eleven pre-war D.N.I.s and their doyen during the war itself, Reginald Hall, was not recaptured until Troup's tenure (D.N.I. 195-1939), with a slow, but systematic build-up of N.I.D.'s activities before war began, and to the time when Godfrey took over. The latter soon recaptured the influence of the pre-1919 era. He writes in his unpublished memoirs: "…both Admirals Backhouse and Pound were alive to the need of an emergency audience for D.N.I. and invariably listened to all I had to say with patience and appreciation."[333]

In a period of peace, such as 1919-1929, when there were no apparent enemies to challenge Britain, strategic planning and tactical evaluations are more difficult, particularly if (continued) Battenburg built up a professional body of intelligence workers. During his tenure, Battenburg was very much the First Sea Lord's right-hand man.

There is no immediate war experience to call upon—the developing strategy of the Royal Air Force in the '20s and '30s had not been tested in war, just as in the contemporary world planning for strategic and tactical nuclear warfare has no foundation in experience. Coupled to this difficulty is the tendency to ignore or under-rate intelligence, one of the sure signs of wishful thinking of those who direct defence. There can be no doubt that a strong nation must be prepared, even during an ostensibly quiet period in world affairs, for a potential enemy to take an unwise or unremunerative course of action.

Before Japan's intentions in the Far East became fairly obvious Britain's knowledge of Japanese naval developments, other than straightforward paper strengths and so forth, was flimsy in the extreme, and, although the Americans were to acquire some valuable data pre-Pearl Harbour and develop their 'magics' to effect,[334] some vital pieces of information about Japanese naval air capabilities

---

[333] Admiral Godfrey's unpublished typescript memoirs. Mss. 66/104. Vol. 5, Part I. p. 45, National Maritime Museum, Greenwich.

[334] The word 'magics' was used to describe the deciphered, Japanese radio signals, and the process whereby they had been deciphered.

went undetected which, coupled to organisational problems, rendered much intelligence ineffectual. Admiral Godfrey has written this:

"Japan, behind an impenetrable security wall, had built up a fighting machine about whose composition and intentions we knew very little. Both we and the Americans erred, and there is hardly anyone who is entitled to say: 'I told you so'."[335] That Britain did eventually tackle this Japanese and other intelligence problems before it was too late does not alter the chronic all-round failure of British Naval intelligence in the '20s and the early years of appeasement, a failure whose surmounting might have produced more realistic planning and even prevented warlike situations developing.[336]

Naval intelligence in the Far East was organised through a joint services body, the Far East Combined Bureau (F.E.C.B.). It was based in Hong Kong until August 1939, when it moved to Singapore. On the purely naval side, there was established an O.I.C. type organisation on the London model, and similar to the one established in Malta for the Mediterranean. In November and December 1941, 'operational' intelligence in the Far East was very good. Aerial, reconnaissance, HF/DF fixes, and cryptanalysis revealed the moves of major Japanese units in S.E. Asia.

However, there was a British intelligence 'blind spot' in the central Pacific area. This was considered an American responsibility and on, in any event, seemingly not directly affecting British interests. Before Pearl Harbour, it is true to say that J.I.C. appraisals in 1941 (based on F.E.C.B. reports) of Japanese intentions were sound in fact and reasoning. However, it is well known that the British government and the C.O.S. feared the consequences of a two-theatre war, which, materially, Britain was incapable of fighting. Above all, she feared a

---

[335] Godfrey Mss., National Maritime Museum, Greenwich. Vol. 5, Part I. p. 77.

[336] As far as Japan was concerned, N.I.D. did not intensify its activities until 1938. See, for example, Adm. 1/9589: Japanese landing operations in the Yangtse Delta—report N.I.D. 01333/1938. P.R.O., and Adm. 1/9587: Military information on the fighting in China and appreciation of Japan's military capabilities. N.I.D. soon realised the dangers of the torpedo in Japanese hands—see Adm. 1/9649—Foreign development of the torpedo as an air weapon. N.I.D. 0520/1938. It also intensified activity to find better ways of resisting possible aerial attacks, from Japan or Germany—see Adm. 1/9713—control of anti-aircraft guns and searchlights by infra-red cell radiation: report on US experiments. N.I.D. 031/1938.

Japanese attack on British possessions which would not necessarily provoke the Americans and therefore not bring them into the war on the British side.

The argument that there was little Britain could do in any case (despite, for example, excellent intelligence reports) must have considerable credence. If criticism is really seriously to be levelled, then it must surely be aimed at the tragic circumstances surrounding the fall of Singapore. Since June 1937, the N.I.D. in London had indicated that there was a strong possibility of a Japanese attack on Hong Kong and Singapore within the next few years.

On the question of the threat to Singapore, ample evidence was afforded of a positive Japanese capability to attack and take Singapore from the landward. The signs were there in 1940 in abundance. On 22 September 1940, the Vichy government in France signed an agreement with the Japanese over Indo-China. Within six days, they had begun to move in. By July 1941, the Japanese occupied Saigon, six hundred miles from Singapore. Where British intelligence slipped up was in its assessment of the Japanese mentality—its ability to do the irrational.

In February and March 1941, the results of combined British, American and Dutch talks show that all three powers believed Japan would not attack because this was mad—she would be taking on far more than she could possibly handle. Of course, this was true. It was also as much a subject of debate in Tokyo as it was in F.E.C.B. in Singapore and the J.I.C. in London. There was a strong faction in Tokyo which considered it a rash move to make a bid for S.E. Asia.

On the straightforward question of intelligence, there can be little doubt that the real failure in the Far East lay in the American camp, not so much at Pearl Harbour but in Washington itself. As late as the summer of 1941 (when N.I.D. sent a delegation to Washington), the O.N.I. had no proper O.I.C., and certainly not one which had full and direct liaison with the Operations Division of the U.S. Naval Staff. Admiral Godfrey noted how much the Americans were against setting up an O.I.D., and he attributed this to a complete inability on the American Naval Staff's part to cooperate with one another.

The rift between O.N.I. and Operations was indeed similar to that between N.I.D. and the Operations Division of the British Admiralty at the time of the Battle of Jutland. The point here is that a better organised, more efficient American O.I.C. would undoubtedly have prevented Pearl Harbour. How far this would have affected Japanese plans for SE. Asia is too speculative to seriously entertain, but it is certainly true that the less aggressive, more cautious faction in Tokyo would have had more of a case with an American fleet seemingly alert and invulnerable to a pre-emptive attack and, therefore, a possible ally for the British and the Dutch in the very early, and crucial, days of Japanese strikes in S.E. Asia.

Peacetime intelligence is more vulnerable to the vagaries of politics than in wartime, when military objectives are more clear-cut and the professional Naval Staff have a greater say in events. At the very worst, of course, there is some danger to the security of the nation—intelligence may be used (or not used as the case may be) in a totally unobjective way, or the very failure to ensure sufficient intelligence is collected may jeopardise Britain's defence.[337] In the event of hostilities without the direction, without organisation, the great risk of defeat is run.

For example, Donald McLachlan has this to say on the chase of the Bismarck and British warships' capabilities of defeating her in a running battle: "Wishful thinking, that ever lurking temptation for politicians dealing with military affairs, and for serving officers involved in politics—is even more conspicuous in this episode than in that of the U-boat sinkings."[338]

The position in 1939 is in marked contrast with that in 1914. For example, between 1912-1914, N.I.D. intensified its work in the Mediterranean—what it produced for the political decision-makers was first class. At a meeting of the C.I.D. on 4 July 1912, to discuss the 'Strategical Position in the Mediterranean', Churchill produced the N.I.D. data.[339]

He made these comments: "In addition to this diagram, members would find on the table a comparative statement prepared by the Naval Intelligence Department at the request of Lord Morley (Lord President of the Council) showing the strength of these powers in armoured ships of all kinds at the present time...," and so he goes on to discuss strategic implications, all in marked

---

[337] A comparison of the area intelligence reports before, and immediately after the Great War, with the sparse data coming into the N.I.D., particularly from Germany, in the '30s soon reveals a lack of political direction. These reflect the run-down in the N.I.D. organisation. For N.I.D. intelligence regarding Germany before and during the Great War see Adm. 137/108-111, 302. An examination of the public records pre-1936 reveals a complete absence of the high-quality area intelligence reports which flowed into N.I.D. pre-1920. For the early period see Adm. 137/2026—intelligence in the Baltic, Adm. 137/2090, 498—intelligence in the Crimea, Adm. 137/382 482—intelligence in the Black Sea, for good and typical examples of N.I.D.'s work.

[338] Donald McLachlan. Room 39. p. 15.

[339] Cab. 38/20.21.

contrast with the state of affairs two years before World War II began.[340] N.I.D.'s technical intelligence pre-1914 was excellent too; it had details of every major German unit, a situation which would have embarrassed the N.I.D. of the late '30s, particularly in the light of McLachlan's comments on the Bismarck above.[341]

Intelligence can only be as good as the organisation which collects, analyses and interprets it. The onus must be divided between both naval and political authorities to ensure that a satisfactory organisation exists. In 1914, although certain techniques were still in their infancy, especially the use of HF/DF and cryptographic intelligence, there was a world-wide network of intelligence officers.[342] Despite the N.I.D.'s failure to locate certain German units in 1914, intelligence on the whole worked well. When war broke out, for example, naval intelligence on the China Station worked like clockwork.

Admiral Jerram, as a result of HF/DF fixes and port intelligence reports from his intelligence officers and British and Australian consuls, knew the general whereabouts of most major German units.[343] In the last two years before World War II, there was a headlong rush to establish some resemblance of an effective

---

[340] For the Mediterranean see Adm. 1/9564, Mediterranean Intelligence Report No. 7. N.I.D. 09786/1938. This reveals the comparatively low standard of intelligence reports in 1938.

[341] See Policy and Operations in the Mediterranean 1912-1914, ed. E. W. R. Lumby, for the Navy Records Society, 1970: p. 353-55—N.I.D. technical intelligence was submitted in evidence at the Court of Enquiry and Court Martial of Rear-Admiral Troubridge, 7 September-9 November 1914, following the escape of the Breslau and Goeben. The data from the N.I.D. files was excellent, especially regarding the fire-control systems and range finders of the German ships.

[342] In the pre-1914 period, the N.I.D. had divided the world into intelligence areas, corresponding approximately, but by no means exactly, to the limits of the naval stations. Each area naval intelligence officer worked in close harmony with Foreign Office officials and the principal officials in British ports. In time of war, port intelligence officers also had to control merchant shipping. Before war, this duty was envisaged as offering suggestions to ships' masters as regards their route and procedure, and the precautions they should take to lessen the chances of capture. They could close trade routes if they deemed them unsafe. Each area naval intelligence officer was under the command of the Admiral commanding the station.

[343] See the Naval Staff Monographs for World War I. Vol. 5. p. 41-43. Naval Library, Empress State building, Earl's Court.

operational intelligence organisation. As already mentioned in Chapter One, its heart became the O.I.C. (Operational Intelligence Centre).[344] Its establishment was followed by a welter of other sections and the development of plans for an expanded N.I.D.[345] Throughout the world, the N.I.D. was having to streamline its organisation and prepare itself for the inevitable war.[346]

This sudden impetus which had to be given to the whole N.I.D. machine reflects the total lack of political and naval foresight as to the great necessity and value of long-range, and immediate, operational intelligence. However, the Americans were not even as well off as the British; Godfrey himself, with Ian Fleming, went to Washington as the representative of the Chiefs of Staff and the Joint Intelligence Committee to persuade them to establish an American O.I.C. and foster cooperation.[347] Fortunately for the later, Allied cause President Roosevelt listened to Godfrey.

---

[344] See Adm. 1/10226—Development of the Operational Intelligence Centre at the Admiralty, N.I.D. 004/1939.

[345] See Adm. 1/9792—Naval Intelligence in Wartime. N.I.D. 89/1939, and Adm. 1/10218—Reorganisation of the N.I.D. to meet wartime conditions. Adm. 1/10224, N.I.D. 01113/1939 gives details of the formation of the N.I.D.'s Information Section, Adm. 1/9525, N.I.D. 001410/1938 deals with the establishment of HF/DF stations covering the important trade routes in the South Atlantic, Adm. 1/10465 covers the appointment of an additional D.D.N.I., and Adm. 1/10471 and Adm. 1/10014 detail the organisation of the N.I.D.'s press and publicity section, and the institution of a press division, and the relationship between this and the Ministry of Information; the increase in personnel in N.I.D. in 1939 and 1940 and the granting of R.N.V.R. commissions (Special Branch) are detailed in Adm. 1/10946.

[346] See, for example, Adm. 1/9567 which deals with the reorganisation of N.I.D.'s intelligence staff in Cape Town.

[347] The Senate enquiry following the disaster at Pearl Harbour was to reveal the confusion over the handling of vital intelligence, which in terms of the quality of collection revealed the excellence of Captain Kirk's O.N.I.—despite the competitiveness and the lack of a unified government policy for G2 (military intelligence), O.N.I. and the F.B.I., and the antagonism shown by the United States' Navy's Operations Division (very reminiscent of N.I.D. at the time of Jutland), it had managed to produce some first class data.

Some Political Ramifications and Aspects of the Role and Work of Naval Intelligence

Intelligence in the Royal Navy always faced the problem of finding the right level at which to aim its data, irrespective of any qualitative analysis of the data. The latter was a problem in itself—the apparently trivial piece of intelligence one day might be the key to a major policy decision the next. The recognition of this was the less difficult of the two. The Americans found this at Pearl Harbour.

Placing information in the right hands so that the right action is taken calls not only for accurate perception that must by nature be intuitive and speculative, rather than logical and grounded in reality, but also for the kind of political organisation which easily becomes sensitive to well-timed intelligence. If it is neither accurate, relevant, or well-timed, the loss of credibility reduces intelligence to the level of crystal-gazing. In the pre-1914 period, when the D.N.I. was the heart of the growing Naval Staff, one can perceive within naval intelligence an obvious ability always to gain a hearing, at the appropriate level, dependent upon the value of the information, whether it was well-ascertained fact or the current opinion of the D.N.I. on British foreign and defence policy.

In the absence of administrative and hierarchical constraints from within the service, the Civil Service and government, the pre-1914 N.I.D. found its own levels of operation and usefulness. Under Hall, the N.I.D. had full reign, and one of the major reasons why it was able to have such a great influence on the war at sea was that it was unfettered by a bureaucratic machine, part of which might offer a challenge to its own autonomy.

With the proliferation of defence organisations which came in the wake of peace, rather than as the forerunners to war, the N.I.D., with diminished power and staff, found it increasingly more difficult to hit the right chords at the right time. The result was the almost total absence of good intelligence, or the recognition of the need to acquire it, in the major political-military decisions affecting the Royal Navy in the inter-war period.

The problem is highlighted by such questions as the role of the Royal Navy in the Far East in the 1920s and the position of Singapore. As early as 1921, the C.I.D. had farsightedly reviewed the possibility of war in the Far East, and they decided Singapore should be used as a naval base. Within ten years, they were to be proven correct with Japan's invasion of Manchuria on 18 September 1931. Singapore, offering facilities as a fuelling and repair base, would be the centre of any concentration of naval power in the Far East.

Certain general facts could be ascertained by the sub-committees of the C.I.D. without expert knowledge, such as it would take the Fleet four to six weeks to reach the Far East in an emergency. Assuming Britain could not permanently keep a large fleet on station in the Far East, and that the Japanese would try to eliminate Singapore once war broke out, some measure of security had to be provided in the western Pacific before Britain could muster stronger forces—C.I.D.'s answer was the stationing of the fast light cruisers and large submarines, with great endurance, on the station.

So, the C.I.D. continued in its speculations and deliberations, the Singapore issue being reviewed annually from 1925 onwards.[348] They made estimates of the number of shore-based maritime aircraft which would be needed in a war in the Far East.

What is significant is the complete absence of intelligence appreciations to support C.I.D. decision-making. Committees such as the C.I.D. could surely draw sound conclusions, made up as it was of distinguished professionals, but despite this, without sound intelligence, it could not justifiably rely on experience and military logic and probabilities, when further data, often quite easily available, would leave no one in doubt, not least of all the politicians. Even when firmly entrenched in the political arena, the fate of intelligence, whatever its quality, will always remain in the balance.

In the mid-30s, intelligence estimated that each year Hitler was spending as much on armaments as the whole British budget, though between November 1936 and February 1938, there were major delays in re-armament. Some, such as Eden, thought re-armament would frighten Hitler. Others disagreed. Intelligence may be accurate, and pertinent, but it does not mean at all that it will influence events.

Whilst the Far Eastern War waged between November 1936 and January 1938, with British and American ships being sunk in the Yangtse in December 1937, Britain's re-armament remained moribund, even though years previous the C.I.D., N.I.D., and any reasonable man with an informed knowledge of British and Japanese naval strengths, might have predicted that Britain just could not afford to send major fleet units to the Far East in the event of disaster. However, could intelligence have made allowances for the extent of Japanese fanaticism, or the peculiar quality of Hitler's mind?

---

[348] See Adm. 116/241b—the 199 meeting of the C.I.D., 2 April 1925.

Furthermore, some facts, even though ascertainable to intelligence, must by nature pose dangerous questions for the politician. It is now known that at the time of Munich, Hitler was concerned about the mobilisation of the British Fleet. Raeder visited him and warned him about the implications of this. How far such information, in the hands of the democracies, could have swayed things, must remain in the realms of historical conjecture. What would seem certain is that such information would have made Chamberlain's task more difficult than it was, in terms of his own outlook and policy towards Germany, rather than those of his opponents.

Chamberlain might have been no better off than the modern historians who still debate the nature of Hitler's power and the German state under the Nazis, such as the interpretations of A. J. P. Taylor, Hugh Trevor-Roper, Elizabeth Wiskemann, and Alan Bullock. The politician, faced with realities, and the necessity to make decisions, uses intelligence as he sees fit. In late 1940s, Admiral Godfrey was able to tell Churchill quite unequivocally that a German invasion was off. Churchill, nonetheless, continued to publicly state it was still highly probable—he hoped to keep British morale high, by the threat of a German invasion, and to help persuade the Americans that Britain dearly needed American help.

The timing of intelligence is vital. At a meeting of the C.I.D. on 23 August 1911, the decision was made to use a continental strategy at the beginning of the war, with the dispatch of the B.E.F., N.I.D. could offer nothing to counter this. By 1915/1916, not only had the shortcomings of that policy been recognised but also the reckless abandonment of pre-war strategic appraisals was finally realised, but regrettably too late to affect Britain's commitment in N.W. Europe.[349] Even if the timing of intelligence is good, others may win the day.

On the question of the capture of Iceland in World War II (10 May 1940), the N.I.D. won the day. Although neutral, Admiral Godfrey considered its possession by the Allies a strategic necessity. The Foreign Office opposed him, arguing that it was too violent a breach of international law. The D.N.I.

---

[349] See the papers of Admiral Sir Frederick Tower Hamilton—intelligence reports, secret and confidential, including summaries of the international situation by the N.I.D. HTN/122©, nos. 12-23, 1915/1916, National Maritime Museum, Greenwich. <u>Tower-Hamilton, Vice-Admiral Sir Frederick</u> b. 1856; entered R.N. 1869; Commander 1892; Captain 1898; Rear-Admiral 1907; commanded fifth cruiser squadron Atlantic Fleet 1909-1911; second and third fleets 1911-1913; Second Sea Lord 1914.

convinced Churchill. Irrespective of such controversy, the worst fate for intelligence is the total disregard by the politicians of the need to keep intelligence well-informed of their next move, or those of their allies. The N.I.D. was never badly ignored, unlike their German counterparts. The Abwehr and the German High Command were given no warning, for instance, of Japan's impending attack on Pearl Harbour, 7 December 1941.

It may now seem a truism to say that it is absolutely essential for the politician to have intelligence to help him make political-military decisions. It was not so in the pre-1945 era. One statesman, Harry S. Truman, has written: "The war taught us this lesson—that we had to collect intelligence in a manner that would make the information available where it was needed and when it was wanted, in an intelligent and understandable form. If it is not intelligent and understandable, it is useless."[350]

British intelligence in the '30s was not merely woefully lacking in itself, but the political arm failed to make demands upon it, and worst still, when presented with intelligence, does not appear to have acted upon it. At the time of the Italian invasion of Albania, Churchill bitterly complained of the dispositions of the Mediterranean Fleet, and on 13 April 1939, he challenged the government in the House of Commons:

"After twenty-five years' experience in peace and war, I believe the British intelligence to be the finest of its kind in the world. Yet we have seen, both in the subjugation of Bohemia and on the occasion of the invasion of Albania, that Ministers of the Crown had no inkling, or at any rate no conviction, of what was coming. I cannot believe that this was the fault of the British Secret Service."

Whatever Churchill's motives, or the weight of his comments in terms of their accuracy, he raises the fundamental issues—the availability or otherwise of intelligence and the use or misuse to which intelligence may be put by politicians. In the same Commons' speech, Churchill made this further critical point:

"It seems to me that ministers run the most tremendous risks if they allow the information collected by the intelligence department and sent to them, I am sure, in good time, to be sifted and coloured and reduced in consequences and importance, and if they ever get themselves into a mood of attaching weight only to those pieces of information which accord with their earnest and honourable

---

[350] Harry S. Truman: Memoirs. Doubleday and Co., 1958.

desire that the peace of the world should remain unbroken."[351] Churchill's words echo the pitfalls for a nation, and the frustrations for the military, if intelligence is abused or ignored.

Churchill seldom erred on this point. His 'Plan Catherine', designed to gain control of the Baltic, frightened the C.O.S. and the Admiralty in particular.

Intelligence soon led Churchill to scuttle his plans—Britain could not operate from any Baltic port (Sweden was neutral), and the menace from German U-boats and mines, and the Luftwaffe, were too threatening to hazard British Naval units.[352]

Throughout the 20s and 30s, there can be seen an apparent failure in the dialogue between intelligence and those in power. No government (made aware of the tactical and strategic advantages of maritime air power, and possessing data on Japanese air capabilities and intentions and despite the Air Ministry-Admiralty disputes, Treasury economy, and government changes) could have delayed the re-equipping and expansion of the Fleet Air Arm. Similarly with the naval treaties and conferences.

Captain Roskill has made this pertinent point about the Geneva Conference: "…neither the State Department nor the Foreign Office seems to have made a thorough study of the basic strategy which was bound to condition the other nation's outlook and attitude when their representatives met at the conference table. Thus, the immediate head-on collision at Geneva apparently took both departments by surprise."[353] There was, in effect, a total absence of intelligence appreciations. The public records do not challenge this conclusion. Pre-1914 the D.N.I. had given, and was expected to give, professional advice and data on all major issues.

In December 1908, Slade represented the Admiralty at the International Maritime Conference in London. In a memo to the First Lord and the First Sea Lord on 16 July 1908, Slade wrote: "It is not safe to embark on any line of action on supposition only, we must have actual knowledge before we can act effectively. Therefore, one of the most important developments that we must make in our organisation is that of the Intelligence service, with special reference

---

[351] This speech is recorded in W. S. Churchill: The Second World War. Vol. I. p. 275-277.
[352] Ibid. p. 363, 551.
[353] S. W. Roskill: Naval Policy between the War. p. 514-515.

to the trade of the country and to the occurrences which are taking place on the trade routes."[354]

Twenty years later, and beyond, Slade's demand was still so patently relevant, but was, after ten years of peace, to be found wanting.

The politician has, by the sheer possession of intelligence, or by, at least, the possession of an intelligence organisation known to be efficient, a political weapon in his hands when dealing with either actual allies, potential allies, or possible enemies. The Americans were greatly impressed with the N.I.D.'s operational intelligence centre in 1940. Admiral Godfrey, assisted by Ian Fleming, played a central role in wooing the Americans before they came into the war.

He met Roosevelt, having convinced Churchill and the Admiralty that if there was to be intelligence cooperation between Britain and the U.S.A., it would be necessary to reveal to Roosevelt and his intelligence staff British Naval secrets and methods. Godfrey saw this as an informal way of cementing Anglo-American relations and making them more effective allies when they must, eventually, enter the war. He felt a working relationship had to be started as soon as possible. Naval intelligence cooperation provided a common ground—the American and British Naval staffs were linked, via their attaches, by a shrewd diplomatic game played by the N.I.D.

Godfrey was able to convert Colonel William Donovan, the founder of the O.S.S., to N.I.D.'s way of thinking and organisation. In the summer of 1941, Donovan presented to the President his first draft for an intelligence organisation incorporating political warfare, sabotage and guerilla warfare, with a special section inspired by what he had seen of the British commandos.

Intelligence between allies will tend to be two-way, by definition. A strong alliance will yield a free and total transfer of information—Godfrey realised this. When he led the mission to Washington in June 1941, he went with the object in mind of complete cooperation between the N.I.D. and the United States Office of Naval Intelligence (O.N.I.), and not just liaison. Godfrey knew that the American cypher experts had cracked the Japanese signals, and equally important, he realised that with America still neutral, her agents could continue to collect information in enemy-occupied Europe.

He aimed at a free exchange, with no 'trading' in intelligence. There is no doubt that Godfrey's visit was one of the forerunners to formal alliance and the

---

[354] The Slade MMS, Reel 3, National Maritime Museum, Greenwich.

first stage in the process towards allied integrated intelligence, which was to reach its zenith in Eisenhower's Supreme Headquarters Intelligence staff. Indirectly, Godfrey inspired the creation of the O.S.S., from which grew, in 1947, the Central Intelligence Agency (the C.I.A.).

Intelligence which is known to be strong by a possible aggressor may, in itself, deter. Not only is it an insurance against surprise but the knowledge that a nation has an effective warning system must also remove from the enemy's hand an ace card. The fact that accurate intelligence is possessed does not guarantee a particular course of action. At worst, it may be married to a current political viewpoint, or it may be ignored, as with the warnings of the impending attack on Pearl Harbour.

The way in which the political arm uses intelligence, as with any other defence data, is ultimately outside of the direct influence of the military authorities. What a Naval Staff may consider disastrous, either in the form of a political decision, or political change, either of party or policy, cannot gain legitimate or legal expression. The totalitarian states found this to be equally true as the democracies. Naval intelligence and a Naval Staff may see things in far different colours than their political masters. This was nowhere more true than with Raeder's Kriegsmarine.

Raeder knew what the Royal Navy's capabilities were, its roles in a future war, its deployment, and how he could hit it hardest. His intelligence and planners were well-tuned to how the Third Reich could best hit Great Britain at sea: "Britain imported about 50M tons of goods annually and her very existence depended on the keeping open of her overseas supply lines. An effective attack on Britain's overseas supplies therefore had to be the main aim of any German naval building programme.

"For this purpose, we needed powerful surface craft capable of operating in the Atlantic…because of our unfavourable geographical position, and our lack of overseas bases…in addition to submarines and cruisers, task forces consisting of battle cruisers and ordinary cruisers were to be used against Britain's overseas supply lines. In this way, the British Navy would have to provide stronger escorts for convoys than the usual light naval forces which were sufficient protection against submarines and auxiliary cruisers. Powerful ships would have to be used and this would mean that Britain's heavy naval units would be spread out."[355]

---

[355] Grand Admiral Raeder: Struggle for the Sea. p. 127-128.

A sound prognosis, retrospectively, based upon what is now known to have been accurate German Naval intelligence data. What Raeder quickly discovered was that his plan for attacking the Royal Navy would have to fit into Hitler's time scale and his wider conceptions and plans for a war in the west. As such, Raeder's intelligence and short and long-term plans, would be thrown to the winds—the type of data which previously had enabled Raeder to soundly advise Hitler and von Ribbentrop on the terms of the Anglo-German Naval Agreement, was ignored.

"I was never drawn into matters of home or foreign policy except when the interests of the Navy were directly concerned, and not always then, as in 1939 when relations with Britain became critical."[356] Raeder's plans for independent naval air power,[357] and his timing for a naval war against Britain, in terms of the German building program (1945 or 1946 certainly not 1939)[358] were ignored. The sound reasoning, derived from some basic, but accurate and very relevant, intelligence, about Britain's naval capabilities, and probable policy, were considered irrelevant by Hitler.

For the senior officer, and particularly the head of an intelligence organisation, such as the N.I.D., bad political decisions must pose the great problem of keeping themselves and the service clear of all political disputes and upheavals, yet at the same time keeping the service going along lines which might be totally anathema to them. At worst, therefore, the Armed Services, with their own knowledge, must be party, constitutionally, to a policy which may prove to be completely detrimental to the interests of the state.

In a system of alliances, the worst aspects of bad political—military decision-making may be avoided. Intelligence can stand on its own, in Godfrey's phrase "…to resist temptation of allowing the truth to be bent by what people would like to hear of what fits in with a policy to which we are committed or a pet project…"[359] The strength of an allied intelligence committee, or many other committees for that matter, lay in its ability to withstand brow-beating and hierarchical pressures (perhaps stemming from the rank structure of the services

---

[356] Ibid. p. 98.
[357] Ibid. p. 89-90.
[358] Ibid. p. 124-126.
[359] Memoirs of Admiral J. H. Godfrey MS 66/104, Vol. 5. Part I. p. 40, The National Maritime Museum, Greenwich.

and the need to obey senior officers) and to maintain therefore in the critical atmosphere of a group of intelligent men an independent viewpoint.

On the topic of Allied intelligence cooperation in World War II, one distinguished intelligence worker, the American Allen Dulles, has written: "On the Allied side, in opposition to the common enemy, there was a collaboration between intelligence services that is without parallel in history and which had a most welcome outcome."[360] John Godfrey was the architect of this. As early as January 1939, he had visited the French D.N.I., Admiral de Villaire, and both had agreed to exchange information about intelligence centres abroad and to devise a simple method of communication.

Godfrey writes: "We were both naturally interested in the movements of German, Italian and Japanese men-of-war and merchant ships. This involved revealing to the French our reporting system in foreign ports—a system of which they must have been conscious for many years."[361] Other emissaries which Godfrey sent from the N.I.D. were equally successful, particularly at convincing the Americans.

Godfrey has this to say about the genius of the U-boat tracking room, Roger Winn, whom he sent to the United States: "So successful was he that it seemed only natural, when the United States became an ally, that he should go to Washington to induce the American Navy to adopt an organisation similar to ours. This he did with remarkable success. He had the redoubtable Ernie King eating out of his hand, and was actually asked by King to go to New York to persuade the American Admiral there to fall in with our ideas. This mission he also brought to a successful conclusion."[362]

Just as in World War I, when most of the results of Room 40's work were conveyed to the French, Russians and Italians, so too in World War II the interchange of intelligence had a strong binding political force. Churchill, for instance, was well aware of the need to exchange intelligence—he knew the Americans could provide Britain with timely data, and vice-versa.

He writes: "From the end of 1940, the Americans had pierced the vital Japanese cyphers, and were decoding large numbers of their military and diplomatic telegrams. In the secret American circles, they were referred to as

---

[360] Allen Dulles: The Craft of Intelligence, p. 34.
[361] Memoirs of Admiral J. H. Godfrey. MSS 66/104. Vol. 5. Part I. p. 15, the National Maritime Museum, Greenwich.
[362] Ibid. p. 12.

'magics'. The 'magics' were repeated to us, but there was an inevitable delay—sometimes of two or three days—before we got them. We did not know therefore at any given moment all that the President or Mr Hull knew. I made no complaint of this."[363] Fortunately for the United States and Great Britain, the U.S. Navy and Army had studied the problems of cryptanalysis since the late 1920s, with particular emphasis on Japan.

By 1941, the year of Pearl Harbour, the important Japanese naval and diplomatic codes and cyphers had been broken. As a result, the U.S.N. and later the Intelligence Staff of Admiral Mountbatten's S.E. Asian Command, Colonel Lamplough, Chief Staff Officer, Intelligence; formerly O.-I.-C. the Far Eastern Section in the N.I.D., and D.D.N.I. (foreign),[364] and the intelligence staff of the British Pacific Fleet, formed much later in the war, were frequently in possession of evidence of imminent Japanese action in the Pacific theatre before it took place. Intelligence cooperation called for a mutual trust and confidence which was, by the very nature of the task and material used, fully demanding and binding on the Anglo-American alliance.

Naval Intelligence and Politics in the Inter-War Period

Before a more detailed analysis is made of specific items regarding political-military decisions and intelligence, it is important that the position, role and work of the N.I.D. in the crucial inter-war period (as they apply to political questions) are now made clear, in addition to what has been said earlier on the general growth of naval intelligence.

Naval intelligence, like every other aspect of defence from the late twenties to the late '30s, suffered from the axe of economy, wielded arbitrarily in the face of principles which had traditionally governed British foreign and defence policies. The contrast with the pre-1914 eras is marked in the extreme. The warnings of men such as Churchill and Hankey, and indeed a forthright First Sea Lord himself, Chatfield, were drowned in a sea of vacillation and military half-measures.

In the atmosphere which prevailed, where politicians were prone to moralise rather than to take actions, which although painful, were absolutely vital in a world going slowly mad, an organisation such as the N.I.D., already decimated

---

[363] W. S. Churchill: The Second World War. Vol. 3. p. 532-533.
[364] Godfrey, p. 14.

after World War I, could not hope to influence until it both possessed the machinery and also until the need for thorough intelligence had been fully accepted by those in power. The Staff College teaching appears to have been intellectually lethargic and largely irrelevant—nothing concrete seems to have merged from the courses, and cooperation between the various Naval staff departments never materialised.[365]

In 1934, the D.N.I., Rear-Admiral Dickens, suggested joint appreciations between Plans and the N.I.D. (Godfrey was D.D. Plans, and Captain G. A. Scott D.D.N.I. at the time), but the whole matter was dropped. The tenor of Godfrey's memoirs for the 1930s is that the Naval Staff just did not wish to be over-concerned with intelligence, insofar as any data which might challenge current political appreciations and naval strategy would not be handled effectively by Downing Street or the Foreign Office. This was particularly true over possible German treachery regarding the Anglo-German Naval Agreement.[366]

The N.I.D. was a backwater, until the real threat of a war shook everyone into action.[367] It was not until the founding of the O.I.C. that the N.I.D. came to play a real role.[368] The N.I.D. prepared, for instance, under Captain John

---

[365] This is certainly the overall impression left by Godfrey's remarks on the Naval Staff College teaching in the inter-war period in several of the volumes of his unpublished Memoirs.

[366] On 23 December 1936, Captain Troubridge, the Naval Attaché in Berlin, sent his annual report to the Foreign Office, via his ambassador, Sir E. Phipps, who submitted Troubridge's work as an enclosure to his own report to Mr Eden, dated 12 January 1937. The D.N.I. and the C.-in-C. Home Fleet received Troubridge's original report (he sent them individual copies), in which he said: "The Anglo-German Naval Agreement was one of the master strokes of policy which has characterised Germany's dealings with her ex-enemies since the war. When the time is ripe, as history shows, it will unquestionably go to the same way as other agreements: but the time is not yet."
Phipps may well have thought that his naval subordinate had overstretched himself and should keep to naval matters, but whatever the reason, he omitted, what in retrospect, were vital comments from Troubridge's report to the Foreign Office. He may surely have been right to censure Troubridge's report. This would not have precluded Phipps drawing the same conclusions and including them in his own report. See Cab. 357/18.

[367] As far as the N.I.D. was concerned, this was confirmed in a conversation with Vice-Admiral Sir N. E. Denning, KBE, CB, on 11 August 1971.

[368] Captain Clayton's team in the O.I.C. was first class. From early on, they plotted enemy submarines, surface craft, and merchant ships. The consular shipping officers in

Creswell's direction, Convoy Instructions and handbooks for Merchant Navy masters and officers in 1937/1938, in keeping with the C.I.D.'s Defence of Trade Report, 2 December 1937. Unfortunately, none of the former documents seem to have survived.[369] Even so, it was too late to re-dress certain failures and deficiencies, the most serious of all being the failure to continue the great work of Room 40's cryptanalysts.[370]

In 1939, Britain did not possess any of the crucial German naval codes. There had been major failures pre-1914,[371] but none can really compare with the paucity of knowledge about German naval codes in 1939.[372]

In light of World War II, the meagre and low-quality intelligence the N.I.D. produced in the inter-war period, certainly pre-1936/1937, had, in any event, little influence upon naval policy, and certainly none at all upon higher defence planning and foreign policy. The last two years of peace, and then the immediate need for operational intelligence when war came, witnessed an unprecedented expansion of the N.I.D. Nothing like it had occurred before, even in the halcyon days of Admiral Hall. Reports began to flow,[373] organisation was expanded, and

---

the ports throughout the world reported details of ships to the N.I.D.—time of departure, destination, possible course, cargo, ship capabilities, weapons, and so on. Hence, the success of the blockade very early on in World War II. In 1945, the O.I.C. War Diary was destroyed, on Admiralty orders—this emerged in conversation with Captain S.W. Roskill on 7 July 1971.

[369] This was confirmed by Captain Roskill.

[370] See Adm. 116/3637—intelligence deficiencies revealed in the 1938 crisis.

[371] HF/DF was still in its infancy in 1914. However, it was rapidly developed, in conjunction with high quality cryptanalysis. In 1914, there were no real plans for a detailed convoy system, and convoy tactics—Hankey had to force this upon the Admiralty, and no work had been done on the use of asdic, or the use of air, sea and shore sightings in the hunt for U-boats.

[372] This statement was fully endorsed in conversation with both Admiral Denning and Captain Roskill.

[373] See, for example, Adm. 1/9552—N.I.D. report. Combined Operations exercises, 5/6 I 1938.

thought given to the intelligence requirements war would bring,[374] and staff recruitment was expanded.[375]

Furthermore, technical intelligence and liaison within N.I.D. mushroomed[376] and N.I.D. concern over any leakage of data, at whatever level, became acute,[377] and with this came an intensification of naval security and the inevitable censorship which total war demanded.[378]

All of these moves reflect the demands of a coming war. They also show, relatively speaking, how inactive the N.I.D. had been for many years. For the first time, since Hall's day, the N.I.D. was being consulted over Fleet dispositions.[379] The documents speak of a new zest, a feeling of purpose, and of the development of an elan, so patently lacking for years, within the N.I.D. The data began to pour in, in a manner and from sources reminiscent of World War I. There were some early bulls scored by the N.I.D.[380] Intelligence rapidly had operational successes.[381]

---

[374] See Adm. 1/10212, N.I.D. 0827/1939—the new intelligence organisation for the Mediterranean station. Adm. 1/10220, N.I.D. 0397/1939, N.I.D. reporting and control work in South America; Adm. 1/10214, N.I.D. 0810/1939—possibility of N.I.D. establishing coast-watching and intelligence organisation in Eire. With war imminent, these documents reflect the rush to fill large and obvious gaps.

[375] See Adm. 1/9679, N.I.D. 001148/1939—officers employed on operational intelligence.

[376] See as good examples of the score of areas N.I.D. began to investigate: Adm. 1/10222, N.I.D. 02258/1939—the use by German submarines of a sonoperophon; Adm. 1/10176, N.I.D. 02137/1939—N.I.D. investigation into the possible use of midget submarines; and Adm. 1/9741, N.I.D. 2057/1938—magnetic telephones in U.S. ships.

[377] See for example, Adm. 1/10227, N.I.D. 00894/1939—Anglo-German Naval Conference; Singapore—leakage of information.

[378] See Adm. 1/10217, N.I.D. 0219/1939—censorship of telephone calls from the Forth and the Clyde areas to Ireland; Adm. 1/10066, N.I.D. 01897/1939, N.I.D.'s proposed censorship of outgoing neutral mails.

[379] See, for example, Adm. 1/9922, initial dispositions of the Mediterranean Fleet in the event of war.

[380] See Adm. 1/10228, N.I.D. 3844/1939—a report of an interview between Field Marshall H. Goring and the Swedish Captain C. Florman; this came via Stockholm on 3 November 1939 to Rear-Admiral H. Boyes, the Attaché in Oslo, to the N.I.D.; and Adm. 1/10958, N.I.D. 4500/1940, N.I.D. interrogation of the crew of the German SS Schoke.

[381] Adm. 1/9759, N.I.D. 02356/1939, intelligence regarding the Battle of the River Plate and the German Battle Cruiser Admiral Graf Spee's refuge in Montevideo Harbour.

N.I.D. began to exert an influence on all aspects of naval planning and operations, as well as numerous joint service committees and organisations. In 1938, a joint Service Committee was set up to work out an amphibious warfare doctrine, and the types of landing craft that would be needed. At this time, amphibious operations were still undeveloped; the N.I.D. had given no thought to them pre-1938.

The spectre of the Dardanelles and the possible use of air power to defeat such operations still hung such operations N.I.D. helped in the formulation of a doctrine,[382] and an Inter-Service Training and Development Centre (I.S.T.D.C.), led by Rear-Admiral I.E.H. Maund, conducted a number of trial assaults, as well as lecturing to the staff colleges and senior officers' courses at Greenwich. Tenders were put out for the design and construction of the various types of craft needed.

N.I.D. played no small part in the development of amphibious warfare, just as it did in the founding of organisations such as the Future Operations Enemy Section (F.O.E.S.) on 1 January 1941. This sprang from the dearth of enemy intelligence after western Europe was overrun in the summer of 1940. This was a joint service body with additional representation from the Foreign Office and the Ministry of Economic Warfare (M.E.W.). One of its first tasks was to provide a forecast from the German point of view of their strategy for the spring of 1941.

F.O.E.S. was later replaced by the Advanced Planning Enemy Section (A.P.E.S.), consisting of the same members, in which N.I.D. had a considerable stake.

Such then was the pace of change within the N.I.D. as crisis after crisis brewed in Europe and war finally came. Naval intelligence emerged from the wilderness to reassert itself, but in a dominantly operational, rather than political-military, or quasi-political way. Fortunately for the Allied cause, Nazi intelligence was following a diametrically opposed course to the N.I.D.'s.

---

[382] In 1938, the doctrine consisted of achieving tactical surprise by small, fast landing craft, landed far off-shore, at night or at dawn, to take and keep a beachhead, to be reinforced by larger L.C.s, artillery and tanks, so as to secure the hinterland, followed by a steady build-up from ships coming close inshore. There was no mention of air cover or naval gunfire support.

Chapter Seven
Naval Intelligence and Specific Political Decisions

It is now commonplace for governments to be greatly dependent upon their intelligence agencies for the supply of data and appreciation to assist them in the formulation of foreign policy and the contingencies this creates for defence planning. One of the most marked contrasts between the N.I.D. of the pre-1919 era and that of the inter-war period is the great influence the former had upon high-level policy-making in the Admiralty, C.I.D., and the Cabinet, and the almost non-existent influence it wielded during the period of peace, appeasement, and the prelude to war. Let us examine this contention in detail.

Foreign Policy, Strategy and Naval Intelligence Pre-1914

Successive D.N.I.s and their staffs from Custance (D.N.I. 1899-1902) until 1919 had a primary role in British policy-making. In 1901, on the question of a Russian threat to the Mediterranean, Custance argued to the First Lord and the First Sea Lord that Britain would have to reconcile herself to facing the Russian Black Sea Fleet in the Mediterranean, rather than blockading the Straits, in order to maintain the route to India. In a memorandum of 21 March 1901, which reached Cabinet level, he wrote: "Great Britain alone, with France actively hostile or even doubtful, cannot at the present time prevent a Russian occupation of Constantinople and the Dardanelles."[383]

Custance also firmly believed that Austria and Italy would assist Britain against Russia, since they had a mutual interest in ensuring the Russians did not

---
[383] Adm. 116/866B.

occupy Constantinople.[384] At the same time as giving Fisher all manner of data and advice as his right-hand man on the emergent Naval Staff,[385] Custance gave Selborne, the First Lord, data for the report he had to submit to the Cabinet with regard to naval policy in the Far East and the implications of an Anglo-Japanese Alliance (1902).

Selborne, along with Fisher, and Custance, and then Battenburg, were able to put up a strong case for the end of isolation and an Anglo-Japanese Alliance, insofar as it would prevent Britain from being outnumbered in battleship strength in the Far East.[386] Nothing is more indicative than the Anglo-Japanese Alliance of the influence of the N.I.D. during these years.

The N.I.D. became deeply involved in British policy towards Morocco. In 1902, the Foreign Office became concerned over the possibility of a German naval base at Tangiers. Neither Battenburg, or his opposite number in the Army, Sir William Nicholson, the D.M.I., were alarmed.

With considerable astuteness, and influence, Battenburg wrote the Foreign Office: "It would seem to be advantageous to this country that Germany should have an interest in the Fez-Tangier section of the railway, because she would act as a counterpoise to France and, as against ourselves, her position there would

---

[384] This point was to be successfully argued by later D.N.I.s until the international situation changed. On 7 February 1903, the D.N.I., Prince Louis of Battenburg, (D.N.I. 1902-1905) argued to the C.I.D. that whether Russia had control of the Straits or whether she had not, she could not hope "to effect anything serious, be it in Egypt or elsewhere, until her fleet has fought and beaten our fleet." Battenburg's conclusions were unanimously accepted and passed on to the Cabinet. Cab. 2/1 2B.

[385] For example, when Fisher required to know what would be involved in the defence of Gibraltar should Spain become hostile, he turned to his D.N.I. for full details, and a plan. Custance furnished it based on 10,000 troops. Adm. 1/7516.

[386] The great fear for the Admiralty in 1902, as indeed in the 1930s, was the problem of providing reinforcements in the Far East at the expense of the forces in European waters. An Anglo-Japanese combination would, by contrast, have a superiority of eleven to nine and might even allow Britain to strengthen her home fleets. See Z. S. Steiner: Great Britain and the Creation of the Anglo-Japanese Alliance. Journal of Modern History. No. 31 (1959).

be weak because we should be between her force in the North Sea and any detachment she might have in the Straits of Gibraltar."[387]

During the Moroccan crisis, April-December 1905, the D.N.I. Ottley (1905-1907) is still seen to be as influential, although he has changed tack. On 1 May 1905, he told Fisher that he was basing his strategic plans upon the expectation that when peace came to be discussed, there would be a confrontation between Britain and Japan on the one side, and Russia, Germany, and France on the other. D.N.I. believed that Britain could well find herself at war with the three continental powers by August.

Lansdowne allowed neither the fear of this nor the complications of the Moroccan crisis to deter him from pursuit of a renewed Japanese alliance.[388] On the question of German intentions and interests on the Moroccan coast, Ottley wrote to the Foreign Office on 10 May 1905: "What Germany wants is coaling stations and undoubtedly our interest is to oppose tooth and nail any such stations being acquired by her. The French should be told that we will support them to the last extremity in resisting any such demands."[389]

The Japanese alliance was concluded in April-May 1905. The Foreign Office consulted both the C.I.D. and the N.I.D. on the naval implications. At the 70th meeting of the C.I.D. on 12 April 1905, Ottley said that if the treaty became operative against one power only, Russia would be discouraged from re-building her fleet to try her hand against Japan a second time. She might be able to out-build Japan; but if she knew that Britain would come in against her in any case, she could well decide that competition was hopeless.[390]

The N.I.D., through its head, had a direct influence upon almost every major political-military decision affecting the Royal Navy or with maritime

---

[387] 28 October 1902. F.O. 99/400. In a memorandum of 7 August 1903, Prince Louis further condemned Lansdowne's Moroccan proposals: "An agreement which would leave the future fate of Morocco in the hands of France and Spain alone is not one which this country could contemplate with indifference, nor could the removal of subjects of dispute between France and England in other parts of the world, as is held out by M. Delcasse, be considered as compensation."

[388] <u>Lansdowne, Fifth Marquess of</u>: b. 1845; Lord of the Treasury 1869-1872; Under-Secretary for War 1872-1874; Under-Secretary for India 1880; Governor-General of Canada 1883-1888; Governor-General of India 1888-1893; Secretary for War 1895-1900; Foreign Secretary, 1900-1905.

[389] F.O. 64/1630.

[390] Cab. 2/1.

implications for the nation, pre-1914. For example, from 1903/1904 onwards, the N.I.D. furnished the C.I.D. with ideas and plans regarding a possible invasion threat. On 31 March 1903, and later that year, on 14 July, the D.N.I., Battenburg, submitted to the C.I.D. papers in which he said the Navy alone could resist invasion.

He demonstrated how—even if the battle fleet was defeated, or away from home waters—Britain's enormous superiority in cruisers and torpedo boats would be sufficient to do this.[391] The N.I.D. made no concessions to the Army, (somewhat ironic in view of the Admiralty's later failure to enforce a maritime strategy on the Cabinet before World War I began). In a memorandum of 1 July 1903, the N.I.D. refuted the Army's point that a force of ninety thousand men was needed at home to resist invasion.[392] C.I.D.'s deliberations on measures to deal with possible invasion always contained well-demonstrated and reasoned evidence from the N.I.D.[393]

Whether it was in the preparation of plans for combined naval and military operations in the event of certain hypothetical war situations, such as those surmised in 1905,[394] or the many plans prepared between 1902-1912 for the protection of ocean trade in war,[395] the N.I.D.'s involvement in C.I.D. business was direct and influential. There can be no doubt that the era of Custance, Battenburg, Ottley, King-Hall and Slade (1899-1909) was unique in N.I.D.'s pre-1945 history, in terms of its active and fertile influence on naval and foreign affairs.

Slade's tenureship bears careful study: he was a brilliant and sophisticated D.N.I. His contingency plans for blockading Germany and the treatment of neutrals and contraband were fully endorsed by the C.I.D. and the Cabinet, as was his paper dealing with possible attacks on Imperial territories. His conclusion on such a threat was: "Against a properly organised defence, based on adequate cruiser squadrons, Germany can do nothing, unless she dispatches regular men-of-war from her home ports to support her vessels in distant waters, and this it is the function of the Home Fleet to prevent."[396]

---

[391] Cab. 3/1, 11A, 16A.

[392] Cab. 31, 14A

[393] See Cab. 17/22—C.I.D. plans for the defence of the United Kingdom.

[394] See Cab. 17.5.

[395] Cab. 17/3.

[396] Slade MSS, Reel 3, p. 7, National Maritime Museum.

On the question of German naval commitments in the Baltic, he told his political masters with dead accuracy: "The amount so held to the Baltic would not in any case be more than would be demanded by a strictly defensive attitude, and, until Russia has restored her Navy, would probably consist merely of some of the older battleships and the flotillas allocated to that coast."[397]

Similarly, he pressed home to the First Lord, First Sea Lord, and the C.I.D. the factors involved in a trade war in distant waters: "Now no increase in the number of battleships and no victories in the North Sea will save us from the danger which threatens our trade in distant waters. Our very existence depends upon, not only the maintenance, but also the increase of this trade in war, and if it is neglected, we should fall more certainly than if we lose in battle."[398]

On every issue the N.I.D. made major contributions—the strategy necessary for a possible war against the United States, the formation of an Australian Defence Force, the impact of wireless telegraphy on naval strategy and tactics, the defence of commerce and so on, and along with the routine analyses the department made—German cruiser strengths, or a breakdown of the manoeuvres of July 1908, or the implications of German possession of the Baltic. On the latter issue, Slade wrote the First Sea Lord:

"…so we may succeed in stopping their trade in the North Sea and in causing damage and loss on the northern coasts, but as long as Germany has the exit from the Baltic open to her and closed to us, which would be the case if we did not attempt to force our way into that sea, she may refuse to listen to overtures of peace until we bring further pressure to bear."[399]

N.I.D.'s influence on operational policy was pronounced—in October 1908, for example, German cruisers were patrolling off the southeast coast of South America. N.I.D. convinced the C.I.D. and the Cabinet this might constitute a possible threat to British trade. British cruisers took up station there until the German presence ceased.

Foreign Policy, Strategy and Naval Intelligence 1914-1939

It is difficult to establish causal relationships between intelligence and policy-making in peacetime. In wartime, when operational intelligence is at a

---

[397] Slade MSS, Reel 3, p. 7, National Maritime Museum.
[398] Ibid.
[399] Slade MSS, Reel 3, p. 7, National Maritime Museum.

premium, real measures of effectiveness and influence are available. In the period 1919/1920-1936, there is virtually no evidence indicating any such relationships between naval intelligence and politico-military decision-making, especially on the issue of foreign affairs. During the classical period of inter-war peace, epitomised by the Ten-Year Rule, not only was the N.I.D. run down to a painfully low level, so as to be virtually ineffective, but also all defence bodies were obviously finding it difficult to make assessments of possible targets.

The pre-1914 routine analyses ceased—peace meant far more between 1919-1931 than it had pre-1914. The significance of intelligence was forgotten, not ignored. There was nothing wilful, or necessarily incompetent in this. Only hindsight allowed Admiral Rufus L. Taylor to write in 1960: "We cannot afford the luxury of leaders who do not understand the business of getting information of the enemy. We must be sure that our educational system for high command does not permit an officer to reach such command without having demonstrated a thorough knowledge of intelligence."[400]

The Foreign Office's post-war attitude to the N.I.D. was natural enough, it was neither politically loaded or insidious. In retrospect, of course, it was tragic, knowing what we do of the '30s, of the absence of machinery and personnel to collect, process and disseminate data to those who made policy. The Naval Staff College's work in the '20s illustrates the profound absence within the Admiralty and defence staff as a whole of concrete objective.[401] [402] It is not surprising, therefore, that intelligence was relegated from the prime position within the naval hierarchy to that of a poor relation.

In theory, it ought to have provided the basis for all serious analysis and planning,[403] merely proving that institutions, however valuable, and well-tried,

---

[400] Admiral Rufus L. Taylor: Command and the Intelligence Process: United States Naval Institute Proceedings. August 1960. p. 27-39.

[401] See p. 347.

[402] See also Cab. 53/14 no. 125. Report by the Commandant of the first session of the Imperial Defence College, January-December 1927. Intelligence was not discussed, in terms of its role in higher defence planning.

[403] As late as 1957, two American scholars, John W. Masland and Lawrence I. Redway, were able to write in their 'Soldiers and Statesmen' (Princeton University Press, 1957), about higher military training in the United States; "study of the full relationship of intelligence to security is neglected in the War Colleges." p. 389. This comment is even more ironic, in terms of the American experience, in the light of the Report of the War

will survive in the naval hierarchy only unless strong action to preserve continuity in all spheres is taken.

The organisation of defence itself, centred on the C.I.D., the new C.D.S. and their sub-committees, particularly the Joint Planning Sub-Committee—this, with the other factors, shifted the balance away from intelligence. It may be argued too that intelligence was in any case badly managed—that N.I.D. never sold itself, or tried to evaluate the effectiveness of intelligence in terms of feedback from the Naval Staff and the Fleet. This point will bear review shortly.

The high period of appeasement witnessed a classic case of intelligence failure—to be the unsleeping hammer of the sleeping, to keep working as a result of its own conviction that it has certain incontrovertible facts that must challenge national policy. It is now appropriate to be aware of the policy and atmosphere in which naval intelligence had to operate during those vital four years.

There were those, such as Eden and Churchill, who favoured re-armament in the light of Italian aggression in the Mediterranean and the Red Sea, Japanese aggression in the Far East, and the growing menace of Germany, indicated by the re-occupation of the Rhineland, re-armament, denunciation of the European status quo, and the failure of the League of Nations to contain the Spanish Civil War. [404] Eden for one argued that British re-armament would help the unemployment problem. [405] The 1935 White paper on re-armament revealed

---

Department Military Education Board on an Educational System for officers of the Army—Washington, D.C., 1946. This report had recommended the establishment of an 'Intelligence School'. The parallels with Britain in the '20s and '30s are striking.

[404] On 9 March, 1935, Germany announced the formation of the Luftwaffe, forbidden by the Treaty of Versailles. On 16 March, compulsory military service was introduced. The 1935 warnings of the British ambassador in Berlin, Sir Horace Rumbold, of the growing Nazi evil, were ignored by the Baldwin government. They now read like accurate prophecies of doom. Hitler had also given £43m. aid to Franco. In the autumn of 1936, ten thousand German troops arrived in Spain. On 31 May 1937, Italy and Germany walked out of the naval talks on non-intervention in the Mediterranean. Italian attacks on English merchantmen continues.

[405] In 1937, there were one and a half million unemployed in Britain. Certainly, the defence budget was greatly increased from 1936-1939, as these figures show:
   1936: £188M.
   1937: £280M.
   1939: £700M.

Baldwin's pacifism, dominated as it was by inaccurate platitudes, such as "the bomber will always get through."

In July 1936, a deputation from the Lords and Commons visited Baldwin and pleaded for an increase in defence expenditure. They made no real impression. Chamberlain was even more emotionally oriented—"all the savings of the old and young wasted in war, a simple philosophy based on the notion that arms cost money, which is a waste, they lead to war, which is bad, and this cannot be tolerated."[406]

In June 1937, Hitler issued his directive, Operation Green, for aggression in the east, and on 5 November 1937, in the now infamous Hossbach Memorandum, to which Admiral Raeder was a signatory, Hitler issued his plans for aggression in the west. On 19 November 1937, Halifax visited Berchtesgaden to propagate Chamberlain's policy of peaceful evolution. In the same month, after a warning from Eden in the Commons, Chamberlain advised him to "go home and take an aspirin."

Intelligence failed in general to penetrate or piece together the weighty evidence indicating German war plans. On the naval side, the N.I.D. remained blissfully ignorant of the major developments (other than from the attachés' reports). The Edens, Churchills and Duff Coopers were totally unaware of the

---

It was not known at the time that when Germany went to war in 1939, her margin of strength was, on paper at any rate, very much less than seemed to be the case at the time. There was certainly an assumption in Bri of Germany's overwhelming strength because of Hitler's tremendous propagandist boastings about his power, and partly because his violent diplomacy suggested confidence based on strength, and this seemed to be confirmed by brilliant German victories in 1939 and 1940. Germany's limitations and deficiencies only became public knowledge in the official survey conducted by the British and American economists immediately after the war.

It was discovered, for example, that her aircraft production in the autumn of 1939 had been about six hundred seventy-five per month, no more than that of Britain; her tank production was less, and she had started the war with only three months' supply of aviation fuel. She had to treble her output of armaments and munitions after February 1942, to meet the demands of war with Russia and America. All these facts merely prove that in 1939 and 1940, Hitler took a calculated risk which brilliantly succeeded, even though he miscalculated later. In Britain, there was no such data on the Third Reich's industrial capability.

[406] See Keith Feiling's 'Life of Neville Chamberlain' for a detailed appraisal of the background and rationale to Chamberlain's appeasement.

real magnitude of Hitler's intentions and planning.[407] British public opinion was strongly pacifist—Churchill's argument that Britain should say that she will fight if the Czechs fight (because otherwise the Germans will gamble on Britain not helping the Czechs and they will take the risk) fell on deaf ears.

Furthermore, there would have been little support for independent French action over the re-occupation of the Rhineland, the Anschluss or Czechoslovakia. Collective security and the naval applications of a blockade and sanctions against Spain, and Italy in Abyssinia, failed. Why then had there been an almost complete breakdown in intelligence in the Admiralty to present the C.I.D. and government with their view of the naval intentions of the major aggressors and how this fitted to the overall position?

At this point, it is imperative to emphasise that it is not the intention here to make comments on what 'might have been'. Indeed, it can be soundly argued, that, however more active and influential the N.I.D. and the other intelligence bodies might have been, there could not have been, and can never be, any guarantee that politicians will make the sort of decisions only uninhibited hindsight interpretations permit. It is surely probable that Chamberlain would have been undeterred.

Whether one examines C.I.D. papers, such as Cab. 16/153—Foreign Policy and defence, 1936, or a speech of Chamberlain's on 24 March 1938, following the Anschluss on the 12 March, in which he said: "Where war and peace are concerned, legal obligations are not alone involved," the major factor emerges of the personal convictions of politicians. In 1775, Edmund Burke wrote: "The concessions of the weak are the concessions of fear."

Chamberlain would have stoutly refuted this, in the Munich context, just as he did Duff Cooper's resignation speech in the House of Commons on 3 October 1938, following Munich: "It was not for Serbia that we fought in 1914. It was not even for Belgium, although it occasionally suited some people to say so. We were fighting then, as we should have been fighting last week, in order that one great power should not be allowed in disregard of treaty obligations, of the laws

---

[407] That he was planning on 'lightning action after an incident' in Czechoslovakia, or Hitler's directive of 30 May 1938, calling for that country's eradication. (D.G.F.P. Vol. 2, no. 221). See the Diplomatic Diaries of Oliver Harvey, 1937-1940, ed. by John Harvey, Collins, 1970, for conclusive evidence of how little the British government knew of German intentions and capabilities. The so-called warmongers made their deductions on fairly conclusive, but very basic, prima facie evidence.

of nations, and decrees of morality, to dominate by brutal force the continent of Europe…for that principle we must ever be prepared to fight, for the day when we are not prepared to fight for it we forfeit Empire, our liberties, and our independence."

Duff Cooper and Chamberlain represent two diametrically opposed views. The question, would better intelligence have altered things, remains an open, speculative question. Questions, such as should Britain have fought in 1938, assuming better intelligence, are more meaningful. Intelligence would have shown that in certain weapon systems and training Germany was two to three years ahead of Britain. However, Britain would have had the initiative and the resources of Czechoslovakia and Russia. Intelligence would have stressed too the significance of a war on two fronts for Hitler in 1938, at a time when his high command was worried and divided over his plans.

Excellent intelligence would have observed a few cold feet. The Third Reich was to benefit more than the Allies from the Munich 'breathing space'.

In the post-World War I period, there was neither the intelligence machinery nor the personnel, other than the attachés and a small headquarters N.I.D. staff to provide the C.I.D. and the Cabinet with detailed intelligence—there was a blithe obliviousness to the value of intelligence in peacetime. As a result of this, intelligence never became strong enough to reassert itself.

The Chiefs of Staff structure excluded the significant role intelligence ought to have played. C.O.S., and then the C.I.D., and ultimately the Cabinet, came to place great dependence on the Joint Planning Sub-Committee (J.P.C.) of the Chiefs of Staff, and the three individual Service Planning Staffs. Naval Plans, in one sense through no fault of its own, gained an unwarranted primacy, since it made plans for the Naval Staff on the flimsiest of intelligence data, or no intelligence at all.[408]

Above all else was the attitude and morale of the Naval Staff generally—it was far from healthy. It was as if the N.I.D. had served its function of bearing the infant Naval Staff pre-1914, had done sterling work during the Great War

---

[408] Admiral Godfrey wrote in his Memoirs: "Plans was concerned with policy-making, with the future, with strategy, and its effect on bases, depots, stores and administration, with logistics (a new word borrowed from the USA) and with the naval aspect of international affairs, treaties and agreements. At a time when we were re-orientating our policy after the Kaiser war, and the abrogation of the Anglo-Japanese alliance, Plans Division had a finger in every pie." Vol. 3. p. 7.

and now, during a period of prolonged peace in a world that could not possibly contemplate total war again, it could safely be put out to graze, and be quietly forgotten.

In the period before the foundation of the Joint Intelligence Committee (J.I.C.), and the resurgence of 'operational' intelligence within the N.I.D. itself, the J.P.C. had the lion's say in every major defence issue when C.O.S. called for advice, data, or a second opinion, (as well, of course, as making plans). An examination of the records from 1926 to 1938 fully supports this view. A review of some of these will illustrate the point.

In June 1927, the C.O.S. called for data regarding the Defence of the Suez Canal, and in October the factors involved in the defence of Hong Kong, with emphasis on the possibility of a Japanese attack. The J.P.C. and the Services' Planning Staffs were consulted. N.I.D. was not consulted.[409] This pattern continued for the next decade. In October 1936, C.O.S. was required to produce an overall appraisal in the event of war with Germany in 1939. In December of the same year, C.O.S. produced for the C.I.D. a report of the implications for sea-borne trade of a war with Germany (it dealt with the types, areas, and scales of possible German attacks, and defence measures).

The work for this was done through the J.P.C. No intelligence evaluations were used.[410] Not surprisingly, the 1936 report of the Commandant of the Imperial Defence College makes no mention of intelligence. Its use was not discussed during the course.[411] However, by late 1936, the tide began to turn. C.O.S. awoke to the value of intelligence. In a report of the 5 January 1937, 'Appreciations of the Situation in the event of war with Germany', the Chiefs of Staff stated quite clearly in recommendation no. 55:

"We draw attention, however, to the 15th and 16th recommendations above, where we point out the need for intelligence arrangements by the appropriate organisations, and we recommend that the Joint Intelligence Sub-Committee and the Sub-Committee on Industrial Intelligence in foreign countries should review the intelligence arrangements for the contingency of war with Germany." (Recommendation no. 15 emphasised the need for air reconnaissance of the North Sea).[412]

---

[409] Cab. 53/14, nos. 101, 117.

[410] See Cab. 53/29, nos. 513, 535.

[411] See Cab. 53/29, no. 539.

[412] Cab. 53/29, no. 540.

Although this document shows the incredibly limited perspective the C.O.S. had of intelligence, it nonetheless helped initiate the swing towards operational intelligence as the sands of time were running out in Europe. By 25 October 1938, the swing was complete. In a signed memorandum headed, 'Revision of Appreciations', the three members of the Joint Planning Sub-Committee submitted (somewhat ironically in view of the previous twelve years) to the C.O.S. among several recommendations on the issue of intelligence, the following points: paragraph 8:

"In order to obtain an agreed political setting, we suggest that the Joint Intelligence Sub-Committee should be instructed to produce a forecast of the political setting in April 1939, in collaboration with the Foreign Office;" paragraph 9: "In addition, we suggest that the Joint Intelligence Sub-Committee should again examine the strength of all the Powers included in the political setting, and prepare a comparative statement of their forces they could maintain in war. Signed V. H. Danckwerts, J. N. Kennedy, J. C. Slessor."[413]

The die was cast. The J.I.C. began to play a role similar to the pre-1914 N.I.D.[414] How every D.N.I. from Custance to Hall would have agreed with Troup and Godfrey that the J.I.C. should have existed when all the momentous decisions of the '20s and '30s were made. There was no Lord Charles Beresford to raise questions on naval policy, whether it was the Singapore naval base, or the use of air power, or the vulnerability of capital ships to air attack.

In the '30s, the Naval Staff placed their faith in the development of asdic, and seemed to believe that the terms and spirit of the Geneva Convention would be observed by enemy submarines in a future war, despite past experience. As a result, the surface threat was still regarded as paramount. In 1937, the Naval Staff stated: "The submarine would never again be able to present us with the problems we were faced with in 1917."[415] Hence the firm belief that Coastal

---

[413] Cab. 53/42, no. 785.

[414] The papers of the Joint Intelligence Committee, housed in the Cabinet Office Library, have still to be released. There is, therefore, no way of accurately assessing its work, and impact on the preparations for war, and World War II.

[415] Churchill made the obvious point in his 'Second World War', when discussing the 1935 Anglo-German Naval Agreement: "The Germans, of course, gave assurance that their U-boats would never be used against merchant shipping. Why, then, were they needed?"

Command's task should consist solely of patrolling the North Sea for surface raiders escaping from the German ports.

Furthermore, no preparations were made for enlarging the convoy escort force of hundred and fifty asdic-fitted destroyers. Many of the latter were World War I vintage. In September 1939, R.A.F. Coastal Command had no aircraft designed, and aircrews trained, for anti-submarine work.[416] As a result of lack of intelligence, and 'operational research', only bitter experience in war brought change.[417]

The one thread which kept the N.I.D. going during its period in the wilderness were the Naval Attachés—they were the strongest link in the chain, but regrettably for British defence, a chain is only as strong as its weakest link. They worked well at the time of the Washington Naval Agreement (1922), the Geneva Naval Talks (1927), the London Naval Talks (1930), and the Anglo-German Naval Agreement (1935). As will be seen later, the N.I.D. and the C.O.S. and government realised that the tonnage allowed Germany would, in any case, stretch her resources to the full.

The situation was well summed up in a Foreign Office letter to Nevile Henderson in August 1938: "At the time of the Agreement, the German government were well aware that 35% of our Navy was probably the most they could hope to achieve for a considerable period."[418] In 1939, the N.I.D. knew Germany was below her allowed tonnage, even in submarines. Although some forty thousand tons of submarines had been announced in their building program by Germany and communicated to the Admiralty, the N.I.D. knew Germany had only thirty thousand tons of complete submarines in 1939, which was below 45% of the British tonnage.[419]

---

[416] It will be remembered that the N.I.D. had not detected Donitz's wolf-pack techniques, and the great range and increased performance of his U-boats.

[417] In February 1942, the Western Approaches Tactical Unit was set up in Liverpool to train escort captains and group commanders in convoy tactics. In March 1943, experience dictated an adjustment of the North Atlantic Convoy Cycle, whereby fewer and larger convoys were sailed each day.

[418] F.O. to Henderson, 17 August 1938. Adm. 116/3378.

[419] Data coming into the Admiralty about the German building program can be found in Adm. 116/3368 and 3369. British tonnage was seventy thousand tons at the end of 1938. 45% of this figure is thirty-one thousand five hundred tons. The total projected submarine tonnage at the end of 1938 was thirty-two thousand tons, and that is why Germany had

Donita himself wrote later: "It was the lack of submarines which prevented Germany from winning a rapid and decisive victory over the British Navy."[420] In other special areas, the attachés played a passive, ineffective role, such as at the time of the Abyssinian crisis, when a minority, headed by Churchill, wanted the Mediterranean Fleet to stop Italy by a fleet action to destroy their communications with Ethiopia.

Before we go on to examine some specific aspects of the N.I.D.'s work in relation to political decision-making, one final factor should be mentioned—the attitude and morale of the Naval Staff in the '30s.

Even in the late '30s the Naval Staff gave the impression of being reticent, almost tardy, in all their major business, and when forced to act, even under the Chamberlain government, seem to be dilatory. The C.O.S. as a body were certainly motivated by a pessimism centred on a possible encounter with a united Germany, Italy and Japan, with Britain being attacked without allies. There were certainly no firm guarantees that the United States would come to British assistance in the Far East.

Chatfield himself was most uncooperative on the question of staff talks with the French, particularly on the issue of arranging air bases in France (both Chamberlain and Eden saw these as part of the fulfilment of Locarno obligations). As late as March 1938, the C.O.S. had no contingency plans for the support of Czechoslovakia and France.[421] The Admiralty were still arguing in late April 1938, that staff talks with the French were unnecessary, as Fleet dispositions could be quickly made at the last minute, almost Fisher-like in their attitude to staff work.

Certainly, the C.O.S.'s attitude on the state of Britain's defence compared with Germany's (which in retrospect is seen to have been based upon incomplete intelligence reports) tended to confirm the Chamberlain government in their belief that they should not give military guarantees to France and Czechoslovakia. On 25 March 1938, Oliver Harvey wrote in his diary: "The General Staffs are defeatist, especially Admiralty."

---

to claim submarine parity. She would otherwise have been unable to lay down any submarines in 1939. Germany had only fifty-five submarines, (only twenty-six of which were ocean-going) at the outbreak of war.

[420] K. Donitz: Memoirs—Ten Years and Twenty Days.
[421] Harvey Diaries, p. 119.

Three days later, 28 April 1938, Harvey gave Sir Maurice Hankey a very cursory write-up: "I cannot help feeling this is satisfactory (Hankey had left the C.I.D. and been granted a sinecure). Hankey, who has been running the C.I.D. since 1912, is tired and now only immersed in the ramifications of his own machinery: he is out of touch and rather reactionary."

Even more significant, Harvey wrote on 9 June 1938: "Discussion in H's (Halifax) room today about bombing in Spain (attacks on British ships in Republican harbours) to discover what we can do to stop it. Admiralty (Admiral Sir William James, Deputy Chief of Naval Staff, 1935-1938 and Rear-Admiral V. A. Dankwerts, Director of Plans, Admiralty, 1938-1940) were present. Admiralty as usual defeatist."

In a letter to *The Times* dated 18 July 1970, Mr John Harvey (Harvey's son), challenging Captain S. W. Roskill's rebuke of his father's attack on C.O.S. and the Admiralty attitudes, wrote: "Obviously, the fundamental weakness was the politicians' fault, but as the Diaries show, the Chiefs of Staff and the C.I.D. under Hankey were as much the vigorous advocates in the Cabinet debate for appeasement as Eden and the diplomats were against it. Their influence upon the politicians was not negligible, and they cannot really claim, therefore, that it was unfair to criticise them."

On this issue, certain factors should be remembered—the French Navy alone was larger than the Italian, the Foreign Office was assuming American assistance in the Far East (it was regarded as their sphere of influence). The documents show that the Foreign Office appreciation of the situation was that the menace of Mussolini was being exaggerated. The C.O.S. did not agree, and they won the day over the Foreign Office when it came to influencing Chamberlain. In the absence of J.I.C. evidence, no assessment can be made of the influence of intelligence. The argument that the C.O.S., and Admiralty in general, were 'realistic' has some merit.

The Royal Navy had a very good idea of what a war on three fronts (and five oceans) could mean for British Naval resources, with many World War I ships, badly defended bases, and insufficient personnel. What they did not possess of course was the total picture (not least of all the strength and willingness of the Czechs to fight, the strength and position of the Luftwaffe, the problems for Germany, and the internal political risks for Hitler, of a two-fronted war, even if the Czechs did last only three months, and so on), and this is where the government must begin to bear total responsibility.

That the C.O.S., and indeed the government must begin to bear total responsibility. That the C.O.S., and indeed the government, were unaware of some fairly basic, but critical facts about German capabilities, was a fault of the system as a whole, not least of all the chronic state of intelligence.

It is patently true looking at the documents that are public that the N.I.D. did not possess any real influence at C.O.S. level. It provided basic facts and figures on fleet numbers and so on, but that was all. Whatever the value of the many interpretations of British diplomacy, the point must remain that the C.O.S. were influential, and that influence, certainly from the naval side, had not been backed by a continuous process of sound intelligence from 1935 onwards. The point here is not to argue cases, such as whether Britain should have fought in September 1938, to "keep Germans out of Germany,"[422] but rather a question of the quality of the data available, and how it was handled.

In a letter to *The Times* of 1 August 1970, Mr Peter Calvocoressi wrote: "The Cabinet's failure to do the job of appraising (correct) military judgments against other factors is seen too in its acceptance of the Admiralty view that it would be fatal to get into war with Italy. Whilst the Admiralty's fears may have been justly grounded in naval arithmetic, the Cabinet forgot to ask itself whether the Italian state was, regardless of the state of the Italian Navy, in a position to make war— which it was not."

There is no evidence to counter Calvocoressi's allegation against the Chamberlain government, and everything points to its self-evidence. What happened, besides the purely personal political affiliations and interpretations, was partly therefore a straightforward communication failure. The Cabinet never saw the wood for the trees, and the C.O.S. (and Admiralty in particular), seeing only part of the wood were strong enough (and some would argue foolish enough) to convince the C.I.D. and Chamberlain, whenever they turned for advice, or facts, that they were, in fact, looking at the whole wood. Nothing could have been further from the truth.

In this sense, the 'realistic' epithet appended to the C.O.S.'s policy must lose some credibility. A man cannot be properly described as 'realistic' if he states opinions based only upon a limited number of the total salient facts. He might, at very best, be described as well-meaning, intelligent, pleasant, but completely misinformed. The C.O.S. were surely in that position over several crucial issues.

---

[422] The Harvey Diaries. p. 182.

The intelligence breakdown of the inter-war period reaped its bitter harvest in war. It was devastatingly apparent in the German U-boat campaign and in the absence of sufficient expert naval air support. Let us look at the latter.

The role of maritime air power had never been satisfactorily appraised by the N.I.D.[423] The long battle between the Royal Air Force and the Royal Navy (with Trenchard's eventual victory for a policy of 'unified air') reflects the ever-present political content of such disputes, irrespective of strategic and tactical considerations, which hindsight says should have formed the basis for all such decisions. Whilst the United States Navy and the Japanese were studying the results of air-sea exercises and developing a carrier policy, Britain, from the earliest days, had other preoccupations.

A sub-committee (Balfour) of the 1923 Salisbury Committee looked into R.A.F.—Royal Navy relations. The Admiralty Board described their findings as "…prejudicial to the efficiency of the Fleet in time of peace, and will invite disaster in time of war."[424] So it went on until Britain was forced to fight a naval war with no real naval air policy, and neither equipment or personnel with which to adequately fight.

The Crete campaign showed how the British government and the C.O.S. still thought that the island could be held by the Fleet, without air support, even though the air was dominated by more than five hundred enemy bombers and dive bombers. Needless to say, when Crete was evacuated, the Mediterranean Fleet suffered heavy casualties from German air attacks. At home, the C.O.S. continued to believe that the R.A.F. and Fleet should accept any losses to prevent German reinforcements arriving.

As Cunningham aptly wrote later: "They failed lamentably to appreciate the realities of the situation." Pound summed up the two decades of inconclusiveness when he was obliged to write Cunningham in the Mediterranean Fleet: "I am afraid you are terribly short of 'air', but I do not see what can be done because, as you will realise, every available aircraft is wanted in home waters. The one lesson we have learnt here is that it is essential to have fighter protection over the Fleet whenever they are within range of enemy bombers. You will be without such protection, which is a very serious matter, but I do not see any way of rectifying it."

---

[423] Details of British Naval Air Policy: tactics, equipment, types of aircraft, and the number of aircraft can be found in Adm. 116/4030.
[424] Adm. 167/68. Board Minute no. 1750, 21 November 1923.

There is no evidence that the N.I.D. had ever investigated, for instance, the variables involved in the arrival of an enemy Air Force (such as Fliegerkorps X's in Sicily) within range of, say, the Mediterranean Fleet, let alone the offensive power naval aircraft would have given in a Crete campaign; they are hypothetical case studies, but it is not unreasonable to say that they should not have gone unnoticed in the exercise planning of the 1930s. The Americans and Japanese were hard at it.

Let us now look at a more concrete area where the N.I.D. was involved—the Anglo-German Naval Agreement.

Whatever the political ramifications of the Anglo-German Naval Agreement, and there were many (such as it acknowledged the right of Germany to re-arm, it overtly revised Versailles, and indirectly and tacitly accepted any future violation of that treaty; furthermore, it was undeniable evidence of intended German aval expansion, and the possibility therefore of its use in war. Both in their attitude to the Germans, and the Agreement itself, the British Naval Staff, spearheaded by people such as Jellicoe in the Lords, reveal themselves as a pertinent factor in the whole negotiations), the role of intelligence, even if solely regarded at the lowliest level as a purveyor of data, bears special analysis.

In the immediate pre-1935 period, it is true to say there was a moderate and sympathetic attitude towards Germany and her Navy in the Royal Navy, though not approving, or often not aware, of Nazi machinations. This was in part related to a firm view of the Anglo-German naval position—that Britain could do little in any event to prevent German naval re-armament. On the diplomatic front, the Washington Naval Agreement of 1922 was due to expire in 1936 in any case. Many saw an agreement as a means of preventing an Anglo-German naval arms race beginning again.

Lord Beatty was quick to stress the latter point in his Lords' speech of 26 June 1935. German good faith was to be given some credence later by her agreement, on 23ʳSeptember 1936, to the 1930 London Protocol, to abide by international law regarding submarine attacks on merchant shipping.

Whatever political analysis shows,[425] the British government was deceived, partly as a result of the failure to listen to intelligence, and partly as a result of the latter's inadequacy. It was known that all the Agreement did was to allow

---

[425] See D. C. Watt: The Anglo-German Naval Agreement of 1935: An Interim Judgment. Journal of Modern History. XXVII. No. 2, June 1956: W. S. Churchill: The Second World War. Vol. I. p. 107-110.

German construction to go ahead at its very maximum that its yards could, in any case permit. In this sense, there was no practical limitation or restraint of any kind imposed upon German naval expansion. They could build as fast as was physically possible. But they could have (and would have no doubt) done this whatever the efforts of British diplomacy.

On the positive side for Britain, it would be a means of knowing exactly what Germany would be doing in hard construction terms, and the very nature of that construction would give some indication of possible policy (i.e., technical details of ships and submarines built). What is more, any positive evidence that all the data was not being revealed would be a further indication of a shift in policy and an obvious target for clandestine intelligence collection. Compared with the Nazis, the British were far too generous with their data.[426] N.I.D. in particular was too gullible.

Nonetheless, some warning was given, but it fell on deaf ears. In his 1936 annual report dated 23 December 1936, the Naval Attaché in Berlin, Captain Troubridge wrote: "The Anglo-German Naval Agreement was one of the master strokes of policy which have characterised Germany's dealings with her ex-enemies since the war. When the time is ripe, as history shows, it will unquestioningly go the same way of other agreements, but the time is not yet." His predecessor, Captain Muirhead-Gould, had written in the same vein to the D.N.I.

Their words were accurate indeed, but even Troubridge was deceived by the Germans regarding the technical details of battleship and U-boat construction. Raeder himself lied to Troubridge. As a result, a totally incorrect appreciation was made of the Bismarck's tonnage and draft. This influenced adversely the design of the King George V class (King George V class had 14" guns and, compared with the Bismarck, low endurance), and certainly in 1936, the British conception of the Germans' naval strategy (Baltic oriented) and therefore, by implication, of her overall policy.

When war broke out, very few ships of the British 1937 and 1938 programs had been completed.

Much of the data exchanged was entirely accurate. Moreover, there is no evidence that the C.I.D. challenged N.I.D. data or was suspicious. The D.N.I.'s

---

[426] See Adm. 116/3929: Supply of forecasts of British naval strength to Germany, under the Anglo-German Naval Agreement, 1935, and Adm. 116/3368 (up to 1937), and Adm. 116/3369 (up to 1939), gives comparative Anglo-German data.

verdicts (Troup's) were firmly accepted.[427] The tragedy was that at the purely naval contact level, Anglo-German naval relations were good.[428] What the N.I.D. missed, and it was no exception, was the overall significance for Hitler, not Raeder or any other outwardly friendly German naval officer for that matter, of the new German Navy under construction.[429]

Politics, the War and Naval Intelligence 1939-1945

As a result of the N.I.D. and Foreign Office failure to acquire all technical data, and even strengths, particularly of the U-boat force, Britain was hard pressed when war was declared. Churchill wrote: "My first Admiralty Minute was concerned with the probably scale of the U-boat menace in the immediate future."[430] Hard, accurate data was lacking—Churchill had to ask for it. On 12 November 1939, when the D.N.I. estimated six out of sixty-six U-boats sunk, the actual numbers were six out of fifty-seven.[431]

It might be argued that the N.I.D. had erred on the side of safety (i.e., in giving an over-estimate), but it still came as a salutary shock to both the Admiralty and the government to be given the probable strength of the long-range, ocean-going U-boat force, and the use to which they would obviously be put. The real point here is that the data was not there before 3 September 1939.

---

[427] See Adm. 116/3377—Troup's letter of 9 March 1936. He firmly believes Raeder is telling the truth about German naval strengths. See also Captain Tom Phillips' letter dated 7 December 1936, Adm. 116/3378, in which he considers that the Germans are showing total good faith. Troup agrees and signs the Naval Staff pack, 18 December 1936. Phillips was Director of Plans, Admiralty.

[428] See for example, D.G.F.P., Series C, Vol. 3, no. 541—an interview between the German naval attaché in London and the N.I.D., and the brief prepared for Admiral Cunningham before he visited Germany in 1938 for the Anglo-German Naval staff conversations—D.B.F.P., Third Series Vol. 3, nos. 429, 438, 450 and appendix 7.

[429] See Saul Friedlander: Prelude to Downfall (Chatto and Windus), and J. B. Compton: The Swastika and the Eagle (The Bodley Head, 1968) for two very clear accounts of Hitler's naval mentality.

[430] W. S. Churchill: The Second World War. Volume I. p. 331.

[431] Admiral Godfrey's Memoirs, Part 2 to Volume 5, National Maritime Museum, Greenwich. Godfrey also writes how Churchill, First Lord, and Pound, the First Sea Lord, tended to exaggerate on the radio, not for propaganda purposes, but because of intelligence inaccuracy. Churchill said on the BBC: "The attack of the U-boats has been 'controlled' and they have paid a heavy toll."

In a note dated 4 November 1939, Churchill wrote the D.N.I.: "Let me have a statement of the German U-boat forces, actual and prospective, for the next few months. Please distinguish between ocean-going and small size U-boats. Give the estimated radius of action in days and miles in each case."

Churchill surely had his finger on the N.I.D. pulse immediately and asked the right sort of questions. As the N.I.D. gained momentum, the First Lord was given the data he required. He wrote in Volume I of his Second World War: "I was at once informed that the enemy had sixty U-boats and that a hundred would be ready early in 1940. A detailed answer was returned on 5, which should be studied. The numbers of long-range endurance vessels were formidable and revealed the intentions of the enemy to work far out in the oceans as soon as possible."

Under the terms of the Agreement, more data could have been acquired, if need be, by resources to clandestine methods. When the long-range ocean-going U-boats, in wolf packs, struck Allied convoys in the mid-Atlantic 'air' gap the full failure of earlier intelligence was realised.

In the Far East, British intelligence was alert from 1938 onwards. This intensified once war with Germany had been declared. Japanese pre-emptive strikes were detected by air reconnaissance, coast watchers, and, to a lesser extent, the American 'magics'. The British assessment of a Japanese attack on Siam, with amphibious strikes against strategic points on the Kra Isthmus, were reported to Washington. The possession of the 'magics' did not prevent Pearl Harbour, even though they showed strength, disposition and intention. At Midway, they gave the United States Navy tactical surprise over the Imperial Japanese Navy. Before Pearl Harbour, they were only of ancillary value to the British. The Americans themselves were not using them properly.

Notwithstanding the 'magics' value, the British commitment in the Far East could at best be very limited—all available major units were required in the European theatre. Port defences were poor—AA guns alone were needed to defend Britain. The Prince of Wales and the Repulse met an almost predictable end to those who had any knowledge of Japanese naval air power, particularly the capabilities of the Zero and the aerial torpedo. Paper strengths were well known in the N.I.D.

What happened was what had been feared for two decades. The problem was not so much one of a paucity of intelligence, but more the non-availability of weapons (and modern ones), and a political will. However, in mitigation, the Far

East had been increasingly regarded as an American sphere of influence. That they should bear most responsibility, and give mutual assistance, was accepted in Britain long before Pearl Harbour. When the British Pacific Fleet was formed it went to the Far East very much under American strategic control. This had always been tacitly understood.

If Japan attacked in full force, Britain realised she could offer little in a two-theatre war without the massive American alliance. British Naval intelligence felt therefore it had only a secondary commitment in the Far East in terms of its more pressing responsibilities in Europe. Britain came to rely on the O.N.I. in the Far East theatre,[432] and did so throughout the World War II, save for in the Southeast Asian Command, which acquired N.I.D. trained personnel, and when the British Pacific Fleet was formed, a British intelligence staff was created in Australia, headed by the former Madrid attaché, Captain Hillgarth, R.N.

Politically then, the N.I.D. had little to offer the politicians on the Far East. It had detected the measure of the Japanese threat—its strength and capability, and probable attack points. The C.O.S. and Cabinet knew though that Britain could offer little in retaliation. Where the N.I.D. (and O.N.I.) fell down was in technical appreciation, though even this would have been of dubious value in hard terms, assuming the government was unable to provide the degree of re-equipment for the European theatre, let alone provide a carrier fleet, and support groups for the Far East (with naval aircraft, for example, at least as good as the Zero).

The political pre-occupation was for European intelligence. With the threat of invasion in 1940, both the J.I.C. and the N.I.D. had their hands full. On 6 July 1940, Prime Minister Churchill wrote Colonel Jacob: "Obtain a most careful report today from the Joint Intelligence Staff of any further indication of enemy

---

[432] In the 1939-1945 War, the Australian Naval Intelligence Department provided an excellent coast-watching service. In the 1914-1918 War, the R.A.N. had a very small intelligence staff. In common with the N.I.D., this began to be disbanded in 1918. By January 1919, only one officer remained, a soldier, who acted as military censor. By 1921, there was no Intelligence Department in the R.A.N. There was a temporary resurrection of the D.N.I. appointment in 1922 but this quickly lapsed. Between 1923-1936, there was no D.N.I., or any intelligence as such, in the R.A.N. From 1936-1939, the Assistant Chief of Naval Staff acted as the D.N.I. too, with an Assistant D.N.I. The R.A.N. N.I.D. made no major contribution to British or American naval intelligence pre-1939. See G. H. Gill: Australia in the War of 1939-1945. Royal Australian Navy. Volume I, Canberra, 1957.

preparation for raid or invasion. Let me have this tonight."[433] The pressure was on, and little regard could be paid to the Far East. On 11 July 1940, the Prime Minister wrote the Secretary of State for Air: "At the present time, a very heavy price may be paid for information by reconnaissance of the conditions in the German ports and German-controlled ports and river mouths…"[434]

In a time of crisis, government must have regard to immediate intelligence needs. Eventually, it paid dividends. Churchill was able to write: "Our excellent intelligence confirmed that the operation 'Sea Lion' had been definitely ordered by Hitler and was in active preparation."[435] However, the early assessments were not good.

William L. Shirer summarised the situation thus: "British intelligence of the German plans was extremely faulty and for the first three months of the invasion threat almost completely wrong. Throughout the summer, Churchill and his military advisers remained convinced that the Germans would make their main landing attempt on the east coast and it was here that the bulk of the British land forces were concentrated until September."[436]

Churchill soon appreciated how woefully weak the British espionage system was in crucial areas in western Europe. On 6 June 1940, he instructed General Ismay to improve British espionage and intelligence on the Danish, Dutch and Belgian coasts.[437] On 23 July 1940, he expressed concern about espionage in Europe and what M.E.W. was doing, and on 5 August 1940, Churchill was so concerned and obviously dissatisfied with intelligence in Europe, he wrote Ismay:

"I am not satisfied with the volume or quality of information received from the unoccupied area of France. We seem to be as much cut off from the unoccupied area of France. We seem to be as much cut off from these territories as from Germany. I do not wish such reports as are received to be sifted and digested by the various intelligence authorities. For the present, Major Morton will inspect them for me and submit what he considers to be of major interest. He is to see everything and submit authentic documents for me in their original form.

---

[433] W. S. Churchill: The Second World War. Volume 2. p. 567.
[434] Ibid
[435] Ibid. p. 261.
[436] William L. Shirer: The Rise and Fall of the Third Reich. p. 914.
[437] W. S. Churchill: The Second World War. Volume 2. p. 217.

"Further, I await proposals for improving and extending our own information about France and for keeping a continued flow of agents moving to and from. For this purpose, naval facilities can, if necessary, be invoked. So far as the Vichy government is concerned, it is not creditable that we have so little information. To what extent are American, Swiss and Spanish agents being used?"[438]

Spurred on in part by Churchill, the J.I.C. must have improved dramatically, such that by the time of the withdrawal from Crete, he was able to write laudatory minutes about the range and accuracy of J.I.C. prognoses,[439] though there were several major disagreements between Churchill and the J.I.C. (as recorded by Churchill), such as that over the estimates of the coastal defences of the Italian ports before Salerno;[440] or that over the nature and future of Russo-German relations in 1941.[441]

Churchill wrote that the "...Chiefs of Staff were ahead of their advisers (the J.I.C.), and more definite." In the absence of J.I.C. evidence, the various controversies cannot be untangled. However, it is certain, even on Churchill's evidence, the C.O.S. had exactly the data the J.I.C. had given them and no more. J.I.C. new of rumours in Europe of German plans, but were not prepared to commit themselves without further evidence. Churchill and the C.O.S. played a hunch which came true.

Churchill's reliance upon intelligence for every major military decision runs throughout his writings. It is in stark contrast with all the major German comments in secondary sources, such as General Westphal (Chief of Staff to Kesselring) who wrote in his *Herr in Fesseln*:

"On 21 January 1944, Admiral Canaris, Chief of the German Intelligence, visited Army Group Headquarters, where he was pressed to communicate any information, he might have about the enemy's intentions in regard to a landing. In particular, we wanted to know about the positions of aircraft carriers, battleships and landing craft. Canaris was unable to give us any details but thought that there was no need to fear a new landing in the near future. This was certainly his view. Not only air reconnaissance, but also the German counter-

---

[438] Ibid., p. 278 and 572.
[439] W. S. Churchill: The Second World War. Volume 2. p. 240.
[440] Ibid., p. 682-683.
[441] Ibid p. 317.

espionage, was almost completely out of action at this time. A few hours after the departure of Canaris, the enemy landed at Anzio."[442]

As we have already seen, German intelligence reached its nadir on D-Day, with the success of the brilliant British deceptions, the failure of the Germans to detect the assembly of the assault groups, and their over-estimation of the number of divisions and the amount of suitable shipping available in England (with the resulting fatal deduction that a second big landing was possible), let alone the overconfidence placed in the bad weather on 5/6 June 1944, to deter an amphibious invasion.

Hitler's failure to use naval intelligence was symptomatic of his general abhorrence of naval advice.[443] In his *The Struggle for Europe*, Chester Wilmot quotes from Donitz's Diary for 12 November 1943: "The enemy holds every trump card, covering all areas with long-range air patrols and using location methods against which we still have no warning…The enemy knows all our secrets and we know none of his."[444] Nothing could be in greater contrast than this with the successes of British Naval intelligence by 1943.

In the United States, the O.N.I. went from strength to strength after Pearl Harbour. The researches of Roberta Wohlstetter have shown conclusively that the O.N.I.'s collection had been excellent, but that the system whereby intelligence was relegated to a dormant position, revoking its right to evaluate and advise War Plans Department and the Secretary of State's Office, prevented the commander on the spot receiving the vital data he needed.[445]

The role of naval intelligence in influencing British foreign policy in the '30s was negligible. There is no evidence in the Admiralty, Chiefs of Staff, or Cabinet papers which suggests anything which might be called 'influential'. The overall effect of the intelligence bodies, with the N.I.D., is of course another matter. In

---

[442] Herr in Fesseln. p. 240.

[443] After the Bad Godesburg Conference, Raeder had pleaded with Hitler not to go to war with Britain. Under the so-called Z-Plan, promulgated at the end of 1938, German naval strength would only begin to approach that of the British by 1945. In the spring of 1939, Germany did not possess the heavy ships to sink the British Navy, even by a surprise attack. See also Fuhrer Conferences on Naval Affairs—Summary records of Hitler's Conferences with the C.-in-C. of the German Navy. London Admiralty, 1947. p. 81-82—Hitler refuses to head the advice of his Naval Staff not to invade Britain on a wide front, as Raeder claimed the Navy could only defend a narrow strip of coast.

[444] p. 152.

[445] See Roberta Wohlstetter: Pearl Harbour. Warning and Decision. Stanford. 1962.

the absence of J.I.C. papers, a speculative element must enter. However, in the absence of cross references in the other public sources in the open period to major J.I.C. influences, particularly in the Chiefs of Staff, it would seem reasonable to suppose that the J.I.C. did not have the impact which might be anticipated, certainly not pre-1939.

In general, it may be concluded that foreign policy tended to develop in isolation, away from the intelligence evidence. Great Britain never experienced a Pearl Harbour which would possibly have precipitated a similar review of the organisation and role of naval intelligence, or intelligence in general.

What now be called the specific naval failures of naval intelligence—the failure to acquire the German naval codes, Donitz's wolf pack techniques, technical details of the German surface raider, the lack of topographical intelligence (found to be so wanting at Narvik early in the war), the need for naval air power in offensive and defensive roles, reconnaissance, and the anti-submarine roles, and most of all to pinpoint every major German unit's location and probable intention on 3 September 1939, and in the first months of war. It is these which are more significant.

It is easy to exaggerate the role naval intelligence might have played in the moulding of foreign policy. British diplomacy was European centred and related essentially to Nazi aggression, which was land dominated and, in the early years, primarily eastward-looking. The maritime element was always played down. Hitler had no personal regard for his Navy and its use in his grandiose designs for Lebensraum. He possessed a modern, well-equipped Navy, but one which, in 1939, was unacceptable to Raeder and Donitz in terms of how they saw Germany's naval role.

This is not to underestimate the German naval threat, but it was not one, unlike in 1914, which would lead to prophecies of doom in Britain provided, and this was the crux, certain fairly basic facts were known.

Where the N.I.D. had a real role to play was in its function of providing intelligence which might forestall German aggression, both in 1914 and 1939, that is by responding to the Kaiser's and Nazis' diplomatic and military moves by the traditional manipulation of British sea power. In 1938 and 1939, for instance, it might have had the salutary effect of unifying Europe in an effective military alliance against Hitler (France, Czechoslovakia, Russia, and Britain) and possibly shaking Hitler's own internal political credibility.

In this context, naval intelligence had (and still does) a real role to play in framing foreign and defence policy. Naval intelligence has, furthermore, a major contribution to make to the total mosaic of intelligence. Pre-1914 it most certainly did, not so in the inter-war period, at least not until the establishment of the J.I.C. (and even thereafter, until war came, there is some equivocation). In both eras, naval intelligence came to play its main role in the 'operational' sphere.

With the decline of the blue-water school of strategy, pre-1914 D.N.I.'s role, along with the rest of the Naval Staff, declined. Ultimately, it was European territorial diplomacy, and a dominantly military strategy in the early period of both wars which determined the major elements of foreign policy.

In fairness to the N.I.D. in the period before both wars, it suffered from the natural effects of periods of prolonged peace, most of all the difficulty task of assessing the effectiveness of ships and weapons in situations of which it had no first-hand experience in war. This very inscrutability of the possible course of enemy naval action, and the nature of British policy, made the whole process very arbitrary. This though is not meant as an argument against intensive monitoring and analysis of all potential enemy naval developments, exercises, movements and so on.

On the question of how effective was intelligence is assisting British Naval power to maintain peace the answer is undoubtedly very little, in fact, virtually zero. Even on the issue of the naval agreements, intelligence did not either directly or indirectly effect the various balances agreed, or the international stability it was hoped would ensue. That the C.O.S. were laying plans in 1936 for a possible war with Germany by the end of 1939 is an indication of some insight and politico-military will. As has been indicated, the N.I.D. had little say in these until war neared.

In any event, the political direction as to how British Naval power might be used in a non-belligerent capacity to deter Fascist and Nazi aggression (Abyssinia and the Spanish Civil War are obvious cases, in retrospect, of the feeble use of British sea power), and indeed would be used in war, was lacking until the high point of appeasement was passed. For intelligence to be really significant in this context, it has to be given clear plans of what one's own forces are doing, or planning to do.

In both 1914 and 1939, when the hour arrived, the Royal Navy assumed a less significant role in the final stages before war was declared, and the whole emphasis tended to swing to the soldiers (and airmen in 1939), not the sailors.

The dialectic between Naval intelligence, the defence planners, and the political decision-makers had ceased to have a profitable outcome for the Navy in the last few years before the Great War, and in the pre-1939 N.I.D., it had never really existed at all.

Whatever the quality of intelligence, and the excellence of the organisation which produces and disseminates it, intelligence workers can only go so far in a democracy. In the 1939 and contemporary contexts, Admiral Hall is judged to have gone beyond the pale in his day. A.D.N.I. had to have a clear picture of his role—Godfrey certainly did. When he visited the French, and later on the Americans, he achieved positive political results, as much for a future lend-lease agreement as Anglo-American intelligence cooperation, yet he did not extend or manipulate his brief according to any personalised view of naval intelligence.

What is more, no intelligence worker can expect, or always hope, to influence politicians, whether one's own or those of the enemy. The German Naval Attaché in London, von Schwerin, reported to Hitler and von Ribbentrop, how good the N.I.D. was. He stressed too that Godfrey had made it clear to him that Britain would honour the Polish agreement if Germany invaded.[446] Neither took any notice. Churchill was more receptive—Plan Catherine was cancelled as a result of pressure from the D.N.I. and the Director of Plans (Captain Charles Daniel), though he was particularly stubborn over the Norwegian campaign, and continued against the D.N.I.'s advice (particularly in the absence of detailed topographical intelligence).[447]

This was the same politician who was able to write the First Lord and First Sea Lord on 22 November 1940: "…the Japanese Navy is not likely to venture from its home bases so long as a superior battle fleet is maintained at Singapore or at Honolulu. The Japanese would never attempt a siege of Singapore with a

---

[446] Admiral Godfrey's unpublished Memoirs. Vol. 5. Part I. p. 18-19.

[447] As a result of the chronic lack of intelligence in Norway (the result of which had been predicted by N.I.D. and the J.I.C.) the C.O.S. instructed the J.I.C. to investigate the state of topographical intelligence on 14 May 1940. The J.I.C. decided the N.I.D. should have responsibility for this and, in June 1940, N.I.D.6—the Topographical Section, was established. This was to have a close liaison with Combined Operations HQ, established in Whitehall on 12 June 1940. In October 1940, N.I.D.6 moved from London first to the School of Geography, and then to Manchester College, at Oxford. (See the Godfrey Memoirs. Vol. 5. Part 2. p. 352-353).

hostile, superior American fleet in the Pacific."[448] Wishfulness in a politician is an ever-present danger, but in a democracy, it must remain such or be replaced by an intelligence system with all the attendant dangers of covert political power. Those who opposed Churchill ran the risk of dismissal. The Director of Plans, Danckwerts, opposed Churchill's Norwegian plans (especially over the possibility of the Luftwaffe devastating the Fleet), and he was sacrificed.[449]

Godfrey wrote: "…at the time, we all felt uneasy that Mr Churchill (still First Lord of the Admiralty) was leading us into a strategical adventure that might culminate in the defeat of the Allies." He does go on to say though: "However, General Ismay said himself, 'No one was in any doubt, in spite of the known hazards, we must do what we could to help poor little Norway'."[450] The point remains that few, certainly not Pound, were prepared to oppose Churchill, even knowing the lack of intelligence.

Oddly, Tom Phillips (Vice-Chief of Naval Staff) supported Churchill on this occasion—he believed, like Churchill, that ships properly armed, would be safe against air attack. Phillips was later removed from the Naval Staff, mainly because he would not play up to Churchill over his belief that an invasion was still possible in 1941.[451] The political mentality which short circuited intelligence would naturally tend not to press for expansion and/or improvements in the intelligence machinery.

Only in a crisis or war did politicians tend to awaken and press for additional intelligence. Roosevelt saw the sense in Colonel William Donovan's case for O.S.S. (Office of Strategic Services), just as Churchill did for the I.S.T.D. (Inter-Service Topographical Department) run by the N.I.D., or a massive increase of photographic reconnaissance of enemy ships and installations, calling as it did for Royal Navy-Royal Air Force cooperation. Senior officers are no less likely to sidetrack intelligence than politicians. Godfrey recounts this extraordinary incident, which highlights this point.

"It was agreed that after approval by the Chiefs of Staff, the abridged text of J.I.C. appreciations should be telegraphed to C.-in-C.s abroad. My subsequent experience in India where, as flag officer Commanding Indian Navy, I served on the C.O.S. (India) Committee has, however, convinced me that whatever may

---

[448] W. S. Churchill: The Second World War. Vol. 2. p. 615.
[449] Admiral Godfrey's unpublished Memoirs. Vol. 7. Part 2. p. 228-229.
[450] Ibid.
[451] Ibid. p. 258-259.

have gone out from the Chiefs of Staff, London, the C.I.G.S. informed C.-in-C. India, of his own views, which were different from those of the J.I.C., although approved by the Chiefs of Staff, of whom the C.I.G.S. was then chairman."[452]

In defence politics during this period, whatever the history of intelligence, certain inalienable facts must be remembered when assessing the impact of intelligence. Not least of these is the inseparability of naval intelligence from the mainstream of British political, economic and social life, insofar as it impinged upon defence thinking and policy. Many well-meaning men laboured hard in the inter-war period in pursuit of goals which were later explicit in the aims and work of the N.I.D.

A man like Hankey, a brilliant doyen of all defence bureaucrats, working incessantly in the British defence interest, exemplifies how politicians, their advisers, and the whole paraphernalia of their supporting system, can labour with the right goals in mind, in the right ways, yet still only achieve a modicum of success. This must surely place intelligence in the right perspective in this period—a much lower-level system, separate by nature and power from those who decided and executed policy.

A question which must remain in part unanswered is who is responsible for ensuring that an efficient intelligence organisation exists. Who educates who in understanding the role of intelligence? Certainly, experience itself should make reasonably self-evident to politicians some fairly clear-cut benefits which intelligence can provide, and how these can be acquired in terms of organisation, staff, methods and so on. The political control, and means of assessing the effectiveness of an intelligence organisation such as the N.I.D. can only be determined in an ad hoc way.

There can be no absolute criteria for assessment. Furthermore, the N.I.D. itself surely had a responsibility to explain to politicians (as well as the Naval Staff, C.O.S. or the C.I.D.), its position, and the role and limitations of naval intelligence. It had an educative responsibility.

Politicians as a body (and it is important to remember that they do not maintain the degree of continuity in office which career service officers do) might then be in a position to put intelligence's house in order should it begin to fall down, as it undoubtedly did in the inter-war period, and, equally important, to maximise its use. The cost-effectiveness of intelligence is something which

---

[452] Godfrey, Vol. 5. Part 1. p. 165.

only a politician, fully aware of intelligence's capabilities and limitations, and in the light of his country's overall commitments, can decide.

D.N.I. had a responsibility to make his and N.I.D.'s position clear to hiss Naval Staff and political masters, especially on the inter-dependence of operations and intelligence. An atmosphere had to be created in which this could occur, so that mutual confidence would exist. Godfrey himself regrets that he never took everyone into his confidence as a body rather than dealing as he did, with people individually. With several qualifications, he writes that in 1942, the time was ripe "…to sweep them all into a sort of alliance with D.N.I."

On the question of operations and intelligence, he writes. "This would have made clear to them all the extent of our resources and how, whether it is collateral intelligence, prisoners of war, P.R.U. (Photographic Reconnaissance Unit), or topographical, the flow of information from operations to the N.I.D. must be as great, if not greater, than in the other direction."[453] The defence politician had a responsibility to preserve this independence of N.I.D. and the D.N.I., and, if need be, protect him and his staff from the hierarchical constraints of service, without of course undermining authority or loosening the political control of intelligence.

The politician must be as free from bias as his intelligence directors and staffs. Nor can he afford to show signs of ignoring intelligence reports (however equivocal) when they might run contrary to current policy, or fail to give a fair hearing to intelligence heads when they feel they have something important to say. Only the senior politician can protect himself against the worst features of the political manipulation or non-recognition of intelligence. Godfrey must have been aware of this, although he does not say so, when he tried to convince Churchill and Air Chief Marshall Harris that the 'strategic bombing' offensive was not having the desired results for the Navy, Godfrey does say this:

"My concern as D.N.I. was to assess the effect on German ships, naval bases and installations using every available means of discovering the truth. I am afraid my reports must have been discouraging and the bombing of the German cities was the declared policy of the government. My reports were not the sort of reports that would give any pleasure to bomber headquarters and, being factual, it was impossible and undesirable to dress him up to look nice. It must have annoyed Harris and he had the ear of the Prime Minister who frequently went over to see Harris from Chequers."[454]

---

[453] Admiral Godfrey's unpublished Memoirs: Vol. 5. Part 2. p. 123.
[454] Admiral Godfrey's Memoirs. Vol. 5. Part 1. p. 107.

The bomber offensive continued, and post-war research has substantiated how it was less successful than was thought at the time. Whatever the impact of Godfrey's reports, and there is no evidence available yet to assess this, the point remains that here is a classic example of where a politician, and a senior officer (C.-in-C. Bomber Command) were faced with a contrary intelligence report. The prima facie evidence is that it was ignored and that the strategy continued.

When a Director of Naval Intelligence possessed information such that it gave the N.I.D. a monopoly of influence with the politicians (either as a result of a request for information on a subject or as a result of ideas or a problem being generated from within the N.I.D.), then the political problems were reduced. Take, for example, Admiral Godfrey's concern about neutral Eire during World War II. A paper was produced within the N.I.D. and presented via the First Sea Lord, to the Cabinet. "Mr Churchill took the matter up vigorously and it was discussed in Cabinet on 23 November 1939."[455]

Godfrey had discussed the problem under three main headings: (1) How to neutralise enemy espionage (2) How to prevent leakage (3) How to obtain information relating to maritime events on the coast of Eire. The British government acted swiftly and, if one accepts Godfrey's comments, this was solely due to N.I.D.'s influence. The Irish government was very cooperative, such that by September 1940, a 'cordon sanitaire' had been thrown round Ireland.[456] N.I.D.'s activities in neutral Eire were completely successful.

These were spearheaded by Commander Slade, K.C., R.N.V.R., D.N.I.'s personal representative. Godfrey writes: "As we now know from German records, no naval activities favourable to the Germans took place in Eirean waters, and there is no evidence of the Eirean coast being used for U-boat, or supply bases. Hempel, the German Minister, was determined to remain quite neutral, in spite of proddings from Berlin. He never meant to return to Germany, and in 1948 was keeping a small sweet shop in Dublin."[457]

The example above again illustrates how in wartime, it is easier for intelligence to gain a satisfactory hearing from politicians, either concerning organisational matters, or straightforward intelligence/operational affairs. Two further cases will suffice to emphasise this point. In 1939-1940, the N.I.D. and the other intelligence bodies pressed for the creation of an organisation tasked

---

[455] Admiral Godfrey's Memoirs. Vol. 5. Part 1. p. 1-2.
[456] Ibid. p. 202-204.
[457] Admiral Godfrey's Memoirs. Vol. 5. Part 1. p. 205.

with analysing the enemy high command's thinking and what his next major moves might be.

The result was the creation in November 1940, of the Future Operations (Enemy) Section (F.O.E.S.), with Captain Troubridge, Royal Navy, as O.I.C. and Donald McLachlan as his assistant.[458] In March 1941, F.O.E.S. became part of the J.I.C. organisation (prior to this it had reported directly to the C.O.S.).[459] Churchill and the Cabinet quickly appreciated the need for such an organisation, just as they listened to and accepted the J.I.C.—J.I.S. initiative for 'Operation Torch' (the Allied landings in North Africa).

Through Captain Baker Cresswell, Royal Navy (the chairman and driving force in J.I.S. at the time), these two committees (using N.I.D. assessments amongst others) were able to convincingly and successfully argue that what the Germans feared most was an Allied landing in North Africa.[460]

Certain pieces of intelligence, because of their highly classified nature, must always remain the preserve of a few, perhaps only the heads of the services, their chief intelligence advisers (and subordinates involved), and the Prime Minister and those ministers he wishes to involve. However, there is one great danger here—if intelligence is only known to a few in a decision-making capacity, then those who have to plan naval operations against an enemy in war, or devise strategy and tactics, procure ships and weapons and so on in peace, may well be denied vital information which might otherwise affect their plans and decisions.

This may seem fairly obvious, but it will be remembered that the Submarine Assessment Book was withheld from all but a selected few from November 1939, to September 1940, to the detriment it may be speculated of several vital bodies, not least of all Headquarters Western Approaches Command in Liverpool, and the C.-in-C. Coastal Command, Royal Air Force. How can senior staff officers plan operations, and commanders execute them, if they are not given some indication of the strength of the enemy's forces?

---

[458] Late in 1941, Donald McLachlan was to take control of N.I.D. propaganda and psychological warfare against enemy naval personnel.

[459] Admiral Godfrey's Memoirs: Vol. 5. Part 1. p. 163-164. The original members of the F.O.E.S. were: Royal Navy-Captain Troubridge, Commander Chatwin; Army-Major-General Mackesy; Royal Air Force-Air Commodore Vachell; Foreign Office—Mr Ivone Kirkpatrick; Ministry of Economic Warfare—a representative.

[460] Ibid. p. 165.

It is these sort of considerations a politician must have in mind when he considers the implications of high-grade intelligence, and it is the senior Naval Staff officer who must advise him. Herein lies one of the great problems for the naval officer. How far can he take the initiative in this politico-military sphere? Let us examine this more closely.

NOTE: On the question of public statements regarding submarine losses, Churchill's early statements on the BBC were due to faulty assessment, but not by the N.I.D. His later statements into 1940 were in part due again to faulty information (which was contrary to what the N.I.D. was saying), but also to Churchill's undoubted desire to make propaganda capital and to raise morale amongst the British people. On 20 January, the First Lord broadcast the nation: "It seems pretty certain tonight that half the U-boats with which Germany began the war have been sunk, and that their new building has fallen far behind what we expected."

This was patently not true, and N.I.D. knew so. It should be noted that it was not until September 1940 that the Submarine Assessment Book, compiled by the Director of Anti-Submarine Warfare and the Directorate of Naval Intelligence was shown to anyone else other than the Prime Minister, First Lord, First Sea Lord, Vice-Chief of Naval Staff and the Assistant Chief of Naval Staff.* The N.I.D. was responsible for much of the propaganda to undermine and destroy the morale of the German Navy.

Some insight into this is given in Sefton Delmar's book, *Black Boomerang*. Delmar worked in the P.W.E. (Political Warfare Executive).

The Naval Intelligence Officer and Politics

A senior officer, with intelligence training and experience, should ensure that the politicians are aware of the extent, and limitations, of the intelligence organisation. A politician not familiar with naval organisation and operations could not be expected to appreciate without advice, the requirements of a naval intelligence organisation. There must be, therefore, a meaningful dialogue so that decisions can be made. In this sense, the senior staff officer (intelligence) has indeed the interests of the state and the security of its people in his hands.

No rules can be laid down. A flexibility of mind and attitudes is required that enables workable solutions to be found. In peacetime, without the concrete operational tasks which war demands, this problem becomes paramount. A classic example, drawn from Admiral Godfrey's experiences, in the inter-war period, will illustrate.

In 1934, the D.N.I., Rear-Admiral Dickens,[461] and the D.M.O. and I., Major-General Dill, propounded the idea that the Naval and Military Intelligence departments should collaborate in producing appreciations of what potential enemies might do in certain circumstances. The three general areas they had in mind were: (a) Enemy's possible course of action (b) Factors which might influence the enemy in the selection of his course of action (c) Enemy's most probable course of action. At the time, the Plans Division in Admiralty (Captain King was Director, Godfrey was Deputy Director) were responsible for all such appreciations—(a) to (c) inclusive.

Plans felt that the N.I.D. should begin to provide them with all the data they both felt was necessary for such appreciations. Unfortunately, Admiral Dickens left office and it was decided between Godfrey and Captain G. A. Scott (D.D.N.I.) to drop the whole idea. It did lapse until, as we have seen, C.O.S. pressed J.I.C. for data, and Godfrey came to the N.I.D. as Director and revived everything.

Nonetheless a mistake had been made, of which he was fully cognizant.[462] It is very easy to use the word 'mistake' in retrospect, but this was undoubtedly a missed opportunity—to unite Intelligence and Plans in achieving a common goal. In the absence of influence from other sections of the Naval Staff (and one would surmise this was a move which would have involved the First Sea Lord, Vice-Chief of Naval Staff and the Assistant Chief of Naval Staff), or the political arena (First Lord), it is easy to see how organisational failures can, over a number of years, have substantial repercussions.

If the political arm had been involved there would have been at least a chance of action being taken. However unlikely this may have been responsibility for such a decision would have been rightfully shared between the naval and political arms.

It is appropriate to conclude this chapter on a warming note—of some of the false assumptions which can be made by defence ministries, if the dialogue between intelligence and the political decision-makers is out of joint in some

---

[461] <u>Dickens, Vice-Admiral Sir Gerald Charles</u>: b. 1879; entered R.N. 1894; Commander 1914; Captain 1919; Deputy Director Plans Division, Admiralty, 1920-1922; Directing Staff, Imperial Defence College, 1926-1929; Rear-Admiral, 1932; <u>D.N.I. 1932-1935</u>; commanding reserve fleet 1935-1937; Vice-Admiral 1936; retired list 1938.

[462] Details of this can be seen in Admiral Godfrey's Memoirs: Vol. 5. Part 1. p. 154-155.

shape or form. A brief catalogue, taken from the experiences of Admiral Godfrey, will show quite clearly how fundamental errors can be made quite unwittingly and could have been avoided if a proper dialogue had existed between intelligence and politicians. He claims that in 1939-1941, the British military and political high command made these errors of judgment when deciding how to fight the war.

By imputation he is saying that intelligence may have helped forestall such errors:

(a) That the invasion of England was still on in late 1940 and 1941.
(b) That Germany had a hidden reserve of twenty or so divisions.
(c) That strategic bombing was accurate and effective.
(d) That AA guns, without fighters, could give ships adequate air defence.

He says that in 1938-1939, British wartime planning wrongly assumed:

(e) That the French Army and Air Force were efficient and well equipped.
(f) That its morale was good.

He says that Germany successfully planted false information that led Britain to believe:

(g) That U-boats were operating in the South Atlantic.
(h) That Britain had destroyed forty U-boats when the actual numbers did not exceed eight.

He states that after Japan joined the Axis at the end of 1941 Britain assumed:

(i) That Germany, Japan and Italy were acting in accordance with a coordinated plan, and this led C.I.G.S. to believe:
(j) That India was threatened by a German-Japanese 'pincer' movement.
(k) That the appearance of two British capital ships at Singapore would scare the Japanese and in some vague sort of way act as a deterrent.[463]

What Godfrey is saying is that it is very easy for politicians and senior service officers to make wrong assumptions after a series of hunches and wishful beliefs. To help lessen the degree of possible error, reference to intelligence is essential. For example, in (j) and (k) above, the J.I.C. was not consulted. Intelligence can

---

[463] Admiral Godfrey's Memoirs: Vol. 8

never be an infallible guide, but it nonetheless provides a critical forum for reviewing decisions and an insurance against wishful thinking.

---

* See Admiral Godfrey's Memoirs: Vol. I. Part 2. p. 270.

Chapter Eight
British Naval Intelligence—A Perspective

Conditions for the Survival and Effectiveness of a Naval Intelligence Organisation

The experience which British Naval intelligence had acquired in this period, 1880-1945, gave the post-1945 defence planners some clear indications of the factors involved in creating, maintaining, and adjusting the intelligence environment. In the age of 'flexible response', a flexible intelligence organisation is desirable. Certain conditions have emerged during this study which are absolutely essential for the survival and effectiveness of a naval or any military intelligence organisation.

Firstly, the need for centralisation at the very end of the intelligence process. Intelligence is goal-centred—to produce information on time for the right people in the right place. However excellent the preliminaries, if intelligence is put across to those who need it in a fragmentary, disordered way, then the chances are they will not draw the correct conclusions from it. On any issue there must be no doubt that all the bits and pieces have been put together, and presented in a palatable form to those who make decisions. Communications must be carefully established and well tried.

Direct lines must exist between intelligence workers and those who need their work. As far as the purely physical side of communications are concerned, these are always in danger from the enemy. Therefore, intelligence has a high responsibility for security. The disaster at Pearl Harbour must surely be the classic case study on this point. The Congressional Committee found that neither the C.-in-C. Pacific (Admiral Kimmel), nor any of his senior staff had the information possessed in Washington by the O.N.I., the Chief of Naval Operations, the Secretary of the Navy, and the Secretary of State.

Various people possessed then A1 intelligence of the Japanese intention to launch a pre-emptive attack somewhere in the Pacific, yet no one suggested or ordered air reconnaissance, the fleet to sea, or took other precautions.

The N.I.D. at Jutland and the O.N.I. at Pearl Harbour could have avoided this sort of problem if established working relations had existed between intelligence and operations. For intelligence to be good, the morale of those who work in it must be high—this can only be achieved if they know they are an integrated part of the naval machine. Intelligence is produced, after all, by people, not machines. They require recognition, continuity and tradition, just as the officers and men of a ship do.

Integration must involve the accepted right to evaluate data (to test its accuracy and synthesise it into a coherent whole with conclusions) and then to pass it on in a formal way as an estimate of probable development or, for instance, as a hard piece of intelligence (e.g., the range of enemy ships and speed at full power). To leave intelligence in the dark is to deny its main function. However, its limits must be fully understood by all concerned. Allen Dulles said that it is, in any case, impossible to provide a system that will be proof against the universal human frailty of intellectual stubbornness.

The limit he places on intelligence is "…to see that we have created the best possible mechanism to get the unvarnished facts before the policy-makers, and to get it there in time."[464] This would seem to place intelligence in its right perspective.

As Dulles says, nothing can override intellectual stubbornness or stupidity in those who occupy high positions. If an intelligence consumer has preconceptions, which he will not reject, then intelligence's task is hopeless. One example of where a service allowed its own preconceptions to work was the Royal Air Force in the 1930s, when it would not accept that the Germans regarded the Luftwaffe as ancillary to the Wehrmacht, because the R.A.F. saw its own role as an independent strategic force.[465]

Similarly, intelligence can never afford to take things for granted—judgments must always be constantly kept under review and, if need be, revised.

---

[464] See the paper by Allen W. Dulles: Memorandum respecting Section 202 (Central Intelligence Agency) to the bill to provide for a united defence establishment, 25 April 1947. Hearings before the Committee on Armed Services, United States Senate, 80th Congress, 1st Session.

[465] See Strong: Intelligence at the Top. p. 18.

This then is the atmosphere in which intelligence must exist. As to its ethics, they cannot be concerned with problems such as reducing the number of casualties in war, or the rightness or wrongness of particular policies, but more the goal-centredness, and integrity, of individual pieces of intelligence work. Hence, the absolute necessity for senior Naval Staff and politicians to be aware of their needs and to be able to assess intelligence's value.

If in peacetime intelligence acts as an insurance—the antennae through which a government receives information, and as a result of which it may make certain decisions, then if that system is considered worthwhile, it must be given protection—against pressure and prejudice, within and without the service and government. Admiral Godfrey's intelligence staff could not afford to have the same loyalties and masters as the service and government they served, in terms of policy. If objectivity in judgments was to be maintained, no departmental allegiances were possible.

At the same time, Godfrey and his heads of sections had to have a thorough knowledge of the decision-making process to see where their work fitted in and could make a real contribution.

On the question of objectivity one danger for the N.I.D. staff, of which both Hall and Godfrey were conscious, was that their staffs might inevitably form their own individual outlooks on particular questions and develop their own loyalty to the N.I.D. point of view. In both World Wars, the N.I.D. tried to build up a balanced staff to help obviate the latter—a mixture of disciplines and experiences—academics, lawyers, financiers, journalists, scientists, and so on. As a result, the N.I.D. did avoid a 'preponderance' of any one point of view on its staff, and there was equal access to data on a 'need to know' basis, and plenty of scope for minority views.

Whatever the checks and balances within the N.I.D. itself, political control in World War II was never lost, though, as we have seen, it was on several occasions during World War I. Churchill became the supreme arbiter of intelligence in World War II. He was, by inclination and temperament, suited to intelligence (furthermore he had an international historian, Professor Arnold Toynbee, preparing intelligence summaries for him and the War Cabinet, from N.I.D., J.I.C., D.M.I., D.A.I., S.O.E., M.E.W., F.O., and M.I. 5 and M.I. 6 sources). Intelligence is not a particularly spectacular affair but rather prosaic, and its art, as Field Marshal Alexander wrote, is "...to sift the wheat from the chaff" and produce "...short, clear statement."[466]

What the study of N.I.D. in the pre-1914 period has illustrated is how intelligence, when it is formally related to the politico-military structure, can act as the middle man between those who decide policy and make plans and those who have to carry them out, a clearing-house for ideas and information. As such, the N.I.D. had responsibility, and attendant authority and accountability, but it was never completely autonomous, though in those early days of a developing pragmatic, Naval Staff organisation, it often had no other option than to work virtually alone because an ideal situation could not be attained overnight.

As was stressed earlier, N.I.D. could not set itself objectives until experience itself dictated what those objectives might be, and no one was or could be sufficiently farsighted to draw up a blueprint for a full-scale naval intelligence organisation which would deal with all peace and wartime contingencies. In the post-World War II era, British Defence Intelligence has achieved as a result, amongst other factors, of N.I.D.'s previous history, the degree of integration and objective organisation necessary at all levels for furnishing information for those who make and execute policy.

What N.I.D.'s pre-1945 history indicates is how continuity and organisation can easily be lost, and even if some decisions may at the time seem reasonable and quite rational (such as N.I.D.'s run-down after World War I), in a transient population such as the Naval Staff, there does not necessarily remain a facility for retaining skills, experience, or even the basic professional outlook which would always come out with questions such as, for example, 'What does N.I.D. think, why, are they right, how does this affect us, what shall we recommend as a result?', and so on.

It is this lack of continuity which can become very dangerous because it means that organisations lapse for the wrong reasons. The history of the N.I.D. is a testimony to this danger. One insurance against it must surely be rigorous staff training and regular reappraisals of roles and organisation.

Naval Intelligence Personnel

The selection and training of intelligence personnel is critical. During this period, there was no systematisation in either of these areas and certainly no

---

[466] Field Marshal the Viscount Alexander of Tunis: Memoirs. Cassell. 1962.

formal procedure for recruitment in wartime. There is no trace of an intensive selection board. Whether this was to the detriment of the effectiveness of the N.I.D. is an impossible question to answer. Certainly, both Hall and Godfrey knew what sort of men they were looking for (implying that they knew what the job demanded), and how to go about finding, interviewing, and deciding about them.

Looking at the staff the N.I.D. acquired, particularly in the two World Wars, and the many functions they performed at the various levels of responsibility, several general points emerge.

Firstly, the high intelligence executive was expected to be able to produce intelligence summaries, stating his views of the general enemy, or potential enemy situation, and how his operations were likely to develop. On this score alone, to reduce a vast amount of data to manageable proportions and then to produce, in a few words, a report, either written or verbal, for a senior officer, required great skill.

The best insurance for the N.I.D.'s top staff was to be sceptical, for in the changing situation of war, with new information arriving every day, no sensible intelligence officer would irrevocably commit himself, unless absolutely certain. The N.I.D. had to avoid being too alarmist (e.g., over the possible threat of invasion in 1940), since when they had a truly alarmist position to report no one might pay enough attention to them.

The intelligence officer who lost his spirit of inquiry, whatever the quality of his judgment, was in danger of jeopardising the whole value of intelligence. He had to be prepared to assess a vast amount of data, sift through it, and then discard most of it if it did not appreciably alter the known or anticipated situation. Fortunately, one single man seldom made a decision—most work was done by groups, and so each man's work and judgment came under the critical eyes of his colleagues and the final scrutiny of his head of section and the D.N.I.

Some writers (Lord Mountbatten for example) have criticised the extensive use of civilians and reserve officers in naval intelligence (mainly because they lack the understanding of the factors involved in large-scale naval operations), but the group nature of intelligence work tended to obviate this, where, in any case, a naval officer, usually a Commander, was a head of section, and naturally had the necessary links with the sea, the operational environment and specialist departments of the Admiralty. The presence of civilians, who were not necessarily always impressed by senior naval officers, did, if anything, tend to help the naval officers.[467]

The judgment and independence of a naval officer in intelligence may be somewhat undermined by the necessity for him to obey his senior officers for most of the time. His whole training, the structure and ethos of the service may inhibit total independent judgment. The question in the mind of a man like Admiral Godfrey was—could a naval officer be reasonably expected to exhibit the same scrupulous, painstaking analysis and judgment which a barrister or scholar from civilian life could? The answer was invariably no. This factor was a serious threat to the integrity of intelligence, as were the career implications for a naval officer appointed to the N.I.D.

Most executive officers considered, quite understandably so in one sense, that commanding ships and giving orders was the most important thing, why they joined the Navy and by which they would be judged. As such, many saw intelligence appointments as a blockage to their careers. In the inter-war period, the whole concept of intelligence disappeared in H.M. ships. A ship's intelligence officer was usually detailed from amongst either the navigating or instructor staff. They were presented with the Manual of Intelligence, which mainly dealt with the security of cyphers. This was the measure of intelligence in the eyes of most naval officers.

Little did most officers realise that in the pre-1914 period and in World War I, and eventually in World War II, senior intelligence officer had and were to enjoy considerable influence and authority, with direct access to supreme commanders and politicians. The pre-1914 D.N.I.'s tended to reach the highest offices after this appointment. General Strong makes this comment on his time as Chief of Allied Intelligence:

"As Chief of Intelligence, I had the right of direct access to Eisenhower and his Chief of Staff, and I could approach them whenever I wished. Above all, under the American system I was a member of the 'inner circle', where policy was decided and planning and other decisions taken. All my experience suggests that this status is vital to the efficient functioning of an intelligence machine."[468]

---

[467] Donald McLachlan recalls how a Commander, R.N.V.R. told a newly appointed A.C.N.S. who entered the U-boat tracking room, "Here, Sir, we ascertain the facts first and do not let the policy influence the intelligence." Few career naval officers would have said this to an A.C.N.S.
[468] Strong: Intelligence at the Top. p. 85.

Many of the officers who served in the N.I.D. in junior positions in both World Wars aspired eventually to the highest ranks.

The Political Appreciation of Naval Intelligence

The political appreciation of naval intelligence is as important as that of the service. Not only must it ultimately exercise the necessary political control but it must pay all the necessary respect to the work of intelligence. Some politicians believe that much intelligence is a waste of time and unimportant. There is obviously some truth in this, but it is very dangerous to arbitrarily separate what appears to be the trivial from the important.

The reason for this is that at the time that much intelligence work is carried out it is not always possible to know what is useful and what is wasteful, to assess what is trivial and what later might become of national importance. There is a danger here for the politician—that he might become complacent, or just develop a desire not to be told.

Similarly, his control over aggressive espionage must be firm. It would be highly dangerous, though equally unlikely, for a repetition of Hall's activities to occur today. The politicians must decide how far it is necessary to keep abreast of all naval developments in territories of potential enemies, and whether or not to tell a potential enemy that one has his secrets. In the modern world, it would seem reasonable to suppose that no potential enemy will declare war on a nation because that nation has stolen its secrets, but it may be deterred from going to war if it is realised that those secrets have been discovered.

Responsibility to the Public

Politicians and Naval Staff have a great responsibility to the public to ensure that naval intelligence is efficient. The public have no measure of its effectiveness, in peace or war. Nor can a British political party make political capital from its naval intelligence. The public is more likely to be affected by the converse—the activities of other nations' intelligence organisations (as revealed, for instance, by spy trials) and the resulting suspicion cast on Britain's own security and intelligence services. The politician must carefully stage-manage, in the interests of the state, any knowledge the public gains of intelligence aims, methods and results.

Naval Intelligence in the Nuclear Age

It is appropriate to conclude this study by taking a brief look at naval intelligence in the nuclear age. The whole concept of naval strategy has changed—the various parameters of the past are now subservient to the primary role of nuclear maritime deterrence. It is this which controls the other variables. The weapons of the super powers attempt, at least, to keep abreast of one another. For naval intelligence, this has always posed one great question, which Professor L. W. Martin has, in another context, aptly described thus:

"In essence, however, since conventional war must henceforth be limited war, the question boils down not to the outcome of such a war, but of how large and unfavourable a conventional war either side would accept before resorting to limited or complete nuclear retaliation. The answer would seem to be that such options would be exercised well before the western war effort faced strangulation. How long before must remain a question for the event. The case is essentially similar to the 'pause' in Europe. NATO doctrine calls for the use of nuclear weapons rather than acceptance of defeat on the ground. Much the same would be true at sea."[469]

The problems for intelligence are, therefore, manifold—the more significant of which are the detection of the danger signs of a pre-emptive nuclear strike and the allied diplomatic and psychological precursors to this the detection and analysis of the use of naval power for political ends without recourse to war (paramount now in the nuclear age), and the question of the psychology of deterrence in terms of naval weapons systems via-à-vis potential enemies. Security in the nuclear age may be more concerned with hiding weaknesses, than strengths.

Intelligence may well advise, for instance, that it may be more advantageous to release performance figures of certain of the best and latest weapon systems to convince a possible enemy that the deterrent remains effective. Nonetheless, data regarding enemy weapon systems is still a primary target of intelligence, along with strengths, tactics, ranges and endurances, deployment and location, the state of morale, training, and fighting efficiency. Knowledge of tactical nuclear weapons is as vital as the deterrent systems, and in the age of the nuclear hunter-killer submarines knowledge of the state of anti-submarine warfare and

---

[469] L. W. Martin: The Sea in Modern Strategy. p. 43.

the capabilities of submarines is equally essential, assuming the possibility of limited, conventional warfare.

An ever-present danger today is the possibility of an enemy gaining arms secrets from those countries to whom Britain sells arms. The danger is that their security may not be satisfactory, or that an alliance or friendship may end before the arms themselves have lost their efficacy. Furthermore, when looking at the forces of possible enemy fleets intelligence must always survey their overall commitments. It may be a very false prophecy indeed which ascribes to enemy fleets a limited number of purposes which the event totally disproves.

It is relevant to reiterate a point made earlier—that naval intelligence cannot be separated from the other intelligence studies which assist in the analysis of the make-up of other nations. The advent of nuclear weapons has destroyed the simple assumptions underlaying the pre-1945 political-military world. What intelligence overall must look for is any shifts in the factors that sustain deterrence—it cannot be assumed to be an immutable balance. Intelligence must still be able to warn, and Britain's defences must remain constantly responsive.

In the event of limited war and the actual or threatened use of tactical nuclear weapons, the availability of accurate intelligence, timely produced, may determine whether or not the fighting escalates. Hence, there is a need to keep pace with the technology of intelligence and to counter the efforts of possible enemies.

In the contemporary world, most people in the west hope that they can rely upon the increasing destructiveness of weapons to prevent total nuclear war, notwithstanding the possibilities of limited conventional war. History has shown though that any theory which claims that war can be made so terrible that all nations will remain at peace has no foundation. It is with this in mind that modern military intelligence should continue its incessant work. The period of this study witnessed how energetic, ambitious, and predatory leaders resorted to war regardless of the consequences of their actions for their nations and the world.

There is no reason to suppose that this danger has gone forever with the advent of nuclear weapons. Intelligence can be one safeguard against the frightening consequences of total nuclear war.

APPENDIX A: An Example of Hard Intelligence Data

Below are listed the ranges of German units in 1939. It was this sort of quite simple, yet invaluable information which the N.I.D. had to acquire quickly if it was to be able to assist Operations in determining the waters in which German units might operate. A ten thousand-ton pocket battleship, for example, with a range of eight thousand nautical miles could be expected to head for the South Atlantic, allowing for neutral waters, and the American security zone, and the need to pass via the Denmark Strait from the north German ports to the Atlantic.

A radius of action for each class would have to take into account outward and homeward passage, and the fuel which might be consumed at full power and when in battle—probably a 20% reserve for these contingencies.

Type	Nautical Miles
Type IX U-Boat	9,600
10,000-ton pocket battleship	8,000
Diesel-driven battleship of the Z-Plan	6,400
Scharnhorst-Gneisenau	4,000
Tirpitz, Bismarck and diesel-driven destroyer of the Z-Plan	3,200
Heavy cruiser	2,700
Type V11C U0Boat	2,600
1914-1918 Battlecruiser and Cruiser	2,400
Type ViiA U-Boat	1,700
1936 Class Destroyer and 1914 Class torpedo boat	1,000

APPENDIX B: Directors of Naval Intelligence 1882-1945

1882-1889: <u>Hall, Captain William Henry</u>: see last part of Appendix C.

1889-1894: <u>Bridge, Admiral Sir Cyprian</u>: 1839-1924; entered R.N. 1853; Captain 1877; <u>D.N.I. 1889-1894</u>; C.-in-C. Australia 1894-1898, China 1901-1904. Wrote two major books—*The Art of Naval Warfare* (London 1907), and *Sea Power and Other Studies* (London 1910).

1894-1899: <u>Beaumont, Admiral Sir Lewis Anthony</u>: b. 1847; entered R.N. 1860; Rear-Admiral 1897; <u>D.N.I. 1894-98</u>; C.-in-C. Pacific 1899-1900; C.-in-C. Australia 1901-1903; Admiral 1906; C.-in-C. Devonport 1905-1908.

1899-1902: <u>Custance, Admiral Sir Reginald</u>: 1847-1935; <u>A.D.N.I. 1886-1890</u>; Naval Attaché Washington and Paris 1892-1895; D.N.I. 1899-1902; second-in-command Channel Fleet; an opponent of Fisher's Dreadnought policy; author of *The Ship of the Line* (London 1912).

1902-1905: <u>Battenburg, Prince Louis, Admiral of the Fleet</u>: entered R.N. 1868; joint secretary naval and military committee on defence, 1894; <u>A.D.N.I. 1900</u>; <u>D.N.I. 1902-1905</u>; second-in-command, Mediterranean 1907; C.-in-C.; Atlantic 1908; Second Sea Lord 1911; First Sea Lord 1912; resigned October 1914.

1905-1907: <u>Ottley, Rear-Admiral Sir Charles</u>: b. 1858; entered R.N. 1871; Captain 1899; Naval Attaché Washington, Rome, Tokyo, St. Petersburg, and Paris, 1899-1904; on staff of the Committee of Imperial Defence, 1904; <u>D.N.I. 1905</u>; Secretary of the C.I.D. 1907-1912.

1907: <u>King-Hall, Admiral Sir George Fowler</u>: b. 1850; entered R.N. 1863; Captain 1891; Rear-Admiral 1904; <u>D.N.I. 1907</u>; Admiral commanding on the coast of Ireland 1906-1908; Vice-Admiral 1908; Admiral 1912; C.-in-C. Australia station 1910-1913; retired 1914.

1907-1909: <u>Slade, Admiral Sir Edmond John Warre</u>: 1859-1928; entered R.N. 1872; Commander 1894; Captain 1899; served in H.M.S. Hecla during the

Egyptian war 1882; May 1904 Director of Senior Officers War Course, R.N.C., Greenwich; D.N.I. Nov. 1907-March 1909; C.-in-C. East Indies 1909-1912; retired 1917; Director of the Anglo-Persian Oil Company.

1909-1912: Bethell, Admiral Hon. Sir Alexander Edward: b. 1855; entered R.N. 1869; Commander 1891; Captain 1893; Rear-Admiral 1908; D.N.I. 1909-1912; C.-in-C. East Indies 1912; Vice-Admiral 1913; Commandant R.N. War College 1913-1914; commander battleships 3 Fleet 1914; commander Channel Fleet, 1915; C.-in-C. Plymouth, 1916-1918; retired 1918.

1912-1913 Jackson, Rear-Admiral Thomas: b. 1868; entered R.N. 1881; Commander 1899; Captain 1905; Rear-Admiral 1916; Naval Attaché, Tokyo, 1906; D.N.I. Jan. 1912-Oct. 1913; Director of the Operations Division, Jan. 1915-June 1917.

1913-1914: Oliver, Admiral Sir Henry Francis: b. 1865; entered R.N. 1878; Commander 1899, Captain 1903; Rear-Admiral 1913; D.N.I. 1913-1914; DCNS and Chief of Admiralty War Staff 1914-1918; Vice-Admiral 1918; Vice-Admiral commanding Home Fleet 1919-1920; Second Sea Lord 1920-1924; Admiral 1923.

1914-1918: Hell, Admiral Sir William Reginald: 1870-1943; son of the First D.N.I., William Henry Hall; entered R.N. 1884; Commander 1901; Captain 1905; naval assistant to the Controller of the Navy, 1911-1913; Captain H.M.S. Queen Mary 1913; B. of Heligoland Bight, 28 August 1914; D.N.I. 1914-1918; CB 1915; KCMG 1918; promoted Rear-Admiral 1917; Vice-Admiral 1922; Admiral 1926; Hon. DCL Oxon. 1919; Hom. LLD Cantab. 1920; MP (Con) West Derby Division of Liverpool 1919; principal agent of the Conservative Party, 1923; MP (Con) Eastbourne, 1925. Retired from politics, 1929. A drawing by Francis Dodd, Imperial War Museum.

1918-1921: Sinclair, Vice-Admiral Hugh Francis Paget: entered R.N. 1886; assistant to Director of Naval Ordnance 1904-1905; Commander of R.N. Barracks, Portsmouth 1906-1909; Director of the Mobilisation Division, Admiralty 1914-1916; Captain H.M.S. Renown 1916-1917; Chief of Staff Baltic cruiser forces 1917-1919; D.N.I. 1919-1921; Chief of Submarine service 1921-1923; retired list 1926.

1921-1924: Fitzmaurice, Rear-Admiral Maurice Swynfen: b. 1870; A.D.N.I. 1910; NID staff and Admiralty War Staff 1912-1914; senior officer on the Yangtse 1914; Captain H.M.S. Triumph 1914-1915; principal naval transport officer, Dardanelles and Salonika 1915-1916; Chief of Staff Eastern

Mediterranean, 1916-1917, Captain HMD Dreadnought 1918; senior naval officer coast of Palestine, 1918; commodore commanding British Aegean squadron 1919; D.N.I. 1921-1924.

1924-1927: Hotham, Rear-Admiral Alan Geoffrey: b. 1876; D.N.I. 1924-1929.

1927-1930: Comvile, Admiral Sir Barry Edward: 1878-1971; entered R.N. 1892; Commander 1909; Captain 1916; Rear-Admiral 1927; Asst. Sec. C.I.D. 1912-1914; Director of Plans, Admiralty, 1920-1922, C.N.I. 1927-1930; Vice-Admiral commanding third cruiser squadron, Mediterranean, 1931-1932; President R.N.C. Greenwich, 1932-1934; Admiral and retired list, 1936.

1930-1932: Usborne, Vice-Admiral Cecil Vivian: b. 1880; Captain H.M.S. Colossus 1913; Deputy Director of Gunnery Division, Admiralty, 1922; Director of the Tactical School 1925; Rear-Admiral 1928; D.N.I. 1930-1932; retired 1933.

1932-1935: Dickens, Vice-Admiral Sir Gerald Charles: b. 1879; entered R.N. 1894; Commander 1914; Captain 1919; Deputy Director Plans Division, Admiralty, 1920-1922; Directing Staff, Imperial Defence College, 1926-1929; Rear-Admiral, 1932; D.N.I. 1932-1935; commanding reserve fleet 1935-1937; Vice-Admiral 1936; retired list 1938.

1935: Scott, Rear-Admiral Malcolm Maxwell: b. 1883; entered R.N. 1898; Captain 1925; Rear-Admiral 1936; Capt.-Supt. of contract-built ships 1929-1931; Captain in charge HM naval base Singapore 1932-1934; D.N.I. 1935; retired list 1936.

1935-1939: Troup, Vice-Admiral Sir James Andrew Gardiner: b. 1883; Commander 1916; Captain 1922; Rear-Admiral 1935; D.N.I. 1935-1939; Vice-Admiral 1939; retired 1939.

1939-1943: Godfrey, Admiral John Henry: 1888-1971; Captain 1928; Rear-Admiral 1939; Vice-Admiral 1942; Admiral 1945; Deputy Director, Plans Division, Admiralty, 1933-1935; Captain H.M.S. Repulse, 1936-1939; D.N.I. 1939-1943; Flag officer commanding Royal Indian Navy, 1943-1946.

1943-1946: Rushbrooke, Vice-Admiral Edmund Gerard Noel: b. 1892; Commander 1918; Captain 1936; Chief of the Intelligence staff, China Station, 1937; Captain H.M.S. Guardian 1939; H.M.S. Argus 1940; H.M.S. Eagle 1941; D.N.I. 1943-1946; Rear-Admiral 1945; retired 1947; Vice-Admiral on the retired list 1948.

The following obituary for Captain William Henry Hall, Royal Navy, appeared in *The Times* on 13 March 1895:

We have to record the death, after a few days' illness, of Captain W. H. Hall, late of her Majesty's Ship Resolution, who was recently appointed Captain-Superintendent of Pembroke Dockyard. He was sub-lieutenant of the Challenger during the Mexican expedition of 1861, including the occupation of St. Juan d'Ulloa, Vera Cruz. The following facts are given as they appear in 'Lean's Royal Navy List':

"It was in 1882 that the Foreign Intelligence Committee was established, mainly at the instance or insistence of one or two men like Sir John Colomb and Lord C. Beresford. Captain W. H. Hall was put in charge, and he had as his assistants one marine officer, two clerks, and a copyist. Up to that time, there was no distinct department of the Admiralty for registering what other nations are doing, can do, and are ready to do in the event of war. Captain Hall took this work in hand, and of the way in which he did it, we may judge when Mr Campbell-Bannerman speaks of it, 'as of the highest importance to the efficiency of the naval service.'

"The four years of the existence of the Foreign Intelligence Committee were four years of arduous labour for Captain Hall. In 1887, it was decided to graft upon the basis of the Foreign Intelligence Committee the larger and more important department to be called the Naval Intelligence Department. The staff was largely increased, and at first it was proposed to place an Admiral at the head of the newly created bureau. It was, however, soon recognised that to displace Captain W. H. Hall would be a grave mistake, and that officer was installed as Director of Naval Intelligence.

"The wisdom of this step has been fully proved, and is recognised by the service generally. To the excellent business arrangements, untiring efforts, and exceptional tact of Captain Hall, the celerity and comprehension which have characterised the execution of the function of the new department are largely due."

Captain Hall held the appointment till January 1889. He was joint secretary to the Royal Commission on Army and Navy Administration in 1888; and received his captain's good service pension in June 1894. He was succeeded in the position of Director of Naval Intelligence by Captain, now Rear-Admiral, Bridge. Captain Hall then commanded the Severn in the China Squadron, and was afterwards appointed to the command of the Vernon as head of the School of Torpedo Instruction at Portsmouth; subsequently, in the manoeuvres of 1893, he commanded the Blenheim.

He was afterwards appointed to the Resolution, and was in command of that vessel when she encountered storm at the end of 1893 which compelled her to put back from the Bay of Biscay He remained in the command of the Resolution until a very short time ago, when he was appointed to succeed Captain Penrose-Fitzgerald as Captain-Superintendent of Pembroke Dockyard. He was on his way to take up that appointment when he was taken ill in the train. He was removed thence to his bed, and died on Sunday.

As Director of Naval Intelligence, he was principally responsible for the schemes of naval manoeuvres from 1887—the Jubilee year—until he was succeeded by Admiral Bridge. Both from the point of view of practical experience and general intelligence, he was a most distinguished officer, and had he survived to be promoted to flag rank, he would probably have attained a very distinguished position.

APPENDIX C: N.I.D. Staff—1942

Heads of Departments and Sections

Section	Area, Department or Section Officers
D.N.I.	Vice-Admiral Godfrey
D.D.N.I.	Vice-Admiral Campbell
D.D.N.I. (Foreign)	Major-General Lamplough, RM
Civil Assistant to the D.N.I.	Mr Johns
Personal Assistant to the D.N.I. Private Secretary)	Mr E. L. Merrett
D.D.I.C. Operational Intelligence Centre	Vice-Admiral N. E. Denning
A.D.N.I. (Security)	Major-General R. Neville RM Colonel Caulfield RM
A.D.N.I. (E) Technical (N.I.D.)	Captain (E) Charley
A.D.N.I. (T) Topographical	Colonel Bassett RM Mr A. F. Wells
Section 1 Germany, etc. Scandinavia, Poland, Low Countries, Occupied France	Lt. Cdr. W. Todd, Commander Gonin, Lord Stradbroke
Section 2 The Americans	Mr Wilding
Section 3 Mediterranean, Africa, The Balkans, M.I. (9) and (19) Prisoners of War	Lt. Col. Cordeaux RM, Major Harris, RM, Lt. Cdr. Rosevere
Section 4 Far East, Pacific, Australia, India, Indian Ocean	Commander Barry, Major Hicks, RM, Lt. Cer. Leggatt.
Section 16 Russian Section	Commander Chatwin, Mr Fletcher-Cooke
Section 20 Unoccupied France, North and West Africa, Spain, Portugal and possessions	Commander Jennings, Lt. Cdr. Rayner, Captain A. H. Hillgarth, Mr Pritchett
Section 5 Geographical Handbooks	Professor Mason

Section 6 Topographical (I.S.T.D.)	Colonel Bassett RM, Captain Law, Mr A. F. Wells
Section 7 Technical	Captain (E) Charley, Eng. Commander Cannan
Section 8 Operational Intelligence Centre Submarines, Germany, Italy and Japan	Vice-Admiral N. E. Denning Hon. Mr Justice Winn, Commander Barrow-Green
Section 9 Communications	Captain J. Loehnis
Section 10 Security	Paymaster Captain Wilson
Section 11 Admiralty Photographic Library	Mr Slessor
Section 12 Intelligence Summaries	Commander Montagu, R.N.V.R.
Section 14 D.N.I.'s Naval Secretariat	Commander Pearce, Miss Cameron
Section 17 Operations and Intelligence, J.I.C. and J.I.S. Cover Plans	Captain Baker Cresswell, Captain Drake, Major Lordon, RM, Commander Montagu, R.N.V.R.
Section 19 Propaganda, Information Section	Lt. Cdr. McLachlan, R.N.V.R. Mrs. J. S. G. Saunders, Miss Marjorie Napier, Commander Robertson-MacDonald.
Section 21 Contacts Section	Lt. Harling, R.N.V.R.
Section 21 (a) Contacts Register	Mr Wannacott

This list is taken from the unpublished Memoirs of Admiral J. H. Godfrey, Vol. 5. Part 2. p. 347.

Sources

1. Unpublished (listed according to their location):
A. The Public Record Office:
Adm. 5: 6074, 1462; Adm. 116:3106; Adm. 1:6505, 6634, 6731, 6772, 6818B, 6868A/B, 6922, 8623/64—creation and organisation of the F.I.C.; creation of the N.I.D.; Adm. 1:7166B—Instructions for the Director of Naval Intelligence, 24 January 1887.
Adm. 137:324, 359, 361—work of the N.I.D. shipping and intelligence officers pre-1914.
Adm. 137:408, 446, 2732, 3045—work of the N.I.D. Trade Division pre-1914.
Adm. 116:3095—the papers of Sir George Clark, Secretary of the C.I.D.
Adm. 137:1100—improvements in the transmission of intelligence, 1915.
Adm. 116:4080—improvements in the N.I.D.'s communications system 1935-1939.
Adm. 137:1630—Rear-Admiral J.C. Ley's Committee on the N.I.D., 1918.
Adm. 137:1630—abolition of the titles D.N.I. and D.D.N.I., 1918; improvements in the N.I.D.
Adm. 116:1842—the N.I.D. in the early post-1918 period.
Adm. 137:713—intelligence at the Dardanelles, 1915.
Adm. 137:1013—intelligence of German intentions and capabilities, 1914
Adm. 137:1080—comparison of the Grand and High Seas Fleets, January 1915.
Adm. 116:2519—defence against air raid attack. N.I.D. data, 1927.
Adm. 116:4030—N.I.D. appraisal of a naval air policy, 1936.
Adm. 137:146, 150, 157, 287, 290, 291, 292, 302, 333, 334—naval air reconnaissance in World War I.
Adm. 137:3060, 2060, 2026—N.I.D. intelligence in the Baltic, World War I.
Adm. 137:174—203—N.I.D. intelligence dockets for the Grand Fleet, 1914-1918.

Adm. 116:3929—British forecasts of British naval strengths under the terms of the Anglo-German Naval Agreement 1936-1939.

Adm. 137:1080, 1629, 1630—Foreign Office (naval intelligence) and attaches' reports for World War I.

Cab. 29:148—Berlin attaché's reports, 1934.

F.O. 371:17765—Paris attaché's report 1934; 18860—Berlin attaché's report 1935; 18738—Berlin attaché's report 1935; 17600—N.I.D. report on Japanese naval activity, 1934.

Adm. 137:1629—N.I.D. data from German deserters in World War I.

Adm. 137: 1629; 1630; 1100; 3060—N.I.D. data from P.O.W.s, survivors, friendly neutrals, and agents' reports in World War I; 1080—N.I.D. foreign press sources.

Adm. 1:8646—Naval Shipbuilding Sub-Committee of the C.I.D. 1920.

Adm. 1:2426—Naval Staff discussion on Singapore, 1923.

Adm. 1:7734—Baddeley Papers—presented to the P.R.O. by Sir Vincent Baddeley.

Adm. 116:886B—Naval Staff memoranda, 1889-1914.

Adm. 1: 9589, 9587, 9649, 9713—N.I.D. intelligence in 1938.

Adm. 137:108-111, 302—N.I.D. intelligence from Germany, 1914-1918.

Adm. 137:2090, 498—N.I.D. intelligence in the Crimea, 19114-1918.

Adm. 137:382, 482—N.I.D. intelligence in the Black Sea, 1914-1918.

Cab. 38:20, 21—Churchill presents N.I.D. data to the Cabinet and C.I.D. 1912.

Adm. 1:9564—Mediterranean intelligence report no. 7, 1938.

Adm. 1:10226—development of the O.I.C.; 9792—naval intelligence in wartime; 10218—reorganisation of the N.I.D. to meet wartime conditions; 10224—formation of the Information Section; 9525—establishment of HF/DF stations; 10465—appointment of an additional D.D.N.I.; 10471, 10014—organisation of the N.I.D. press and publicity section; 10946—increase in N.I.D. personnel and granting of R.N.V.R. commissions 1938-1940; 9567—re-organisation of N.I.D. intelligence staff in Cape Town, 1939.

Adm. 116; 241B—199 meeting of the C.I.D., 2 April 1925.

Cab. 357:18—Captain Troubridge's annual report to the D.N.I. and F.O. from Berlin, 1936.

Adm. 116:3637—intelligence deficiencies revealed in the 1938 crisis.

Adm. 1:9552—N.I.D. reports on Combined Operations exercises, 1938; 10212—intelligence organisation on the Mediterranean station; 10220—N.I.D.

control work and reporting in South America; 10214—possibility of the N.I.D. establishing coast-watching and intelligence organisation in Eire, 1939; 9679—officers employed on operational intelligence; 10222—the use by German submarines of a sonoperophon; 10176—N.I.D. investigation into the use of midget submarines; 9741—N.I.D. investigation into magnetic telephones in US ships; 10227—Anglo-German Naval Conference, Singapore—leakage of information; 10217—censorship of telephone calls from the Forth and the Clyde areas to Ireland; 10066—N.I.D.'s proposed censorship of outgoing mails, 1939; 9922—initial dispositions of the Mediterranean Fleet in the event of war, 19139; 10228—an attaché's report, 1939; 10958—N.I.D. interrogation of a German merchant crew, 1940; 9759—intelligence and the Battle of the River Plate, 1939.

Cab. 2:12B—D.N.I. (Battenburg) to the C.I.D. 1903.
Adm. 1:7516—Custance to Fisher.
F.O. 99:400—Battenburg to the F.O. 1902.
F.O. 64:1630—Ottley to the F.O. 1905.
Cab. 2:1—C.I.D. meeting 12 April 1905.
Cab. 3:1—11A, 16A—Battenburg to the C.I.D. 1903.
Cab. 3:1—144A; Cab. 17:22, 5, 3—the N.I.D. and the C.I.D. and the question of an invasion threat and planning for the defence of trade.
Cab. 53:14—Report of the Commandant of the Imperial Defence College, 1927.
Cab. 53:14—J.P.C. 1927; 29-J.P.C. 1936; 29—Report of the Commandant of the Imperial Defence College, 1936; 42—J.P.C., 1938.
Adm. 116:3378—F.O. to Henderson, August 1938.
Adm. 116:3368, 3369—N.I.D. data concerning German building programme, 1936—1939.
Adm. 167:68—Admiralty Board Minutes, 1923.
Adm. 116:3378—Captain Tom Phillips' letter about Germany's naval intentions, December 1936.
Cab. 3:1, 16A—the D.N.I. to the C.I.D., July 1903.
Cab. 16:3A—the D.N.I. and the question of invasion threats, 12 December 1907.

B. The National Maritime Museum, Greenwich:

The Naval Memoirs of Admiral J. H. Godfrey, in typescript.
N.I.D. report no. 835, June, 1908—technical intelligence.
N.I.D. report no. 944, January 1914.

The Slade Papers—a series of letters, memoranda and Slade's Diary (which he was encouraged to keep by Corbett). The correspondence with the First Lord and First Sea Lord is the most valuable.

Papers of Sir Frederick Tower-Hamilton—intelligence reports, secret and confidential, (including summaries of the international situation) by the N.I.D., 1915, 1916.

C. University of London:
Ph.D. thesis (1970)—N.W. Summerton (King's College): The Development of British Military Planning for a war against Germany, 1904-1914. (Department of War Studies)

D. University of Oxford:
D. Phil. Thesis (1967)—B. McL. Ranft (Balliol College): The Naval Defence of British Sea-Borne trade, 1860-1905.

E. Captain S. W. Roskill:
Papers in the private possession of Captain Roskill: CB 0938—Naval Staff Appreciation of the Battle of Jutland; signals and letters of W. F. Clarke (staff of Room 40, World War I); correspondence from Sir Eugen Millington-Drake, Admiral Sir William James, and Donald McLachlan. Verbal information from Captain Roskill proved invaluable.

F. Ministry of Defence Library (Navy):
Selected parts of the Naval Memoirs of Admiral J. H. Godfrey, unavailable at Greenwich.

G. Vice-Admiral Sir N. E. Denning:
Parts of the Naval Memoirs of Admiral J. H. Godfrey, unavailable elsewhere. Verbal information from Admiral Denning proved invaluable.

2. Published:

A. Primary

1. **HMSO**: Cmd. 2097—Mr Peter Thorneycroft's White Paper on the Central Organisation of Defence.

Cmd. 6775 1946—The Official Report on the escape of the Scharnhorst, Gneisenau, and Prinz Eugen from Brest to Germany.

Documents on German Foreign Policy, Series C, Vol. 3.

Cmd. 2029—Findings of the Salisbury Committee, 1923.

Documents on British Foreign Policy, Third Series, Vol. 3.

2. **Navy Records Society**: P. J. Kemp—The Papers of Admiral Sir John Fisher, Vol. 2, London, 1964. Ed. E. W. R. Lumby: Policy and Operations in the Mediterranean, 1912-1914. Ed. Captain S. W. Roskill—Documents Relating to the Naval Air Service, Vol. 1, 1908-1918.

3. **Admiralty**: Naval Staff Monographs for World War I, a complete set of which may be found in the Ministry of Defence Library (Navy).

Führer Conferences on Naval Affairs—Summary records of Hitler's Conferences with the C.-in-C. of the German Navy. London, 1947.

4. **Miscellaneous**: Harvey, J. (ed) (1970) *The Diplomatic Diaries of Oliver Harvey, 1937-1940*, Collins.

W. S. Chalmers, W. S. (1951) *The Life and Letters of David Earl Beatty*, Hodder and Stoughton. The Times, 13 March 1895, Ministry of Defence (Navy) Library.

B. Secondary

Abshagen, K. H. (1956) *Canaris*, Translated by A. H. Brodrick, London: Hutchinson.

Admiralty (1947) 'Führer Conference on Naval Affairs', Admiralty, *HMSO*.

Admiralty White Paper 2710 (1926) *Report on Lord Kitchner's Death*.

Agar, Captain A., V.C., D.S.O., R.N. (1963) *Baltic Episode,* Hodder and Stoughton.

Alexander, Field Marshal the Viscount of Tunis, North, J. (ed) (1962) *Memoirs: 1940-1945*, Cassell.

Alsop, S., Braden, T. (1946) *Sub Rosa. The OSS and American Espionage*, New York: Reynal and Hitchcock.

Arnold, H. H. (1949) *Global Mission. By the Chief of the Army Air Forces 1938-1946*, New York: Harper.

Assman, K. (1959) *Deutsche Seestrategie in Zwei Welkriegen*, Vowinckel Heidelberg.

Aston, Sir George. (1939) *Secret Service*, London: Faber and Faber.

Auphon, Rear-Admiral Paul, Mardal, J. (1959) *The French Navy in World War II*, Translated by Captain A. C. J. Sabalot, USN.

Bacon, R. H. (1936) *Earl Jellicoe*.

Barraclough, G. (1964) *An Introduction to Contemporary History*, Watts.

Barry and Creasy (3 July 1947) 'Attacks on the Tirpitz by Midget Submarines, September 1943', *London Gazette*.

Bedell Smith, W. (1956) *Eisenhower's Six Great Decisions*, London: Longmans, London.

Behrens, C. B. A. (1955) 'Merchant Shipping and the Demands of War: In a History of the Second World War', U.K. Civil Service, *HMSO*.

Bennett, G. (1964) *The Battle of Jutland,* Batsford.

Blackburn, D., Caddell, W. W. *Secret Service in South Africa*.

Bragadin, M. (1957) *The Italian Navy in World War Two*, Annapolis: U.S. Navy Institute.

Bradley, O. N. (1951) *A Soldier's Story*, New York: Holt.

Brassey's Naval Annual, 1948 (8 May 1946) 'Loss of H.M.S. Glorious, from House of Commons', *Parliamentary report*, Hansard. Ships of the Royal Navy in Losses During the Second World War, 1947.

U-boat casualties during the war (1946) German, Italian and Japanese. Particulars of destruction, Cmd. 6843.

Report of the Escape of the Scharnhorst, Gneisenau, and Prinz Eugen from Brest to Germany (1946) Cmd. 6775.

Brodie, B (1959) *Strategy in the Missile Age,* Princeton, N.J.: Princeton University Press.

Brown, N. (1964) *Strategic Mobility*, Chatto and Windus.

Bryant, Sir Arthur (1957-1959) *Field Marshal the Viscount Alanbrooke, Memoirs, Vol. I—The Turn of the Tide, 1939-1943, Vol II—Triumph in the West, 1943-1946*, London: Collins.

Buckmaster, Col. M. J. (1952) *Specially Employed*, London: Batchworth; (1958) *They Fought Alone*, London: Odhams.

Bullock, J. (1963) *M.I. 5: The Origin and History of the British Counter— Espionage Service*, London: Arthur Baker.

Bullock, J., Miller, H. (1961) *Spy Ring: A Story of the Naval Secrets case,* Secker and Warburg.

Burrough (3 July 1947) 'Final Stages of the Naval War in N.W. Europe', *London Gazette*.

Busch, H. (1955) U-Boats at War, London: Clowes.

Bywater, H. C., Ferraby, H. C. (1932) *Strange Intelligence*, Constable and Company. Their Secret Purposes. Drama and Mysteries of the Naval War, London: Constable.

Belot, R. (1951) *The Struggle for the Mediterranean, 1939-1945*, London: O.U.P.

Campbell, I. M. R. (16 January 1946) Russian Convoys, 1941-1945, Royal United Service Institution Lecture.

Carter, D. (1959) *The Fourth Branch of Government*, Boston: Houghton Mifflin.

Chalmers, W. S. (1951) *Life and Letters of David Beatty;*

(1954) *Max Horton and the Western Approaches*, London: Hodder and Stoughton;

(1959) *Full Cycle: The Biography of Admiral Sir Bertram Ramsay*, Hodder and Stoughton.

Chatfield, Lord (1942) *The Navy and Defence*, Heinemann.

Churchill, W. S. (1923-1931) *The World Crisis, 1911-1918,* London: Thornton Butterworth;

(1948-1953) *The Second World War*, Six volumes, London: Cassell.

Clark, A. (1962) *The Fall of Crete*, New York: Morrow.

Clark, M. W. (1950) *Calculated Risk, 1940-1947*, New York: Harper.

Collier, R. (1961) *The Sands of Dunkirk*, New York: Dutton.

Collins (7 July 1948) 'Battle of the Java Sea, 27 February 1942', *London Gazette*.

Colornb, J. C. R. (1882) 'Naval Intelligence and the Protection of Shipping in War', *RUSI Journal XXV*, p. 553-590.

Colvin, I. (1951) *Chief of Intelligence*, London: Gollanz.

(1964) 'Committee of Imperial Defence', Papers to 1914, *HMSO*.

Connolly, C. (1952) *The Missing Diplomats*, London: The Queen Anne Press.

Corbett, Sir J. S. (1920-1931) History of the Great War based on official documents: Naval Operations, Five volumes, Last two volumes by Sir H. Newbold, London: Longmans Green.

Cowier, J. S. (1949) Mines and Minelaying, Oxford University Press.

Craven, J. P. (April 1966) 'Seapower and the Sea-bed', *Proceedings of the U.S. Naval Institute.*

Creasy, Rear-Admiral G. E. (5 December 1945) The Navy's Part in the Victory in Europe, Royal United Service Institution Lecture.

Creswell, J. (1967) *Sea Warfare, 1939-1945*, University of California Press.

Cross, C. (1968) *The Fall of the British Empire,* Book Club Associates.

Cunningham, Admiral of the Fleet the Viscount of Hyndhope (7 July 1948) 'Action off Calabria, 9 July 1940', *London Gazette*;

(4 July 1947) 'Fleet Air Arm Operations against Taranto, November 1940', *London Gazette*;

(31 July 1947) 'Battle of Matapan, arch 1941', *London Gazette*;

(12 May 1948) 'Action against a Convoy, 15/16 April 1941', *London Gazette;*

(24 May 1948) Battle of Crete, May 1941', *London Gazette;*

(23 March 1949) The Landings in North Africa, November 1942', *London Gazette*;

(25 April 1950) Control of the Sicilian Straits, July 1943', *London Gazette*;

(2 May 1950) 'Operations in the Gulf of Salerno, September 1943', *London Gazette*;

(1952) *A Sailor's Odessey*, London: Hutchinson.

With Somerville, Curteis, and Syfret (11 August 1948) 'Mediterranean Convoy Operations, 1941-1942', *London Gazette*.

Dalein, D. J. (1955) *Soviet Espionage*, Oxford University Press.

Dalton, H. (1957) *The Fateful Years*, London: Frederick Muller.

Deacon, R. (1969) *A History of the British Secret Service*, Muller.

Denning, Lord (Sept. 1963) 'Report', *HMSO*.

Derry, T. K. (1952) 'The Campaign in Norway', *HMSO*.

Donitz, K. (1959) *Memoirs: Ten Years and Twenty Days*, Translated by R. H. Stevens in collaboration with D. Woodward, Weidenfeld and Nicolson.

Driberg, T. (1956) *Guy Burgess,* London: Weidenfeld and Nicolson.

Dukes, Sir Paul (1938) *The Story of ST25*, Cassell.

Dulles, A. (1963) *The Craft of Intelligence,* New York: Harper and Row.

Ehrmann, J. (1958) *Cabinet Government and War 1890-1940,* C.U.P.

Eisenhower, D. D. (1948) *Crusade in Europe*, New York: Doubleday.

(1946) 'The Operations in Europe of the Allied Expeditionary Force, June 1944 to May 1945', Report of the Supreme Commander to the Combined Chiefs of Staff.

Ellwood, Air Vice-Marshal A. B. (16 April 1947) Coastal Command in the Victory in Europe, Royal United Service Institution Lecture.

Evans-Lombe, E. M. (16 April 1947) The Royal Navy in the Pacific, Royal United Service Institution Lecture.

Everitt, *British Secret Service during the Great War*, Hutchinson.

Ewing, A. W. (1939) *The Man of Room 40: The Life of Sir Alfred Ewing*, London: Hutchinson.

Falk, S. L. (1966) *Decision at Leyte*, New York: Norton.

Field, J. A. (1947) *The Japanese at Leyte Gulf: The Sho Operation*, Princeton University Press.

Fleming, P. (1957) *Invasion 1940*, London: Harte-Davis.

Foote, A. (1949) *Handbook for Spies*, Museum Press.

Foot, M. R. D. (1964) *S.O.E. in France*, London: HMSO.

Forbes (2 October 1947) 'St. Nazaire, March 1942', *London Gazette*.

Frank, W. (1955) *The Sea Wolves*, Weidenfeld and Nicolson.

Fraser (7 August 1947) 'Sinking of the Scharnhorst, December 1943', *London Gazette*;

(2 June 1948) 'British Pacific Fleet in the Conquest of Okinawa, March to May 1945', *London Gazette*.

Friedman, W. F., Mendelsohn, C. J. (1938) 'The Zimmermann Telegram of 16 January 1917, and its cryptographic background', *War Department, Office of the Chief Signal Officer, Washington, D.C.: U.S. Government Printing Office*.

Fuchida, M., Okumiya, M., Pineau, R., Kawakami, C. (eds.) (1955) *Midway, the Battle that doomed Japan: The Japanese Navy's Story*.

Fuller, J. F. C. (1948) *The Second World War 1939-1945: A strategical and tactical history*, Eyre and Spottiswoode.

(1956) *The Decisive Battles of the Western World*, Volume 3, Eyre and Spottiswoode.

Gibbs, N. H. (1955) *The Origins of Imperial Defence*, O.U.P.

Graham, G. S. (1965) *The Politics of Naval Supremacy*, Cambridge University Press.

Grant, R. M. (1969) *U-boat Intelligence, 1914-1918*, Connecticut: Hamden.

Green, R. L. (1952) *A. E. W. Mason*, London: Max Parrish.

Greenfield, K. R. (ed.) (1959) *Command Decisions, Prepared by the office of the Chief of Military History*, New York: Harcourt-Brace.

Grettan, Sir P. (1965) *Maritime Strategy*, London: Cassell.

Grey, Lord, *Twenty-Five Years*.

Gouzenko, I. (1948) *This Was My Choice*, Eyre and Spottiswoode.

Guigand, F. de (1947) *Operation Victory*, Hodder and Stoughton.

Halifax and Whitworth (3 July 1947) 'First and Second Battles of Narvik, April 1940', *London Gazette*.

Halsey, W. F., Bryan, J. (1947) *Admiral Halsey's Story*, New York: Whittlesey House.

Hankey, Lord (1927) 'The Committee of Imperial Defence', *Army Quarterly Review*, Vol. 14.

'The Supreme Command'.

Harvey, J. (ed.) (1970) *The Diplomatic Diaries of Oliver Harvey, 1937-1940*, Collins.

Haugh, R. (1969) *First Sea Lord: An Authorised Biography of Admiral Lord Fisher*, George Allen and Unwin.

The Hunting of Force Z.

Hendrick, B. J., *Dr Walter Page*.

Hezlett, Vice-Admiral Sir A. (1969) *Aircraft and Sea Power*, Peter Davies.

Higham, R. (1963) *Armed Forces in Peacetime, Britain 1918-1940: A Case Study*, Foulis.

Hilsman, R., *Strategic Intelligence*.

Hinsley, F. H. (1951) *Hitler's Strategy*, C.U.P.

(1953) History Division of the Chief of Naval Operations, Navy Department, Washington: U.S. Government Printing Office, United States Naval Chronology, World War Two.

Hoare, Rt. Hon. Sir Samuel, Viscount Templewood (1946) *Ambassador on a Special Mission*, London: Collins.

Hobbes, T., *Leviathan*.

Holmes, W. J. (1966) *Undersea Victory: The influence of submarine operations on the war in the Pacific*, New York: Doubleday.

Hoore, G., *The Missing Macleans*, London: Cassell.

Harwood (18 September 1947) 'The Battle of Sirte, 22 March 1942', *London Gazette*.

Howarth, D. (1959) *Dawn of D-Day*, London: Collins.

Hughes-Hallet (14 August 1947) 'The Dieppe Raid, August 1942', *London Gazette*.

Hunt, Sir David (1966) *A Don at War*, London: Kimber.

Hyde, M., *The Quiet Canadian*.

Jacobson, H. A., Rohwer, J. (1965) *Decisive battles of World War II: The German View*, Translated from German by Edward Fitzgerald, London: Andre Deutsch.

James, Admiral Sir W. (1956) *The Eyes of the Navy*;

(Spring 1965) 'Room 40', *Edinburgh University Journal*, 22, p. 50-54;

(1956) *A Great Seaman: The Life of Admiral of the Fleet Sir Henry Oliver*, Witherby.

Jellicoe, Earl (1919) *The Grand Fleet*;

(1920) *The Crisis of the Naval War*.

Jessel, R. F. (19 November 1952) The Bismarck Operation: The German Aspect, Royal United Service Institution Lecture.

Johnson, F. A. (1960) *Defence by Committee: The British Committee of Imperial Defence, 1880-1959*, O.U.P.

Joubert de la Ferte, Sir P. B. (1955) *The Third Service. The story behind the Royal Air Force*, London: Thames and Hudson.

Kahn, D. (1966) *The Codebreakers*, Weidenfeld and Nicolson.

Kaznachev, A. (1963) *Inside a Soviet Embassy,* Robert Hale.

Kemp, P. K. (1957) *Victory at Sea, 1939-1945*, London: Muller.

Kendall, W. (July 1949) 'The Functions of Intelligence', *World Politics*.

Kent, S. (1949) *Strategic Intelligence for American World Policy*, Oxford University Press.

Kerr, Admiral Mark (1934) *Life of Prince Louis of Battenburg*, Longmans Green.

King, E. J., *U.S. Navy at War, 1941-1945;*

With Whitehiel, W. M. (1952) *Fleet Admiral King: A Naval Record,* New York: Norton.

Kirkpatrick, L. B. (1970) *Captains Without Eyes*, Hart-Davis.

Korbel, J. (1959) *The Communist Subversion of Czechoslovakia, 1938-1948*, Oxford University Press.

Kurzman, D. (1963) *Subversion of the Innocents*, New York: Random House.

Layton (26 February 1948) 'Loss of the Prince of Wales and Repulse, December 1941', *London Gazette*.

Leahy, W. D. (1950) *I was there: The personal story of the Chief of Staff to Presidents Roosevelt and Truman*, New York: Mcgraw-Hill.

Leighton, R. M., Coalsley, R. W. (1955) 'Global logistics and strategy, 1940-1943, in: U.S. Army in World War Two', The War Department, Washington: Office of the Chief of Military History.

Lewis, N. (1964) *The Honoured Society*, London: Collins.

Liddell-Hart, Captain Sir B. H. (1954) *Strategy: The Indirect Approach*, London: Faber and Faber;

(1951) The Other Side of the Hill, London: Cassell;

(1965) Memoirs, Two volumes, London: Cassell;

(1930) *The Real War: 1914-1918*, Boston: Little Brown and Co.

Lockhart, Sir Robert B. (1932) *Memories of a British Agent*, London: Putnam.

Lockhart, R. (1967) *The Ace of Spies*, London: Hodder and Stoughton.

Ludendorff, General, *My War Memoirs*.

Machiavelli, *The Prince*.

Macintyre (1956) *U-boat Killer*, Weidenfeld and Nicolson.

(1971) The Naval War Against Hitler, Batsford.

Mahan, A. T. (1890) *The Influence of Sea Power Upon History*.

(1892) *The Influence of Sea Power Upon the French Revolution and Empire*.

(1905) *Sea Power in its relation to the war of 1812*.

Marcell, P. Lt. Cdr. R.N. (July 1970) Naval Rivalry Renewed, The London Naval Conference 1935-1936, and the Anglo-German Naval Agreement, 1935, Copy in the Staff College Library, Royal Naval College, Greenwich.

(September 1970) The Anglo-German Naval Agreement 1935, Copy in the Staff College Library, Royal Naval College, Greenwich.

Marder, A. J., *From the Dreadnought to Scapa Flow*, Five volumes, Oxford University Press.

(1940) *The Anatomy of British Sea Power*, Alfred Knopf.

Marti, L. W. (1967) *The Sea in Modern Strategy*, London: For the Institute of Strategic Studies, Chatto and Windus.

Matloff, M. (1959) Strategic Planning for Coalition Warfare, 1943-1944, Washington: Office of the Chief of Military History.

Maund, L. E. H.: (1949) *Assault from the Sea*, Methuen.

McCormick, D. (1959) *The Mystery of Lord Kitchener's Death*, London: Putnam.

McLachlan, D. (1968) *Room 39: Naval Intelligence in Action, 1939-1945*, Weidenfeld and Nicolson.

Millington-Drake, E. (1965) *The drama of the Graf Spee and the Battle of the River Plate: A documentary anthology, 1914-1964*, Peter Davies.

Minott, R. G. (1964) *The Fortress That Never Was*, New York: Holt, Rinehart and Winston.

Monat, P. (1961) *Spy in the U.S.*, New York: Harper and Row.

Montagu, E. E. S. (1953) *The Man who never was*, Evans Brothers.

Montgomery, B. L. (1958) *The Memoirs of Field Marshal the Viscount Montgomery of El Alamein*, London: Collins;

Normandy to the Baltic.

Moorehead, A. (1952) *The Traitors*, Hamish Hamilton.

Morgan, F. (1950) *Overture to Overlord*, London: Hodder and Stoughton.

Morison, S. E. (1948-1962) *History of United States Naval Operations in World War Two*, Fifteen Volumes, Boston: Little Brown;

(1958) *Strategy and Compromise*, Boston: Little Brown;

(9 October 1946) Mountbatten of Burma, Admiral of the Fleet the Viscount: The Strategy of the South-East Asia Campaign, Royal United Service Institution Lecture.

Norman, A. (1952) *Operation Overlord, Design and Reality: The Allied Invasion of Western Europe*, Harrisburg.

Nicolai, Colonel W., *The German Secret Service*, Translated by G. Renwick.

Nicolson, H. (1957) *Journey to Java*, London: Constable.

O'Connor, R., *The Japanese Navy in World War II*.

Oliver, Rear-Admiral G. N. (20 November 1946) Carrier Aircraft in Support of Major Landings, Royal United Service Institution Lecture.

Orlov, A. (1963) *Handbook of intelligence and guerrilla warfare*, Cresset Press.

Oxford, Lord, *The Genesis of the War*.

Pack, S.W.C. (1961) *The Battle of Matapan*, Batsford.

Patton, G. S. (1947) *War as I knew it*, Boston: Mifflin.

Pawle, G., *The Secret War*, Harrap.

Pearson, J. (1966) *The Life of Ian Fleming*, London: Jonathan Cape.

Petter, G. S. (1946) *The Future of American Secret Intelligence*, Washington, D.C.

Petrov, Vladimir and Evdokia (1956) *Empire of Fear*, Andre Deutsch.

Philby, K. (1968) *My Silent War*, New York: Grove Press.

Power, A. (29 April 1948) 'Naval Operations in Ramree Island Area, June-February, 1945', *London Gazette*.

Powers, R. D. (August 1958) Blockade for Winning Without Killing, Proceedings of the United States Naval Institute.

Pratt, F. (1939) *Secret and Urgent: The Story of Codes and Cyphers*, London: Robert Hale.

Progue, F. C. (1954) *U.S. Army in World War II: European Theatre of Operations*, The Supreme Command, Washington D.C.: Department of the Army.

Puleston, W. D. (1947) *The Influence of Sea Power in World War Two*, Yale University Press.

Raeder, E. (1959) *Struggle for the Sea*, Translated by Edward Fitzgerald, London: Kimber.

Ramsey (17 July 1947) 'The Evacuation from Dunkirk, May-June 1940', *London Gazette*;

(30 October 1947) 'Assault Phases of the Normandy Landings, June 1944', *London Gazette*.

Ransom, H. H. (1958) *Central Intelligence and the National Security*, Oxford University Press.

Richmond, Sir H. (1946) *Statesmen and Seapower*.

Rintelen, Captain Franz von (1933) *The Dark Invader*, London: Peter Davies.

Rosere, T., *United States Submarine Operations in World War II*.

Roskill, S. W. (1954-1961) 'The War at Sea, 1939-1945', Three Volumes, *HMSO*.

Hankey (1969) *Man of Secrets*, Collins.

(1968) *Naval Policy Between the Wars*, Vol. I, Collins.

Rowan, R. W. (1938) *The Story of Secret Service*, Miles;

Thirty-Three Centuries of Espionage, London: Royal Institute of International Affairs;

Chronology of the Second World War and other selected readings.

Ruge, F. (1957) *Sea Warfare, 1939-1945: A German Viewpoint*, Translated from German by M. G. Saunders, London: Cassell.

Ryan, C. (1960) *The Longest Day: 6 June 1944*, New York: Simon and Schuster.

Scheer, Admiral (1920) *Germany's High Seas Fleet*.

Schelling, W. R. (1962) *Strategy, Politics, and Defence Budgets*, New York: Columbia University Press.

Schull, J. (1952) *The Far Distant Ships: An official account of Canadian Naval Operations in the Second World War*, Ottawa: Ministry of National Defence.

Schurman, D. M. (1867-1914) The Education of a Navy: The Development Of British Naval Strategic Thought.

Sillitoe, Sir Percy (22 November 1953) 'My answer to critics of M.I. 5', *Sunday Times*.

Sims, Admiral (1930) *Victory at Sea*.

Slessor, Sir J. (1956) *The Central Blue: Recollections and Reflections*, London: Cassell.

Smith, P. C. (1959) *Task Force 57: The British Pacific Fleet, 1944-1945*, William Kimber.

Somerville, Admiral (5 May 1948) 'Action off Cape Spartivento, 17 November 1940', *London Gazette*.

Spencer, J. H. (1952) *Battle for Crete,* London: Heinemann.

Spruance, Admiral R. A. (30 October 1946) The Victory in the Pacific, Royal United Service Institution Lecture.

Stein, H. (ed.) (1963) *American Civil-Military Decisions*, Birmingham, Alabama: University of Alabama Press.

Steinhauer, G., Felstead, S. T.: *The Kaiser's Master Spy.*

Strong, Major-General Sir Kenneth (1968) *Intelligence at the Top*, Cassell.

Syfret (4 March 1948) 'Capture of Diego-Sumarez, May 1942', *London Gazette*.

Taylor, A. J. P. (1963) *The First World War*, Hamish Hamilton.

Terrell, E. (1958) *Admiralty Brief,* Harrap.

Thomson, Sir Basil (1935) *The Story of Scotland Yard*, London: Grayson and Grayson.

Tuchmann, B. W. (1958) *The Zimmermann Telegram*, New York: Viking Press.

Tovey, Admiral (3 June 1948) 'Raid on the Lofoten Islands, March 1941', *London Gazette*.

(16 October 1947) 'Sinking of the Bismarck, May 1941', *London Gazette*.

(25 May 1948) 'Carrier Aircraft Attacks on Kirkenes and Petsamo, July 1941', *London Gazette*.

(5 July 1948) 'Raid on Vaagso Island, December 1941', *London Gazette*.

(15 October 1950) 'Convoys to North Russia, 1942', *London Gazette*.

Toye, F. (1948) *For What We Have Received: An Autobiography*, New York: A.A. Knopf.

Toynbee, A. (ed.) (1952) *Survey of International Affairs, 1939-1946*, Oxford University Press.

U.S. State Department, 'Intelligence, a Bibliography of its Functions, Methods and Techniques', Part I, December 1948. Part II, April 1949.

Watt, D. C. 'The Anglo-German Naval Agreement of 1935: An Interim Judgment', *Journal of Modern History XXVII*, No. 2, June 1956.

Waters, D. W., *A Study of the Philosophy and Conduct of Maritime War, 1815-1945*, Parts 1 and 2, Published privately, Copies in the Ministry of Defence (Navy) Library and National Maritime Museum, Greenwich.

Wemyss, D. E. G. (1948) *Walker's group in the Western Approaches*, Liverpool Post and Echo.

Werner, H. A. (1969) *Iron Coffins: A Personal Account of German U-boat battles of World War II,* Arthur Barker.

Westphal, General, *Herr in Fesseln.*

Wheatley, R. (1958) *Operation Sea Lion: German Plans for the Invasion of England, 1939-1942,* Oxford Clarendon Press.

Willis (11 October 1948) 'Naval operations in the Aegean, September-November 1943', *London Gazette.*

With Somerville (12 July 1948) 'Actions Against Raiders, 1941-1942', *London Gazette.*

Wilmot, C. (1952) *The Struggle for Europe,* London: Collins.

Wohlstetter, R. (1962) *Pearl Harbour, Warning and Decision,* Stanford.

Wolin, S., Slusser, R. M. (1957) *The Soviet Secret Police,* Methuen.

Wood, D., Dempster, D. (1961) *The Narrow Margin,* London: Hutchinson.

Woodburn-Kirkby, S. (1957) 'The War Against Japan', Volume I, *HMSO.*

Woodward, C. V. (1947) *The Battle of Leyte Gulf,* MacMillan.

Zimmerman, B. (1956) *France, 1944 in: The Fatal Decisions,* London: Michael Joseph.

Zimmerman, J. L. (1949) *The Guadalcanal Campaign,* Washington: US Marine Corps.

Anthony Wells' Publications

Literary Awards:

In 2013 & 2017, the United States Submarine League presented Dr Anthony R. Wells with Literary Awards for Articles in *The Submarine Review*.

Books:
German Public Opinion and Hitler's Policies, 1933-39. 1968. Electronic version available at Durham University Library, UK—access www to Durham University Library and enter data base with title and/or author name. Electronic and hard copy versions available.

Studies in British Naval Intelligence, 1880-1945. 1972. Electronic version available via the www British Library (ETHOS), and also King's College, London—www and then enter the data base with title and/or author name. Electronic and hard copy versions available. Also simply enter title, and by Anthony Roland Wells and a www edition is available on line.

Training and the Achievement of Management Objectives, the Solution of Management Problems, and as an Instrument of Organisational Change. 1974. The London School of Economics and Political Science.

Technical Change and British Naval Policy. Edited by Bryan Ranft, Hodder and Stoughton, London, 1977, and Holmes and Meier, New York, NY.

War and Society. Edited by Brian Bond and Ian Roy, Croom Helm, London, 1977, and Holmes and Meier, New York, NY.

Soviet Naval Diplomacy. Edited by B. Dismukes and J. McConnell, Pergamon Press, 1979.

The Soviet and Other Communist Navies. Edited by James George, US Naval Institute Press, Annapolis, Maryland, 1986.

Black Gold Finale. A novel. Dorrance Publishing Company, 2009.

The Golden Few. A novel. Dorrance Publishing Company, 2012.

A Tale of Two Navies: Geopolitics, Technology, and Strategy in the United States and the Royal Navy, 1960-2015. US Naval Institute Press, Annapolis, Maryland, January 2017.

Between Five Eyes. Casemate Publishers, Oxford, UK & Havertown, Pennsylvania, September 2020.

Room 39 and the Lisbon Connection. A novel. Xlibris, Bloomington, Indiana, June 2021

Crossroads in Time Philby & Angleton. A Story of Treachery. A novel. Palmetto Publishing, Charleston, South Carolina, 2022 and Austin Macauley Publishers, London 2022.

Gone to Earth A Young American Woman Disappears in the South Pacific. Based on a true story. A novel. Xlibris, Bloomington, Indiana, 2022.

How Strategic Airpower has Tipped the Balance on the Global Stage From the 100th Bomb Group to the Falklands and Beyond. With Commander Nigel 'Sharkey' Ward, DSC, AFC, Royal Navy (Retired). To be published in 2023.

Guarding against Extremism in the 21st Century A Lesson from the Past German Public Opinion and Hitler's Policies 1933-1939. XLibris, Bloomington, Indiana, 2023. The subject of a PBS broadcast in June, 2023 that was broadcast nationwide in the United States, and globally, including China.

Intrepid's Footsteps Sustaining US-UK Intelligence in an Era of Global Challenges. A Personal Memoire. XLibris, Bloomington, Indiana, 2023.

From Blinker Hall to Room 39: British Naval Intelligence 1880-1945. To be published in 2025.

Never Too Late A Story for Every Parent. To be published in 2024/2025.

Articles

Admirals Hall and Godfrey: Doyens of Naval Intelligence (Two Parts). The Naval Review, 1973.

Staff Training and the Royal Navy (Two Parts). The Naval Review 1975, 1976.

The 1967 June War: Soviet Naval Diplomacy and the Sixth Fleet: A Reappraisal. Centre for Naval Analyses, Arlington, Virginia. Professional Paper 204, October 1977.

The Centre for Naval Analyses. Professional Paper Number 197, December 1977. Department of the Navy, Washington DC, Centre for Naval Analyses.

The Soviet Navy in the Arctic and North Atlantic. National Defence, February 1986.

Soviet Submarine Prospects 1985-2000. Submarine Review, January 1986.

A New Defence Strategy for Britain. Proceedings of the United States Naval Institute, March 1987.

Presence and Military Strategies of the USSR in the Arctic. Quebec Centre for International Relations, Laval University, 1986.

Real Time Targeting: Myth or Reality. Proceedings of the United States Naval Institute, August 2001.

Missing Magics Machine Material. New Insights on 7 December 1941 and Relevance for Today's Navy. The Submarine Review, April 2003.

US Naval Power and the Pursuit of Peace in an Era of International Terrorism and Weapons of Mass Destruction. The Submarine Review, October 2002.

Transformation: Some Insights and Observations for the Royal Navy from Across the Atlantic. The Naval Review, August 2003.

They Did Not Die In Vain. USS Liberty Incident: Some Additional Perspectives. Proceedings of the United States Naval Institute, March 2005

Royal Navy at the Crossroads: Turn the Strategic Tide. A Way to Implement a Lasting Vision. The Naval Review, November 2010

The Royal Navy is Key to Britain's Security Strategy. Proceedings of the United States Naval Institute, December 2010

The Survivability of the Royal Navy and a New Enlightened British Defence Strategy. The Submarine Review, January 2011

A Strategy in East Asia that can Endure. Proceedings of the United States Naval Institute, May 2011

A Strategy in East Asia that can Endure. The Naval Review, August 2011. Reprinted by kind permission of the United States Naval Institute.

The United States Navy, Jordan, and a Long-Term Israeli-Palestinian Security Agreement. The Submarine Review, Spring 2012

Admiral Sir Herbert Richmond: What would he think, write and action today? The Naval Review, February 2013—Lead article in the Centenary Edition of The Naval Review.

Postscript to Missing Magics Machine Material—Tribute to a Great Submariner: Captain Edward Beach, US Navy. The Submarine Review, 2013.

Jordan, Israel, and US Need to Cooperate for Missile Defence. USNI News, 26 March 2013.

A Tribute to Admiral Sir John 'Sandy' Woodward. USNI News, 8 August 2013.

USS LIBERTY Document Centre. Edited by Anthony Wells and Thomas Schaaf. A web site produced by SiteWhirks, Inc., Warrenton, Virginia. September 2013. In April 2017, this website was transferred to the Library of Congress for permanent safekeeping for the use of future scholars and researchers.

The Future of ISIS: A Joint US-Russian Assessment. With Dr Andrey Chuprygin. The Naval Review, May 2015

The Zimmermann Telegram: 100th Anniversary. The Naval Review, February 2017 & The Submarine Review 2017.

Put The Guns in a Box: With Captain J W Phillips, US Navy retired. Proceedings of the US Naval Institute, June 2018.

Quo Vadis China? A View from Across the Atlantic. Part 1. The Naval Review. November 2019.

Quo Vadis China? The Submarine Review, December 2019.

USS Amberjack and the Attack on USS Liberty: With Mr Larry Taylor, ST1 USS Amberjack. US Naval Institute Naval History Blog, 7 January 2020.

USS Amberjack & the Attack on USS Liberty. With Mr Larry Taylor. The Submarine Review. March 2020.

The UK's Strategic Defence & Security Review, A US Perspective. The Submarine Review. June 2020.

The United Kingdom Needs a Maritime Strategy. The Naval Review, August, 2020.

Submarines and the Ring of Fire in the Indo-Pacific Theatre: A Strategic Analysis. The Submarine Review, December 2020.

UK's Defence & Security Review—Some Final Observations: The Naval Review. Autumn 2020.

A Brave New World of Next Generation Technologies: Warship World: Volume 17, Number 2, January/February 2021.

To Honour The Last Nuremburg Prosecutor: Proceedings of the United States Naval Institute May 2021, Annapolis, Maryland.

The United Nations Convention on the Law of the Sea and the United States Navy: US Naval Institute Blog, June 2021.

Is There a Need for a New Generation of Submarine Officers who are Intelligence-Trained and Experienced beyond Current Levels? & How Might We Learn from the Past? The Submarine Review, June 2021.

Behind the Five Eyes: Counsel Magazine (Justice Matters: Spotlight section), the monthly magazine of the Bar of England & Wales, London, UK, July 2021.

Letter from The Plains: A monthly article in the Middleburg Eccentric, Virginia, since 2016 to November 2022.

Reports:

NATO and US Carrier Deployment Policies. Centre for Naval Analyses, Arlington, Virginia, February 1977.

NATO and US Carrier Deployment Policies, Formation of a New Standing Naval Strike Force in NATO. Centre for Naval Analyses, Arlington, Virginia, April 1977.

Sea War '85 Scenario. With Captain John L. Underwood, USN. Centre for Naval Analyses, Arlington, Virginia, June 1977.

Submarine Construction Program for the State of Sabah, Malaysia. RDA Contract TR-188600-OOl, December 1984. Chief Minister of Sabah, Malaysia and Government of Malaysia.

The Application of Drag Reduction and Boundary Layer Control Technologies in an Experimental Program. January 1985. For the Chief Naval Architect, Vickers Shipbuilding and Engineering Ltd, Barrow-in-Furness, UK.

The Strategic Importance and Advantages of Labuan, Federal Malaysian Territory, as a naval base with Special Reference to its Capabilities as the Royal Malaysian Navy Submarine Base, March 1985. Chief Minister of Sabah, Malaysia and Government of Malaysia.

Preliminary Overview of Soviet Merchant Ships in Anti-SSBN Operations and Soviet Merchant Ships and Submarine Masking. (Department of the Navy Contract N00016-85-C-0204).

SSBN Port Egress and the Non-Commercial Activities of the Soviet Merchant Fleet: Concepts of Operation and War Orders for Current and Future Anti-SSBN Operations. (Department of the Navy Contract 136400).

Overview Study of the Maritime Aspects of the Nuclear Balance in the European Theatre (Department of Energy Study for the European Conflict Analysis Project). October 1986.

Soviet Submarine Warfare Strategy Assessment and Future US Submarine and Anti-Submarine Warfare Technologies (Defence Advanced Research Projects Agency, March 1988), RDA Contract 146601).

Limited Objective Experiment ZERO, July 2000. The Naval Air Systems Command, US Navy, Department of Defence. 2002.

Operational factors Associated with the Software Nuclear Safety Analysis for the UGM-109A Tomahawk Submarine-Launched Land Attack Cruise Missile Combat Control System Mark I. United States Navy and Logicon Inc., 1989.

Operation Bahrain, March 2003. The Assistant Director of Central Intelligence, the Central Intelligence Agency.

Distributed Data Analysis with Bayesian Networks: A Preliminary Study for Non-Proliferation of Radioactive Devices, December 2003 (with F. Dowla and G. Larson). The Lawrence Livermore National Laboratory, Livermore, California, December 2003.

FIBRE REINFORCED PUMICE PROTECTIVE BARRIERS—To Mitigate the Effects of Suicide and Truck Bombs. Final Report and Recommendations. United States Navy, Washington DC. With Professor Vistasp Kharbari, Professor of Structural Engineering, University of California, San Diego. August 2006.

WEAPON TARGET CENTRIC MODEL: Preliminary Modules and Applications, in Two Volumes. United States Navy, Principal Executive Officer Submarines, Washington DC, August 2007.

TACTICAL DECISION AID (TDA): Multi-intelligence capability for National, Theatre, and Tactical intelligence in real time across geographic space and time. The National Intelligence Community, Washington DC, May 2012.

SUBMARINE INDUSTRIAL BASE MODEL: Key industrial base model for the US VIRGINIA Class nuclear powered attack submarine, Principal Executive Officer Submarines, Washington Navy Yard, Washington DC, October 2012.

Manuals:

Astro-Navigation: A Programmed Course in 6 Volumes for Training UK and Commonwealth Naval Officers in the Use of Astronomical Navigation at Sea. Royal Navy, Ministry of Defence, UK, 1969.

The Battle of Trafalgar: A Programmed Course in one Volume in Naval Strategy and Tactics. Royal Navy, Ministry of Defence, 1969.

The Double Cross System: A Programmed Course in One Volume for British, Foreign and Commonwealth Naval Officers Attending the Royal Naval Staff College, Greenwich, UK. Royal Navy, Ministry of Defence, 1973.

Unclassified Titles for Technology and Operational Areas—Covering Classified Programs—and Publications—Generic Areas.

Airborne Mine Clearance
Streak Tube Imaging LIDAR
Magic Lantern Program
Tritium Micro-sphere Technology
Classified Applications of the Naval Simulation System
Naval Surface Fire Support and the Extended Range Guided Munition (ERGM)
Non-Acoustic Anti-submarine Warfare
Battlefield Awareness and Data Dissemination (BADD Program)
Joint Stars Program Special Applications
Naval Fires Network
Littoral Surveillance System
Fleet Battle Experiment Operations (Technical Director FBE Alpha and FBE Bravo) Third Fleet, US Pacific Fleet
Ocean Surveillance (radar and optics)
Multi-Spectral Applications
Space Based Sensors and Surveillance
Microwave Radiometry Applications
Detection, Locating and Tracking
Clandestine Operations and Intelligence Collection Operations
Support to Special Forces
Special Submarine Operations
Tagging Tracking and Surveillance
Battlespace Shaping and Real Time Targeting
Covert and Clandestine Operations Against Weapons of Mass Destruction and Other Major Threats to US Security
Special Sensor Technology
Covert & Overt Operations Planning and Execution
Reports and MOUs for Commander-in-Chief and Secretary Level Actions
Airborne Infrared Measurement System
Stealth and Counter Stealth

Counter-Intelligence Operations
Tactical Exploitation System and Joint Fires Network
Asymmetric Warfare Initiative, 2003
Hairy Buffalo Program
Tracking of the al Qai'da Terrorist Network and Operations
Tactical Decision Aid (TDA) for Submarine ISR operations
Advanced Cyber Attack and Defence Technologies and Operations
Shrouded Lightning Special Program
Non-Linear Junction Radar and Adaptive Regenerative Controller Special Program
Special Program in Jordan
Special Program in Malaysia
Special Program in Bahrain
Special Program in Abu Dhabi
Special Program in Saudi Arabia
Special Program with Commander United States Pacific Fleet
Special Tests at the US Naval Air Station Patuxent River, Maryland, September 2012
LISAC Special Program
Applications of the Robust Laser Interferometry (RLI) system and technology
Special Support to a combined Cheltenham UK and Maryland US Group
Special Support for Indo-Pacific Operations

Classified Titles and Publications

From 1968-2018, Anthony has been the author, lead author, or a key author of multiple highly classified Codeword documents at the Top Secret SCI level in both the United Kingdom and the United States.